VISUAL QUICKSTART GUIDE

PICTURE IT! 7

FOR WINDOWS

Steve Schwartz

Peachpit Press

Visual QuickStart Guide

Picture It! 7 for Windows

Steve Schwartz

Peachpit Press
1249 Eighth Street
Berkeley, CA 94710
510/524-2178
800/283-9444
510/524-2221 (fax)

Find us on the World Wide Web at: http://www.peachpit.com
To report errors, please send a note to errata@peachpit.com
Peachpit Press is a division of Pearson Education

Editor: Suki Gear
Production Coordinator: Gloria Márquez
Copyeditor: Steve Schwartz
Compositor: Steve Schwartz
Indexer: Emily Glossbrenner
Cover Design: The Visual Group
Cover Production: Nathalie Valette

Notice of Rights

Notice of Liability

Trademarks

ISBN 0-321-19390-3

9 8 7 6 5 4 3 2 1

Printed and bound in the United States of America

Dedication

To caffeine and nicotine, an author's best friends.

Special thanks

To Suki Gear, Rebecca Ross, Lisa Brazieal, and Marjorie Baer of Peachpit Press, as well as all the wonderful Peachpit employees who were kind enough to contribute photos for the book; Gloria Márquez; Emily Glossbrenner; Lisa Sokulski of Edelman Public Relations; and Matt Wagner of Waterside Productions.

Table of Contents

INTRODUCTION

Welcome to the *Picture It! 7 for Windows: Visual QuickStart Guide*. This book is a visual, step-by-step guide to the four programs in the Picture It! 7 software line: Express, Photo, Photo Premium, and Digital Image Pro.

These four programs share the same menu structure and interface. The important differences between the four are explained below:

- *Express* is useful for basic picture editing and correction but lacks batch-editing capabilities (simultaneously correcting multiple images), artistic filters, and features for creating photo projects (such as greeting cards and calendars).
- *Photo* and *Photo Premium* are identical. However, the latter has three times as many project design templates. Both have advanced image-editing features, such as the ability to auto-adjust levels, apply artistic filters, and use other touch-up tools. You can also do batch editing and create photo projects.
- *Digital Image Pro* is the high-end program in the line. In addition to the features of Photo and Photo Premium, Digital Image Pro lets you manually adjust levels, change the lighting, apply new touch-up features and more than a dozen additional special effects, use Adobe Photoshop filters, and make flipbooks and Web animations.

Picture It!'s extended family

In addition to the four programs explicitly covered in this book, the Picture It! software family includes Greetings, Greetings Workshop, Home Publishing, and Publishing. Collectively, there are eight Picture It! products—each with a slightly different focus and feature set. If you have one of the 2002 version programs, you may still find this book useful; many of the features in version 7 also existed in the 2002 software. Note, however, that the menu structure is different in the 2002 versions. To apply the material in this book to your 2002 program will require that you explore the menus.

How to use this book

If you've never read a *Visual QuickStart Guide*, you'll note that this book has some distinctive differences from other computer books.

First, each chapter is written as a self-contained unit. For example, if you just want to learn about printing, you can turn directly to the chapter on that topic. Thus, although you *can* read this book in chapter order, there's no requirement that you do so.

Second, chapters are laid out in a consistent fashion—one which the series designers created for presenting information in a way that makes digesting it as simple as possible. Every page is laid out as two columns. The outer column contains the text and the inner column has illustrative screen shots (which are referred to by number in the text). Major headings always begin at the top of a column, enabling you to quickly see where you should start reading to learn about a program feature. Minor headings can appear anywhere, but are always subtopics of the major heading that precedes them.

About the author

Steve Schwartz has been a computer industry writer since the days of the early micros. He has written for dozens of major magazines and is the author of almost 50 computer and game books, including the following *Visual QuickStart* titles: Microsoft Office v. X, CorelDRAW 10 and 11, Entourage 2001, Internet Explorer 3 and 5, and Quicken 6. Steve has a Ph.D. in psychology and lives with his sons and faithful pets in the fictional town of Lizard Spit, Arizona. He can be reached via his official Web site at *http://www.siliconwasteland.com*.

Picture It! Essentials

1

It doesn't matter whether this is your first version of Picture It! or an upgrade, whether you're graphics savvy or a beginner, or whether you are a new computer user or an old hand. You got Picture It! to address a need—that of making images (such as digital photos and scans) look their best. So let's get cracking!

In this chapter, you'll get a quick introduction to putting Picture It! to work for you, including:

- Launching Picture It!
- Using the Startup Window
- Understanding the Picture It! interface
- Opening image files
- Changing the view by showing/hiding parts, panning, and zooming
- Using menus and keyboard shortcuts
- Using the Common Tasks list, Tray, Stack, and toolbar
- Undoing actions
- Printing
- Saving edited files
- Getting help
- Closing files and quitting Picture It!

In later chapters, many of these same topics will be covered in greater detail. You should consider this chapter an overview.

About Picture It!

Image editing is Picture It!'s primary function. Using Picture It!, you can resize, crop, brighten, fix the contrast, and touch up digital images—regardless of where the images originated. You may have taken photos with a digital camera or scanned a drawing with your scanner, for example. You may have downloaded image files from the Internet and received others as email attachments. You can use Picture It! to view and correct any of these kinds of images.

In addition to the basic cleanup work that is needed for many digital images, you can use most versions of Picture It! to embellish your images in a number of other useful ways:

- Rotate an image (or just a specific part, such as a text title) to a different angle
- Apply filters to change an ordinary image into artwork
- Add other pictures, artistic shapes, and text
- Surround an image with a decorative frame or mat
- Create *projects*, such as business cards, holiday greeting cards, and calendars

The latter capabilities set Picture It! apart from most other inexpensive Windows image-editing applications. Not only can you use Picture it! to clean up your photos and scans, you can also use it to create artistic collages and just-for-fun projects. And as you'll learn as you read this book, much of the fun stuff (**Figure 1.1**) is simple enough for any family member to create!

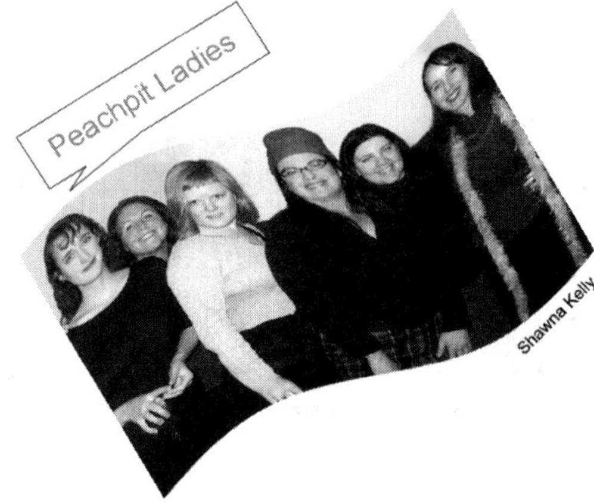

Figure 1.1 It's easy to create a stylized version of a photo, as well as add text and other enhancements.

Launching Picture It!

As with other Windows programs, there are several ways to launch Picture It! and start an image-editing session.

To launch Picture It!:

- *Do one of the following:*
  - ▲ Choose the Picture It! program from the Start > Programs menu.
  - ▲ Click (or double-click) the Picture It! icon or a Desktop shortcut for the program.

    You click or double-click depending on your installed operating system and how it's configured.
  - ▲ If you've created a shortcut for Picture It! and installed or dragged it onto the Quick Launch bar (found to the right of the Start button), click its icon.
  - ▲ If you have Windows XP and have recently run Picture It!, click the program's name in the Start menu (**Figure 1.2**).

✔ Tips

- You can simultaneously launch Picture It! and open selected images by dragging their file icons onto the Picture It! icon or Desktop shortcut.
- To automatically launch Picture It! when a particular type of image icon is clicked (such as one for a JPEG or TIFF file), you must *associate* that file type with Picture It! To accomplish this in Windows XP, right-click an icon of the desired file type and choose Properties from the pop-up menu that appears. Click the Change button in the Properties dialog box (**Figure 1.3**), choose Picture It! 7.0 from the Open With dialog box (**Figure 1.4**), click OK, and then click OK again.

  This procedure is more complex with earlier versions of Windows. See Windows Help (Start > Help) for instructions.

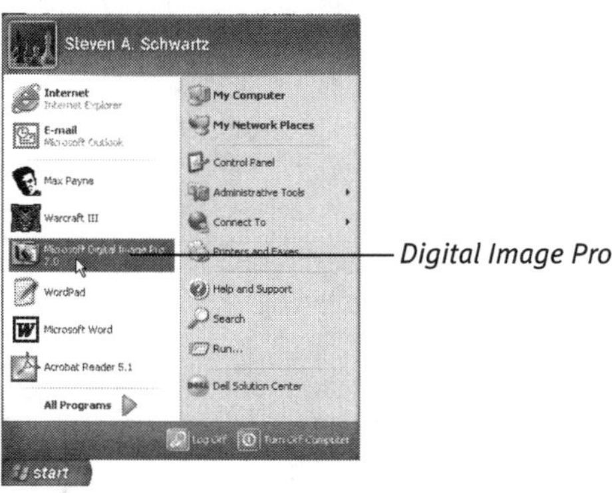

Figure 1.2 Windows XP lists all recently run applications.

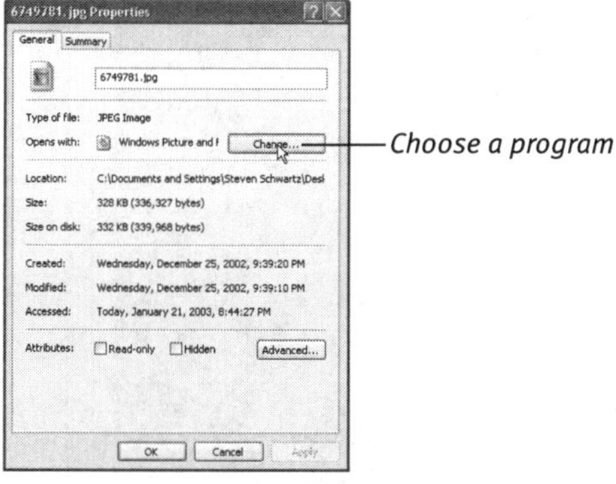

Figure 1.3 Click Change to pick a program with which to associate this file type.

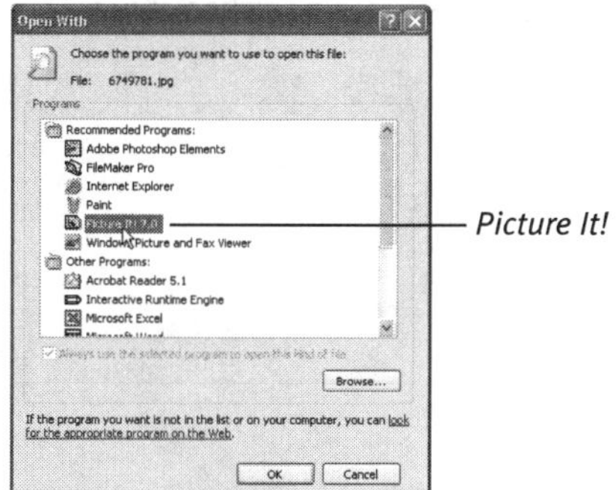

Figure 1.4 Select Picture It! and then click OK.

Using the Startup Window

Unless you've disabled it, the Startup Window (**Figure 1.5**) automatically appears each time you launch Picture It! By clicking icons, text, or images in this window, you can perform common Picture It! tasks.

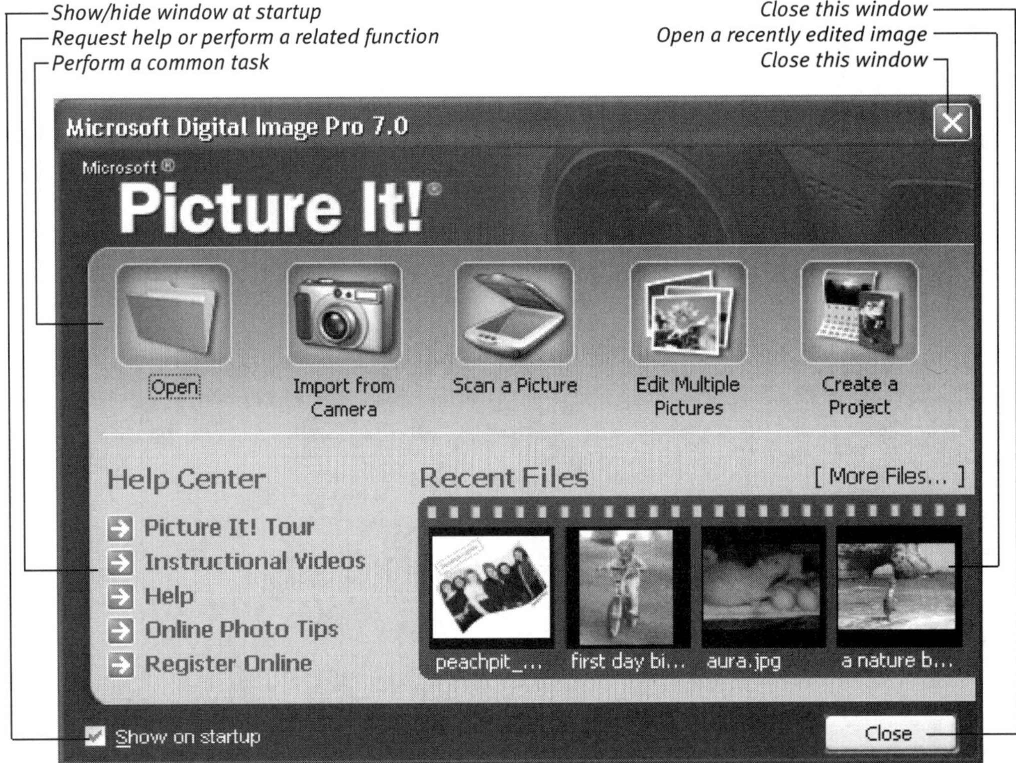

Figure 1.5 The Startup Window.

To use the Startup Window:

- *You can do any of the following:*
  - Click one of the top icons to open an image file from disk, download photos from a connected digital camera or memory card reader, scan an image, open the Mini Lab to edit multiple images, or create a project.

    Picture It! Express only displays the first three icons, rather than all five.
  - Click a Help Center link to get help with the program, taking pictures, or registering.
  - Click an image in the Recent Files area to open a file on which you've recently worked.
  - Click More Files to open a different image file. (This is the same as clicking the Open icon.)
  - Click to add or remove the checkmark from the Show on startup check box.

    Remove the checkmark if you want to prevent the Startup Window from automatically appearing on future start-ups.
  - Click the Close button or the X in the upper-right corner to dismiss the Startup Window.

✔ Tip

- You can summon the Startup Window at any time during an editing session by choosing File > Startup Window.

Starting from Scratch

Most of the time, you'll start Picture It! by opening an image or a previously saved project. However, you can also begin with a blank page. If you're creating a collage of photos, for example, this enables you to set the desired canvas size rather than having it automatically defined by the dimensions of the first image that you open.

To create a blank project, choose File > New or press Ctrl N. In the Resize pane, choose an orientation (portrait or landscape), specify the page size, and choose a resolution that matches what you intend to do with the resulting project. (You might choose 72 pixels per inch for a Web image or one that is meant only to appear onscreen. Use 150 pixels per inch or higher for one that you intend to print.) To complete the process, click Done.

The Picture It! Interface

After choosing an option from the Startup Window (such as opening an image for viewing or editing), you'll see a screen similar to the one in **Figure 1.6**.

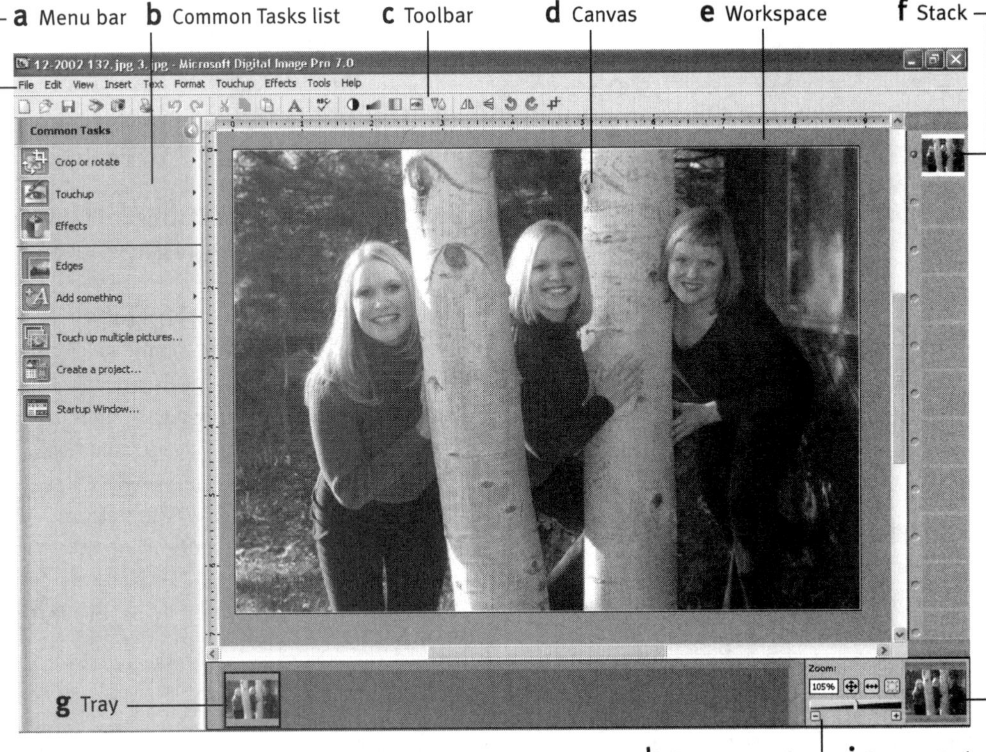

Figure 1.6 The parts of the Picture It! interface

Here's what the various interface parts are for and what you can do with them:

- **a** **Menu bar.** As in other Windows programs, you can choose commands from the menus at the top of the window.
- **b** **Common Tasks list.** Click any of the top icons to choose a common editing or embellishment procedure from a pop-out menu. Clicking any of the lower icons (the ones not followed by a triangle) causes the clicked command to execute immediately.
- **c** **Toolbar.** You can perform many common commands by clicking one of these icons. To learn what an icon does, rest the cursor over it for a moment. A pop-up tooltip will appear, such as Fix Red Eye.
- **d** **Canvas.** This white area marks the portion of the workspace that will be printed.
- **e** **Workspace.** The gray area surrounding the canvas. If you like, you can work on non-printing or temporary items here.
- **f** **Stack.** From top to bottom, items shown here represent the layers of your current project. If you add some text to a photo, for instance, the text layer would appear above the photo in the Stack.
- **g** **Tray.** Displays a thumbnail for every open image. To change the active image, click another thumbnail.
- **h** **Zoom controls.** Use the slider, icons, or text box to change the current magnification.
- **i** **Pan control.** Click and drag in this area to change the part of the image you're viewing.

Opening Files on Disk

As mentioned in the discussion of the Startup Window, Picture It! can open image files stored on disk, download them from a connected digital camera or card reader, or create them using a scanner attached to your PC. The latter procedures are discussed in Chapter 2.

If you're like most users, the bulk of your images will already be on disk—downloaded from a camera, created from scans, received from friends as email attachments, or saved/downloaded from the Web.

To open an image file from disk:

1. *Do one of the following:*
   - ▲ Click the Open icon or [More Files] in the Startup Window.
   - ▲ Choose File > Open (or press Ctrl O).

   The File Browser window appears (**Figure 1.7**), open to the folder you most recently worked on in Picture It!
2. Click items in the Folders area of the File Browser to select the drive and folder that contains the image you want to open.
3. Select the image's thumbnail or file name and then click Open. (You can also open the file by double-clicking its thumbnail or file name.)

   The image opens in the workspace, and its thumbnail appears in the Tray and Stack (see Figure 1.6).

✔ Tips

- To open an image you've recently worked on, click its thumbnail in the Recent Files area of the Startup Window or choose its file name from the list at the bottom of the File menu (**Figure 1.8**).
- You can also open an image by dragging its file icon into the Tray.

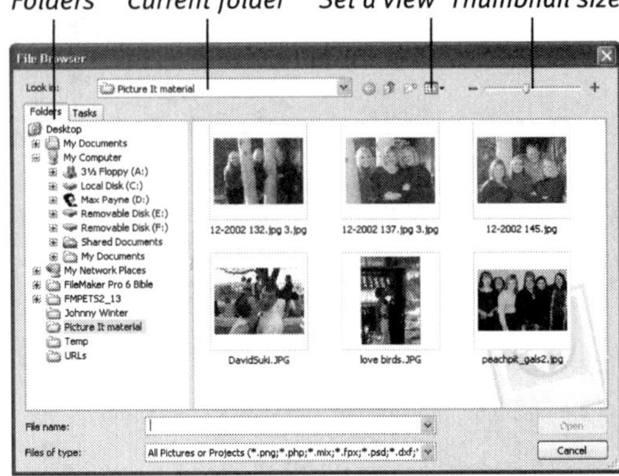

Figure 1.7 Picture It! presents a visual File Browser (rather than an Open dialog box), making it easy for you to locate and open your image files.

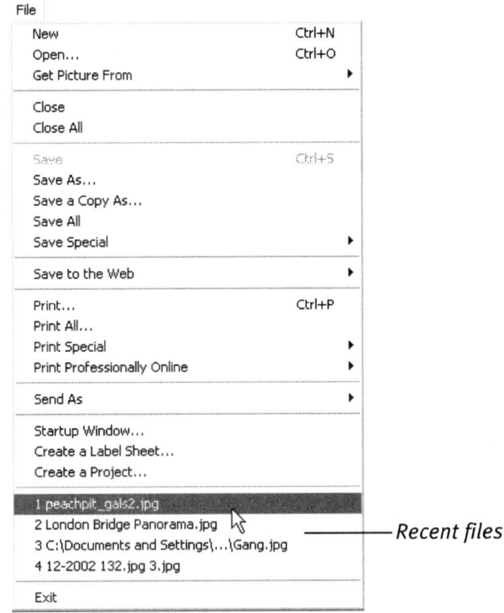

Figure 1.8 Recently opened image files are listed in, and can be chosen from, the bottom of the File menu.

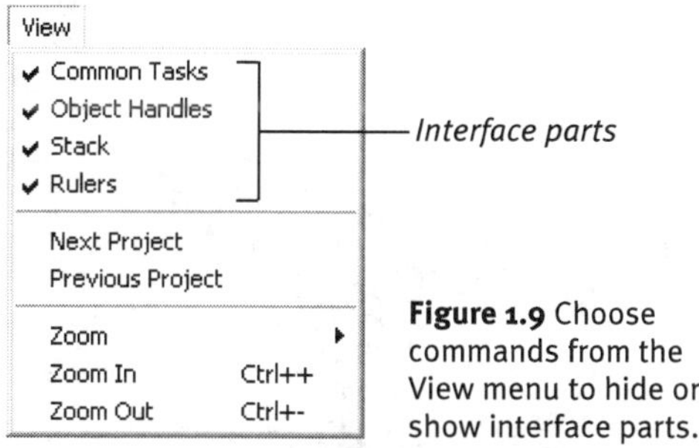

Figure 1.9 Choose commands from the View menu to hide or show interface parts.

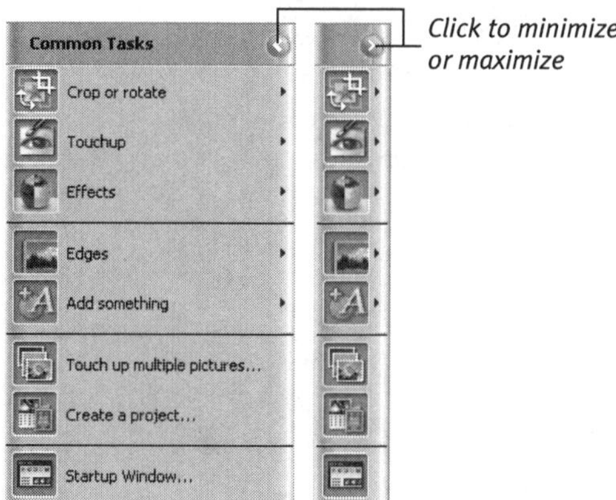

Figure 1.10 Click the arrow icon to maximize (left) or minimize (right) the Common Tasks list.

Showing and Hiding Parts

By choosing commands from the top section of the View menu (**Figure 1.9**), you can show or hide/collapse parts of the interface. Hiding or collapsing a part can be useful when you need more room to edit a large image, for example. Checked parts appear in the interface, while unchecked parts are hidden or collapsed. When you choose a checked part's command, the part will be hidden.

✔ Tips

- Choosing Common Tasks collapses the area rather than hiding it. You can also show/collapse this part by clicking the arrow icon to the right of the Common Tasks title (**Figure 1.10**).
- If you hide object handles, you can still move a selected object, but you won't be able to resize it by dragging an edge or corner. On the other hand, this *will* help you avoid inadvertently resizing objects.

Panning

You already know one way to move around in a document window—by using the scroll bars at the right and bottom edges of the window (**Figure 1.11**). You can click a blank area of a scroll bar, click the arrows at either end, or drag the scroll box to a new position. Click or drag in the *opposite* direction that you want the image to move. For example, clicking the arrow on the right end of the horizontal scroll bar moves the image to the left.

Picture It! also has a dedicated Pan control (see Figure 1.6), found in the lower-right corner.

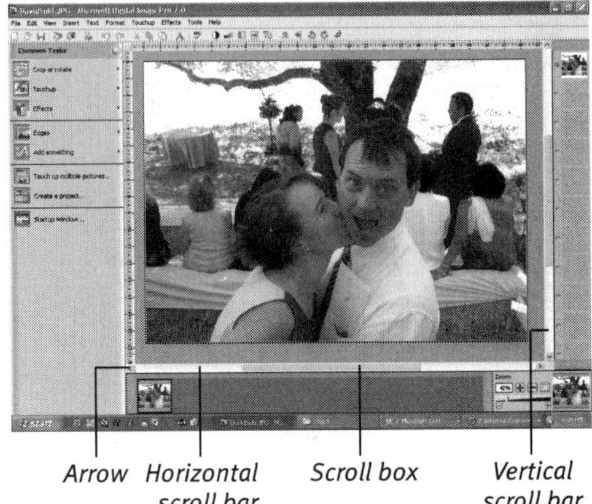

Figure 1.11 You can use the vertical and horizontal scroll bars to move an image around in the workspace.

To pan using the Pan control:

- *Do one of the following:*
  - In the Pan control, click the part of the image that you want to center in the document window.
  - Click and drag in the Pan control. As you drag, the gray frame corresponds to the placement of the image within the window.

✔ Tip

- You can also press Pg Dn or Pg Up to move the image up or down in the window.

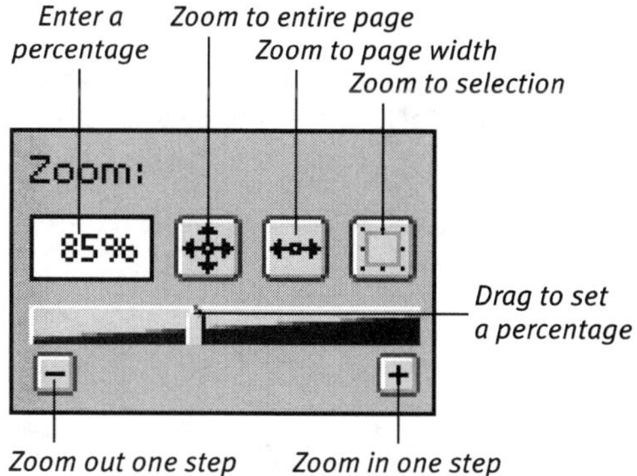

Figure 1.12 The Zoom controls enable you to quickly set a new magnification level.

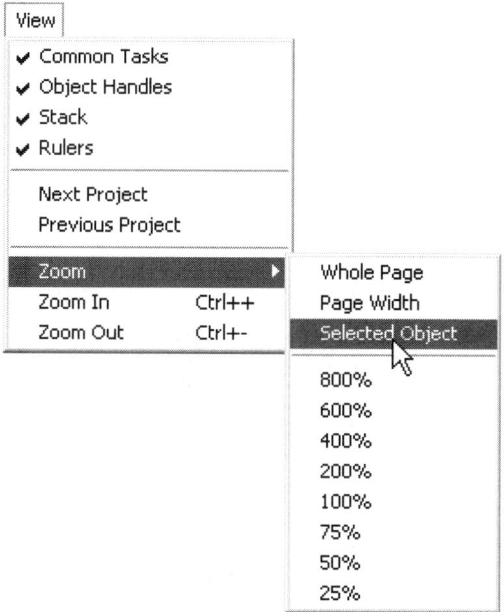

Figure 1.13 Zoom commands can also be found in the View menu.

Zooming

To *zoom* means to change the magnification. Using the Zoom controls (**Figure 1.12**) or the View > Zoom (**Figure 1.13**) commands, you can zoom in to do detailed touch-up work, zoom out to see the entire layout of a complex project, or fill the screen with a selected object.

To change the current magnification:

- *Do one of the following:*
  - To zoom to a specific magnification, choose a percentage from the View > Zoom submenu, drag the Zoom slider, or type a number in the Zoom text box and press Enter.
  - To zoom in one step, choose View > Zoom In, press Ctrl+, or click the + icon in the Zoom controls. To zoom out one step, choose View > Zoom Out, press Ctrl-, or click the - icon in the Zoom controls.
  - To view the entire page in the editing window, choose View > Zoom > Whole Page or click the Zoom to Entire Page icon in the Zoom controls.
  - To zoom to the full width of the page, choose View > Zoom > Page Width or click the Zoom to Page Width icon in the Zoom controls.
  - To fill the window with a selected object, choose View > Zoom > Selected Object or click the Zoom to Selection icon in the Zoom controls.

Working with Menus

Like most Windows programs, the majority of the most important commands can be chosen from the ever-present menu bar (**Figure 1.14**) at the top of the Picture It! window.

To choose a command from a menu:

1. Click the menu title, such as File or Edit.

   The menu drops down (**Figure 1.15**).

2. *Do one of the following:*
   - ▲ Click to choose the desired command.
   - ▲ If the command is followed by a triangle, move the cursor over the command to expose a pop-out (or *hierarchical*) submenu (**Figure 1.16**). Click to choose the desired command.

   The command executes.

✔ Tips

- This technique is also used to choose commands and procedures from the Common Tasks list.
- When chosen, command names that are followed by an ellipsis (such as *Print...*) will present a dialog box or pane, enabling you to set relevant options.
- Some commands require that an object or text string first be selected. For example, if you want to delete an object, you must select the object *before* choosing Edit > Delete.
- In general, commands can only be chosen when they are appropriate for what you're currently doing. In the previous example, the Delete command would be *grayed out* (see Figure 1.15) if you didn't have something selected. (If an object or text isn't selected, there is nothing for Picture It! to delete.)

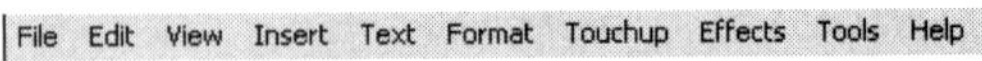

Figure 1.14 Every Windows program has a menu bar that stretches across the top of the document window.

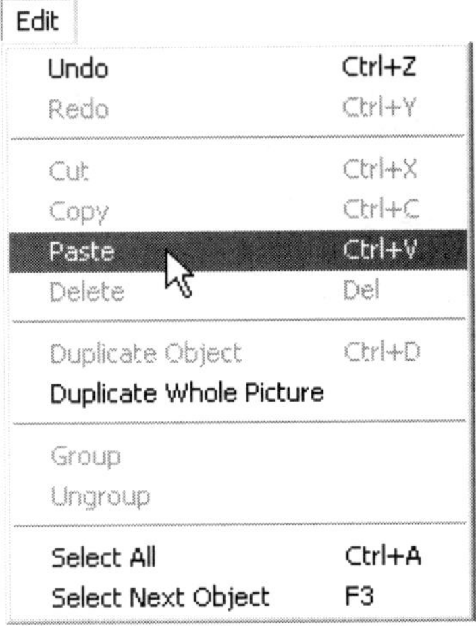

Figure 1.15 When you click an item in the menu bar (such as Edit), the menu drops down.

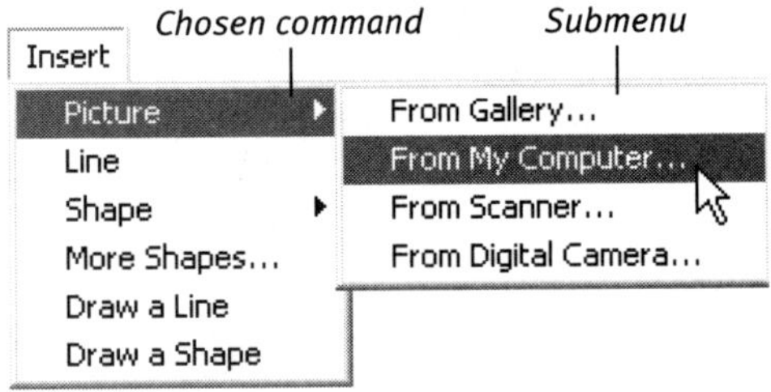

Figure 1.16 Click a command that's followed by a triangle to expose its pop-out submenu.

Using Keyboard Shortcuts

Many commands can also be issued by pressing a key or combination of keys known as a *keyboard shortcut.* If a shortcut is available for a command, it is usually listed in the menu to the right of the command, such as Ctrl V for Edit > Paste. (Refer to Figure 1.15 for some examples.) To type a keyboard shortcut that consists of two keys, hold down the modifier key (such as Ctrl) and then tap the second key (typically a letter).

Here are some tips for using Picture It! keyboard shortcuts:

- Single-key keyboard shortcuts consist mainly of the function keys (F1 to F10).
- You can also choose commands using only the keyboard. First, press Alt or F10. An underlined letter appears in each menu title. Press the key that corresponds to the letter (such as V for View) to open the menu. Then press the key corresponding to the underlined letter of the desired command (such as R for Rulers).
- After a menu has been opened, you can also choose a command by pressing the arrow keys (↑, ↓, ←, and →). When a command is highlighted, press Enter to execute it.
- Picture It!'s keyboard shortcuts are listed in the Help file. To view all keyboard shortcuts, choose Help > Microsoft Picture It! Help, click the Index tab, and double-click the "keyboard shortcuts" entry. If you want to print the list as a reference, click the Options icon and choose Print from the menu that appears.

Keyboard Shortcuts: Why Bother?

No, you don't *have* to use keyboard shortcuts...ever! If you're more comfortable using the menus, you are free to continue doing so.

However, the point of keyboard shortcuts is that they save time, as well as wear and tear on your wrists. There is little point in memorizing all of a program's keyboard shortcuts. Instead, memorize only the short list of ones that you use frequently. Think of the time you can save by knowing that Del or Delete deletes the selected object—rather than having to use the mouse to move all the way to the top of the screen and choose Edit > Delete.

As a bonus, you'll find that the keyboard shortcuts for many of the most common commands (such as Print, Open, Save, Cut, Copy, and Paste) can also be used in almost every other Windows program.

Using the Common Tasks List

Depending on the function you choose from the Common Tasks list (**Figure 1.17**), it may be executed immediately, the Common Tasks pane may change and dedicate itself to the selected task, a wizard may appear to step you through the task, or a new window may open.

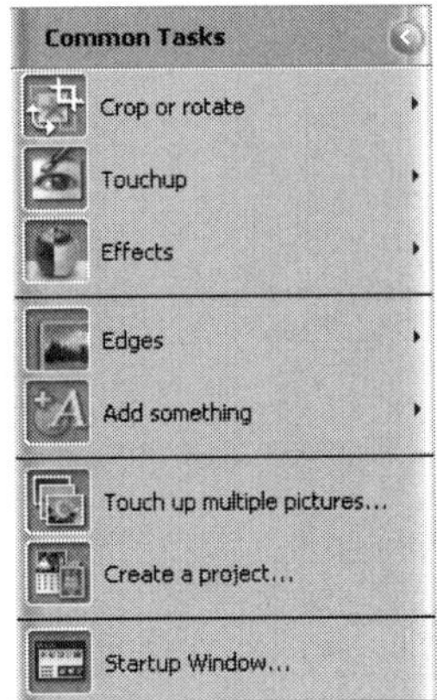

Figure 1.17 Frequently used commands can be found in the Common Tasks list.

To use the Common Tasks list:

- *Do one of the following:*
  - ▲ Click to choose a command from one of the hierarchical (pop-out) menus.

    Some commands, such as adding a shape, are executed immediately. Others, such as Touchup > Brightness and contrast, change the Common Tasks pane so it presents buttons, sliders, and other options (**Figure 1.18**). Set options as desired (the image or selected object changes automatically to match the new settings), and then click Done.

    Still others, such as Edges > Frames and mats, lead you in step-by-step fashion (**Figure 1.19**). Click Next after completing each step to your satisfaction. Click Done following the final step.
  - ▲ Choose Touch up multiple pictures (not available in Picture It! Express) to simultaneously make corrections to multiple image files.
  - ▲ Choose Create a project (not available in Picture It! Express) to step through the creation of a calendar, business card, greeting card, and the like.
  - ▲ Choose Startup Window to open the Startup Window which you normally see each time you launch Picture It!

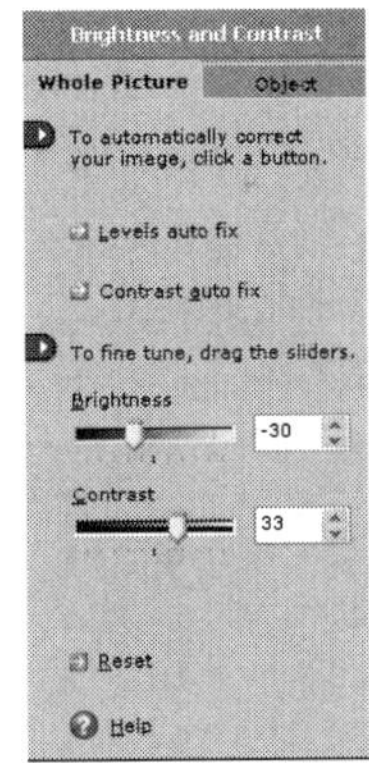

Figure 1.18 Many commands chosen from the Common Tasks list change the pane to present sets of controls.

✔ Tip

- ■ The commands in the Common Tasks list can also be chosen from Picture It!'s menus.

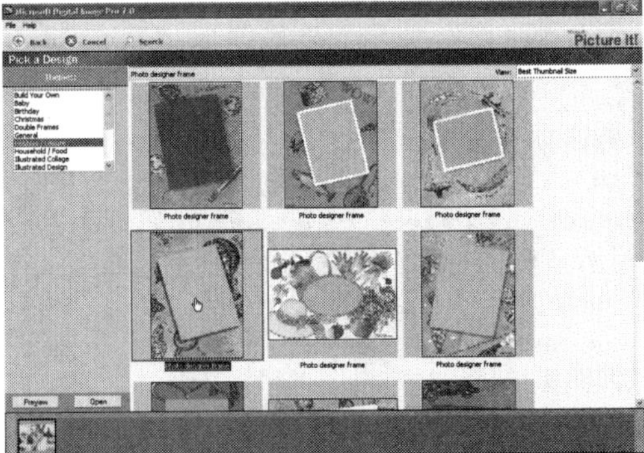

Figure 1.19 Other commands in the Common Tasks list present a multi-screen wizard that steps you through the process.

Figure 1.20 The Tray displays a thumbnail for each open project or image.

Using the Tray

The Tray (**Figure 1.20**) extends across the bottom of the workspace and displays thumbnails for all open images and projects. Whenever you open or create an image, its thumbnail is automatically added to the Tray. You can use the Tray to switch between images and projects, add an image to the current project, or load a new image without using the Open command.

To use the Tray:

- *Do any of the following:*
  - To make a different project or image the active one (in order to view or work on it), click its thumbnail in the Tray.
  - To add an open image to the current project, drag its thumbnail from the Tray into the workspace. The dragged image appears as a new layer or object in the Stack.
  - If there are more items in the Tray than can be displayed simultaneously, scroll through the Tray's contents by clicking the scroll arrow icon at either end.
  - To reorganize items in the Tray, click an image or project thumbnail, drag it to a new position, and then release the mouse button.

✔ Tip

- In addition to using the Open command, you can load a new image by dragging its file icon from your Desktop or a folder into the Tray.

Using the Stack

The Stack displays a thumbnail for each object and layer in the currently active project. (You'll learn more about working with layers in Chapter 6.) The Stack makes it easy for you to select and reorganize the images, shapes, and text strings you've added to a project. As you add items to a project, each one automatically appears as a new element in the Stack (**Figure 1.21**). Because each newly added item is a separate layer in your project, you can edit or delete them without fear of altering items on other layers.

Note that each new item creates a new layer *above* the previous item/layer. Thus, the higher an item is displayed in the Stack, the nearer it is to the top or front.

To use the Stack:

- *Do any of the following:*
  - ▲ To work with a particular object, click its icon in the Stack to select it. (A selected item is indicated in the Stack by a surrounding colored rectangle and a lit radio button.)
  - ▲ To change the layering order of an object, drag its icon up or down in the Stack and release the mouse button.
  - ▲ To change the ordering of items, select an item (in the Stack or the workspace) and then choose a command from the Format > Move Forward or Backward submenu (**Figure 1.22**).
  - ▲ To hide or show the Stack, choose View > Stack.
  - ▲ To delete a selected item in the Stack, press Del, Delete, or Backspace.

✔ Tip

- You can also delete or move an item in the Stack by right-clicking it and choosing a command from the menu that appears (**Figure 1.23**).

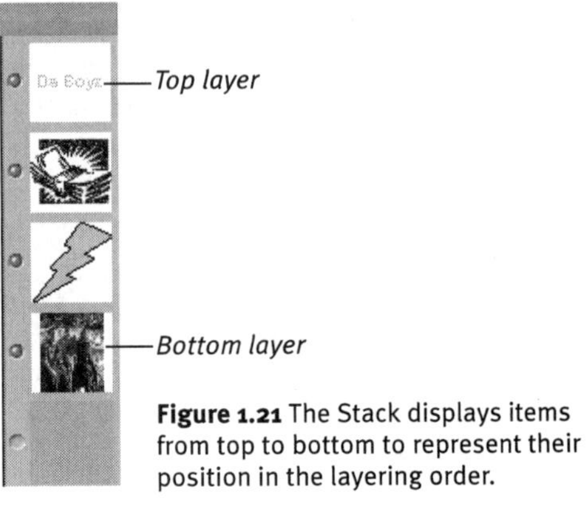

Figure 1.21 The Stack displays items from top to bottom to represent their position in the layering order.

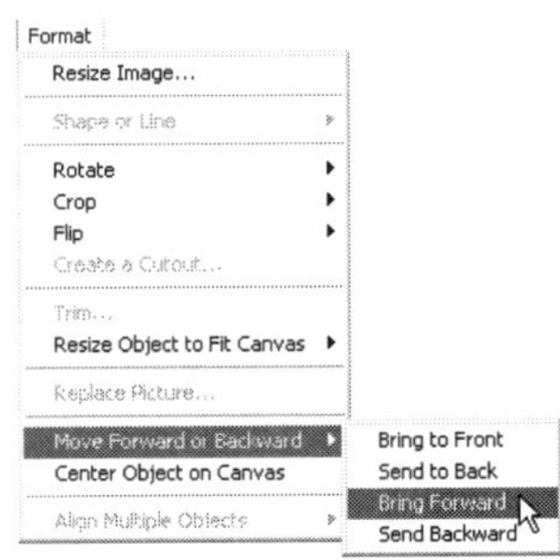

Figure 1.22 After selecting an object, you can change its layer by choosing a command from this submenu.

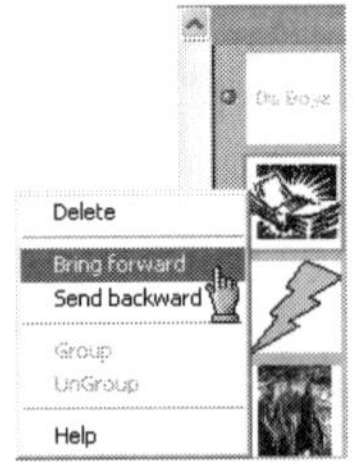

Figure 1.23 Right-click an item in the Stack to reveal this pop-up menu of useful commands.

Using the Stack

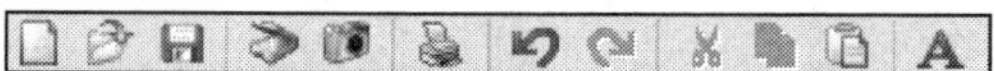

Figure 1.24 Part of a Picture It! toolbar.

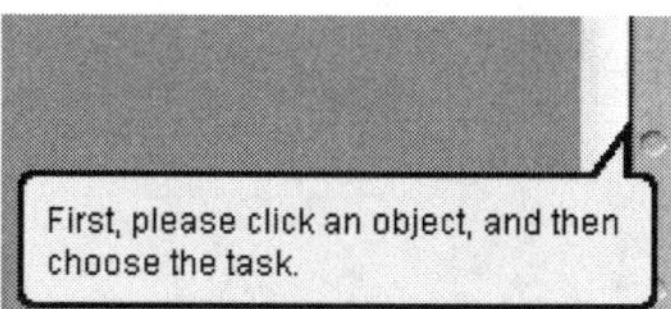

Figure 1.25 This pop-up message may appear if you neglect to select an object before clicking a particular toolbar icon.

Using the Toolbar

The toolbar (**Figure 1.24**) can be found at the top of the screen, immediately below the menu bar. Its purpose is to give you ready access to Picture It!'s most common commands.

Each icon represents a command. The icon set changes to match what you're doing at the moment, such as working with a picture or editing text.

To execute a command, click the appropriate toolbar icon. Depending on the icon clicked, a dialog box may appear, the Common Tasks list may open, or a drop-down menu may expand, for example.

✔ Tips

- To find out what a toolbar icon does, rest the cursor over it for a moment. A pop-up tooltip (such as Rotate Clockwise) will appear.
- You must select one or more objects prior to clicking certain icons. If no object is selected, some icons—such as Copy and Cut—will be temporarily grayed out (unselectable). In other cases, a pop-up balloon will appear (**Figure 1.25**).

Undoing Actions

Mistakes happen. For example, you may decide that you don't like the new brightness setting, the effect of an applied filter, or the font you've just chosen. Using a variety of techniques, you can undo your most recent action. The options available to you depend on whether or not you are correcting an action performed directly in the workspace or one guided by the Common Tasks pane. (In the latter case, the normal program menus are temporarily removed.)

To undo an action:

- *Do one of the following:*
  - If the action was made directly on material in the workspace (such as moving an item or inserting text), choose Edit > Undo or press Ctrl Z.
  - If the action was performed under the guidance of a Common Tasks pane, click Reset or the Cancel button (**Figure 1.26**).

    Click Reset to try different settings in the current pane, or click Cancel to close the pane and ignore all changes.

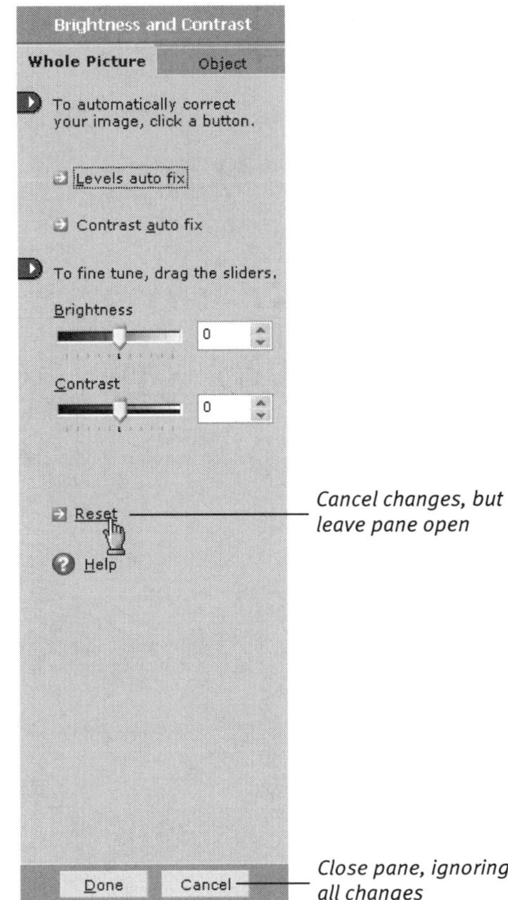

Figure 1.26 To undo actions in the Common Tasks pane, click Reset or Cancel.

✔ Tips

- After performing an action in the Common Tasks pane and then exiting by clicking the Done button, you can still undo the action by choosing Edit > Undo or pressing Ctrl Z.
- After undoing an action, you can reinstate the action by immediately choosing Edit > Redo or by pressing Ctrl Y.
- Another way to issue the Undo or Redo command is by clicking the appropriate toolbar icon.
- You can step back through your actions and make multiple corrections by issuing the Undo command as many times in a row as necessary.
- You cannot undo a Save.

Printing

Although there's no requirement that you print your photos or projects, printing is often useful. For example, when you want to give your folks a picture of your kids, a print on high-quality photo paper is often more appreciated than an email attachment.

In most Windows programs, a standard Print dialog box appears when you issue the Print command. In Picture It!, however, print options are set in the area normally reserved for the Common Tasks list (**Figure 1.27**). Changes that you make to the various print settings are instantly reflected in the preview area.

continues on next page

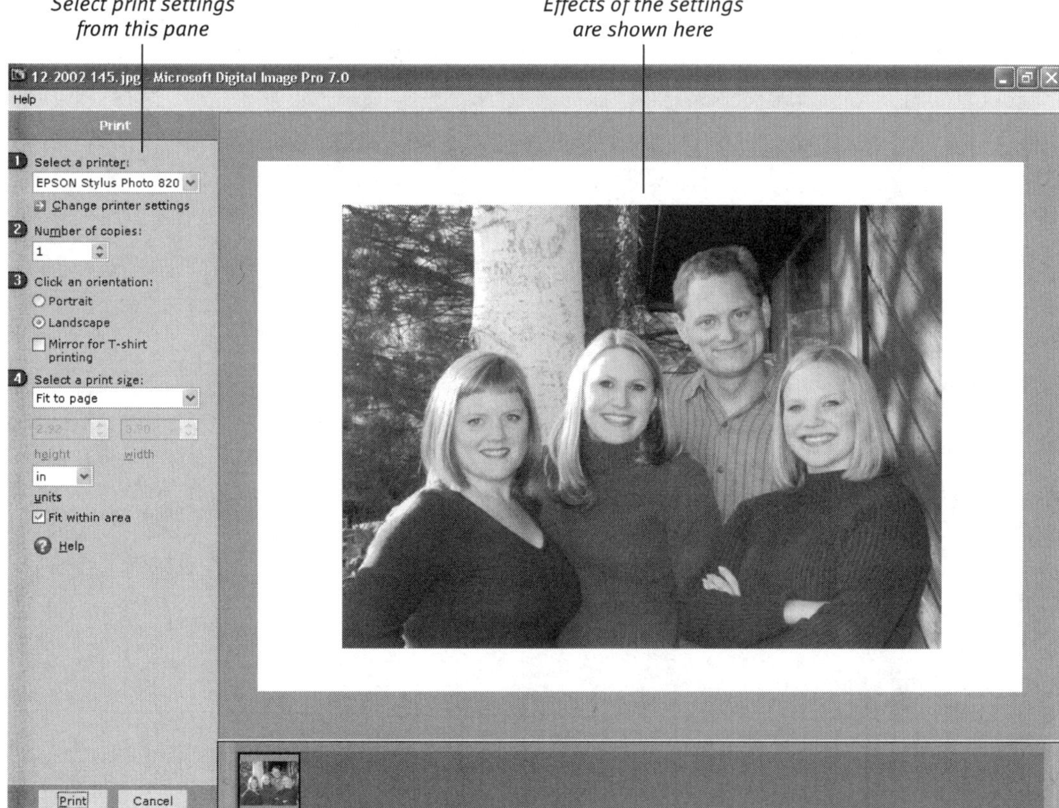

Figure 1.27 Set options in the Print wizard, and then click the Print button.

To print a picture:

1. Choose File > Print, press Ctrl P, or click the Print toolbar icon.

   The Print wizard appears (see Figure 1.27).
2. Choose a connected printer from the Select a printer list.
3. *Optional:* To modify the current printer settings, such as the print quality or the type and size of paper to be used, click Change printer settings.

   A dialog box specific to the chosen printer appears (**Figure 1.28**). Make the appropriate changes and click OK.
4. Select a printing orientation by clicking a radio button: Portrait (normal) or Landscape (sideways).
5. *Optional:* When printing on transfer paper (to iron onto a T-shirt, for example), you'll normally want to flip the picture from left to right. Click the Mirror for T-shirt printing check box.
6. Select a print size from the drop-down list.
7. To resize the image so it will fit on the paper size specified in Step 6, click the Fit within area check box.

   If the image is larger than the specified paper size and the check box isn't checked, the image's edges will be cropped as necessary to make it fit.
8. Be sure that the chosen printer is turned on and ready to print. Then click the Print button.

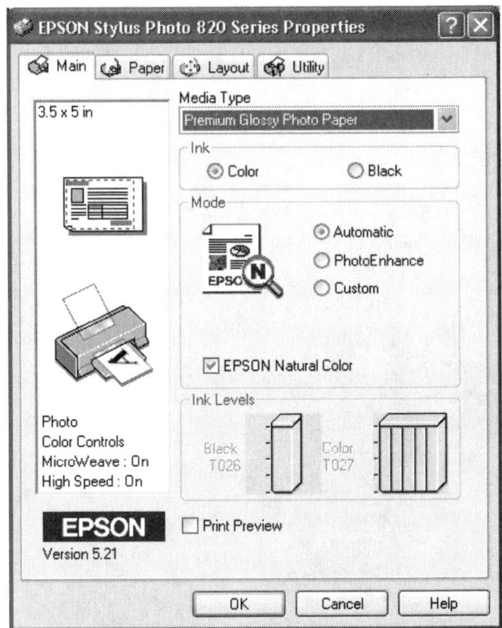

Figure 1.28 Set options for your printer and click OK. (The options vary from printer to printer.)

✔ Tip

- Picture It! can also print multiple copies of a single picture, labels, or an index that shows thumbnails and file names for a set of images. For instructions, refer to Chapter 11.

Saving Images

If you like the changes you've made to an image or project, you'll want to save them. (Unless you save your changes—either to the same file or by creating a new file—they'll disappear the moment you close the file or Picture It!) Like most programs, Picture It! provides two commands for saving files:

- *File > Save.* Used to save an edited version of an image, replacing the original file with the edited version.
- *File > Save As.* Used to save an image using a new name, file type, and/or location on disk (**Figure 1.29**).

continues on next page

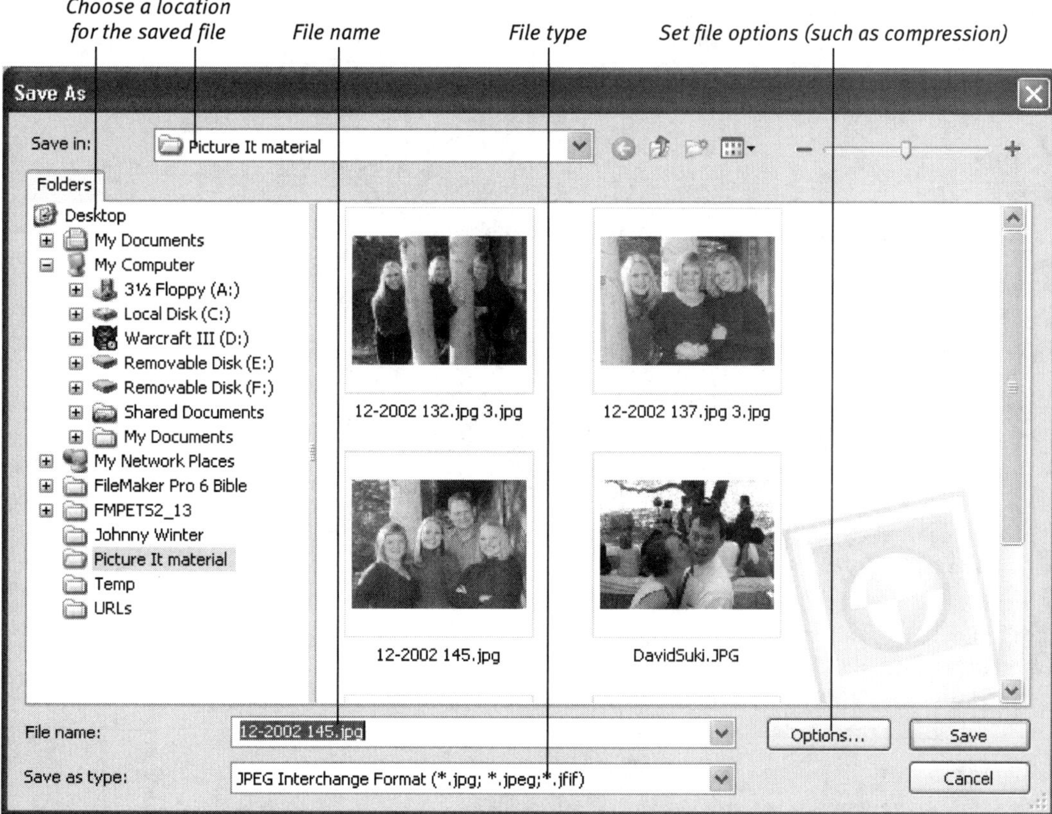

Figure 1.29 Use the Save As dialog box to rename, change the type, save to a new location, or create a backup copy of a file.

To save a file to disk:

- To save a file by *overwriting* (replacing) the original file on disk, choose File > Save, press Ctrl S, or click the Save toolbar icon.

  Use this option when you're sure you'll no longer need the original file. A save of this kind records all changes made to the file, while keeping the original file name and type. No dialog box appears; the save happens without your intervention.

- To save a file using another name, as a different file type, or to a new location on disk, choose File > Save As.

  The Save As dialog box appears (see Figure 1.29). By default, the original file name is suggested. Use the Folders section of the dialog box or the drop-down Save in list to choose a location on disk in which to save the file. You can optionally change the file name, file type, and type-related settings.

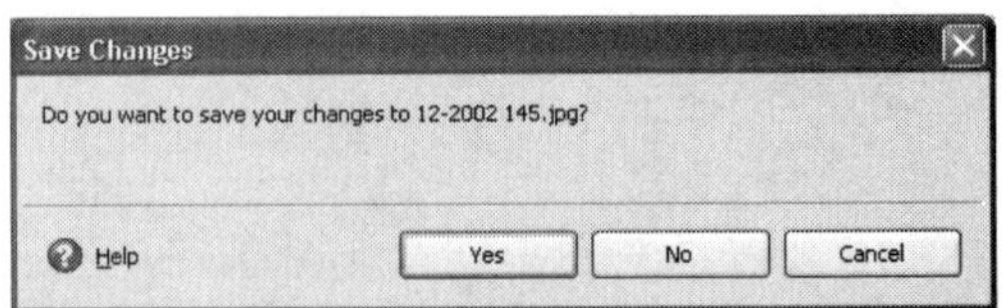

Figure 1.30 If you attempt to close a modified image without saving your changes, this dialog box appears.

✔ Tips

- If you're merely *viewing* an existing image, there's no need to save it. Just close the file.
- If you don't want to save the modifications made to a file, you don't have to do so. When you close the file or quit Picture It!, you'll be given an opportunity to save your changes (**Figure 1.30**). Click the No button.

  If you *do* wish to save the changes, click Yes. The file will be saved just as if you'd issued the File > Save command; that is, the original file will be overwritten, using the same file name, type, and disk location.
- After making a backup copy of a file with the Save a Copy As command, you may prefer to close the original file and then open the copy for editing (rather than modify your original file).
- Picture It! has other useful Save options, such as making backup copies of files. You'll learn about them in Chapter 3.

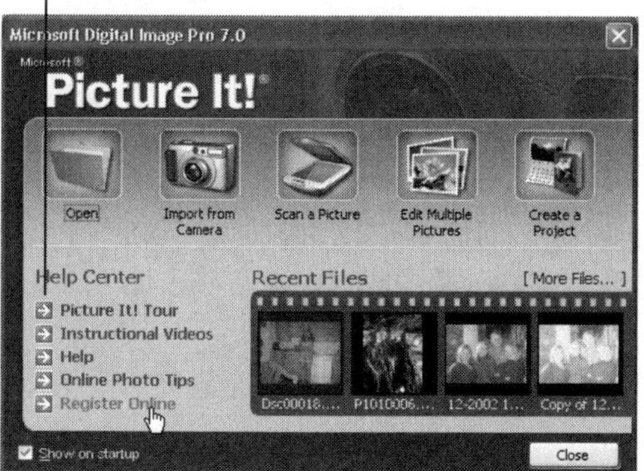

Figure 1.31 You can request help by clicking an option in the Help Center section of the Startup Window.

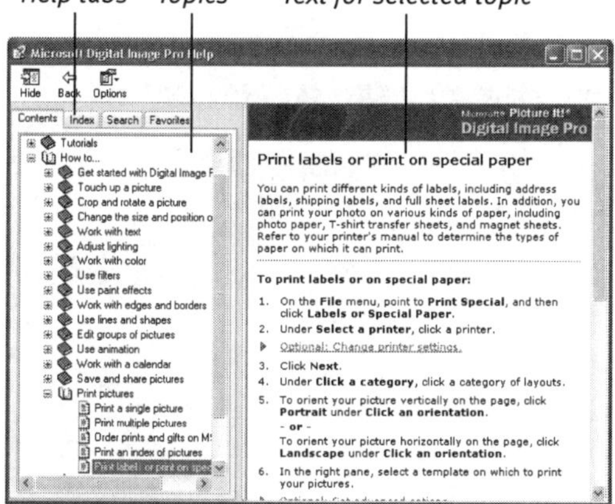

Figure 1.32 The Contents tab of the Help system.

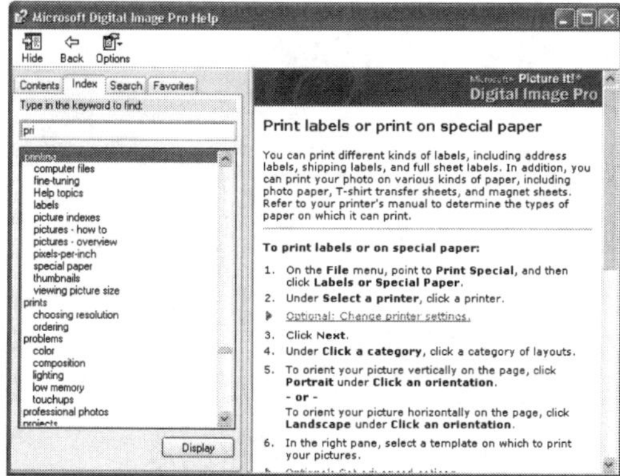

Figure 1.33 The Index tab of the Help system.

Getting Help

Picture It! provides several sources of help for using the program and creating better pictures. Help can be summoned either from the Startup Window (**Figure 1.31**) or from the Help menu. Help options include the following:

- *Microsoft Picture It! Help.* Picture It's Help file/system.
- *Picture It! Tour.* A brief introduction to Picture It!'s features.
- *Instructional Videos.* Video tutorials for some basic editing procedures.
- *Online Photo Tips and Picture It! on the Web.* Helpful tips from the MSN Web site.

Most of your help, however, will come from the Help system. To open Help, choose Help > Microsoft Picture It! Help, press F1, or click the Help icon in the Startup Window. The Help window appears (**Figure 1.32**), open to the tab you most recently used.

The Help System tabs are as follows:

- **Contents tab.** This tab (see Figure 1.32) displays information organized by topic.

  Click plus (+) and minus (-) icons to expand or collapse topics, click a topic to view its Help text, and click underlined Help text to view definitions of terms and play videos.

- **Index tab.** This tab (**Figure 1.33**) displays an alphabetical list of terms in the Help file.

  Scroll through the list, select the entry that interests you, and click Display. To quickly move to an entry, begin typing a keyword in the text box. As you type, the window scrolls to highlight a possible matching term.

  After selecting an entry and clicking Display, a Topics Found dialog box sometimes appears and lists several possible topics for you to explore. Highlight the topic you want to read about and click Display.

continues on next page

- **Search tab.** Use this tab (**Figure 1.34**) to search for all matching entries in Help.

  Type a keyword in the text box, and click the List Topics button to display all possible matching Help topics. Select a topic and click Display.

- **Favorites tab.** Help topics that you want to refer to later can be saved on this tab (**Figure 1.35**) as *favorites*.

  While viewing a useful Help topic, click the Favorites tab and then click the Add button to save the topic as a favorite. To later view this topic again, switch to the Favorites tab, highlight the topic, and click the Display button. To delete a favorite you no longer wish to save, highlight it and click Remove.

✔ Tips

- You can collapse the tab section of the window by clicking the Hide icon at the top of the window. To restore the tabs, click Show.
- Click the Back icon to step back through recently viewed Help screens. After clicking Back several times, you can move forward through the same Help screens by choosing Forward from the Options drop-down menu.
- To print the current Help topic, choose Print from the Options drop-down menu.
- To print only some of the Help text rather than the entire topic, highlight the text, choose Print from the Options drop-down menu, and click the Selection radio button in the Page Range area of the Print dialog box (**Figure 1.36**).
- Context-sensitive help is available when conducting wizard-directed procedures, such as printing or applying a filter. Just click the Help icon.
- You can resize the Help window.

Enter a keyword

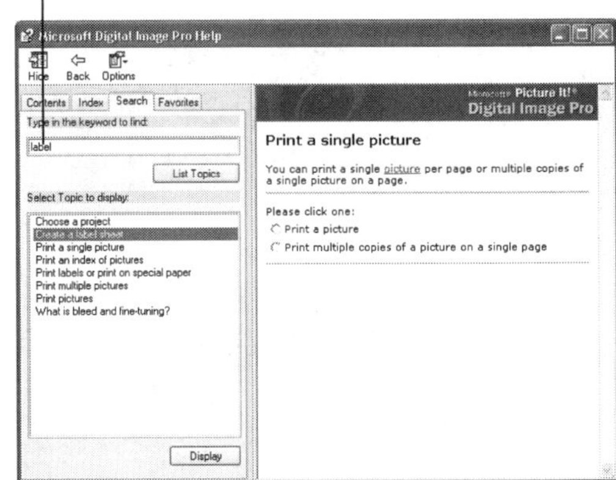

Figure 1.34 The Search tab of the Help system.

Saved favorites

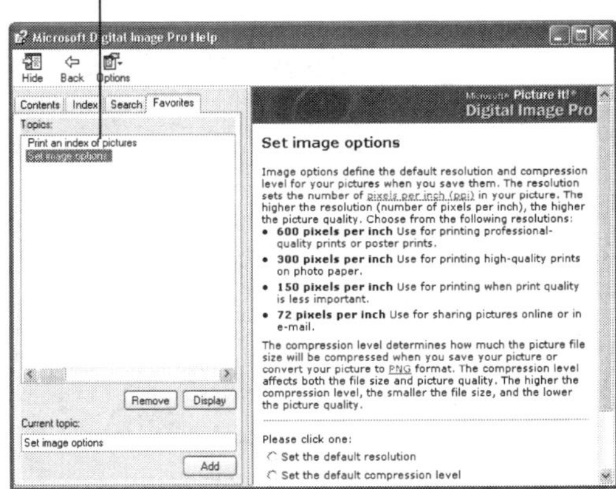

Figure 1.35 The Favorites tab of the Help system.

Print selected text

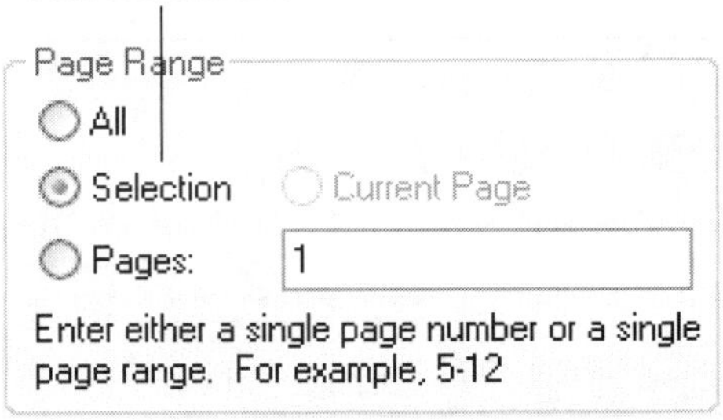

Page Range

All

Selection Current Page

Pages: 1

Enter either a single page number or a single page range. For example, 5-12

Figure 1.36 You can print selected Help text by clicking the Selection radio button.

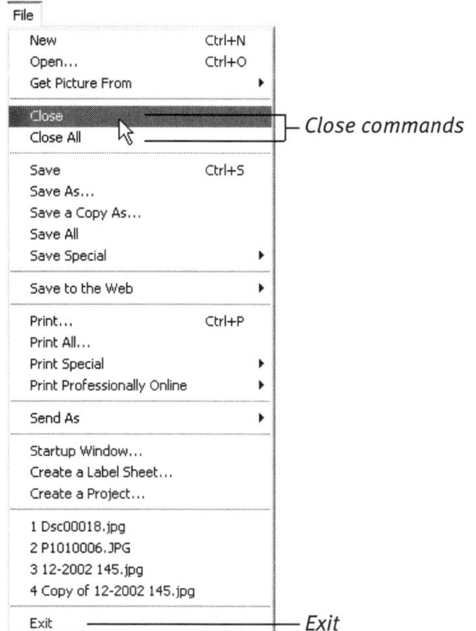

Figure 1.37 Commands for closing files and quitting are found in the File menu.

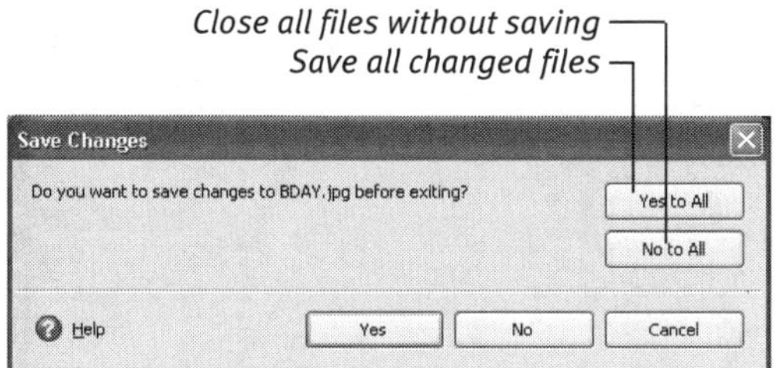

Figure 1.38 To save changes to all open files, click Yes to All. To step through all open files one at a time, click Yes or No for each one.

Closing Files and Quitting

When you're done editing or viewing a picture or project, you're free to close the file. Closing a file clears it from the Tray and frees memory for working with other pictures.

Similarly, when you're through using Picture It!, you can quit or exit the program. The memory that was reserved for running Picture It! will then be available to your computer for running other programs.

To close a file:

◆ *Do one of the following:*
  - ▲ Make the file *active* (the one that's currently displayed) by clicking its icon in the Tray. Then choose File > Close (**Figure 1.37**).
  - ▲ To simultaneously close all open files, choose File > Close All.

To quit Picture It!:

1. *Do one of the following:*
   - ▲ Choose File > Exit or press Alt F4.
   - ▲ Click the close box (the large X in the upper-right corner of the window).
2. If any of the open images have been modified, a Save Changes dialog box will appear (**Figure 1.38**). Click buttons to specify the changed files you want to save.

✔ Tips

- Documents in most programs generally have a close box (an X) in the upper-right corner that you can click to close the window. Picture It!, however, doesn't work this way. To close an image file, you must choose the File > Close command.
- You're never *required* to close image files. If memory isn't an issue and you're able to manage all of the currently open files, feel free to leave them open.

2

Opening and Importing Images

Unless you are content with working with the bundled clip art, shapes, and photos, you can't really *create* images in Picture It! Virtually everything that you'll do in the program will require you to obtain and open images from other sources.

In this chapter, you'll learn how to open or import images:

- From your hard disk, CDs, and other types of drives and media
- From the Gallery
- From a digital camera or card reader
- From a connected scanner
- From the MSN Photos Web site
- Downloaded from the Web or newsgroups
- Received as email attachments

From Disk

The bulk of your images are likely already on your computer's hard drive—either downloaded from a camera, created from scans, received from friends as email attachments, or downloaded from the Web. Even if you downloaded or scanned some images directly into Picture It!, part of the process is to save the images on disk. Later, you may want to open the same images again—to view them, include them in projects, or to do some additional editing.

To open an image file from disk:

1. *Do one of the following:*
   - ▲ Click the Open icon or [More Files] in the Startup Window (**Figure 2.1**).
   - ▲ Choose File > Open (or press Ctrl O).

   The File Browser window appears (**Figure 2.2**), open to the folder you most recently used in Picture It!
2. Click items in the Folders area of the File Browser to select the drive and folder that contains the image you want to open.
3. Select the image's thumbnail or file name and then click Open. (You can also open the file by double-clicking its thumbnail or file name.)

✔ Tips

- To open an image you've recently worked on, click its thumbnail in the Recent Files area of the Startup Window or choose its file name from the list at the bottom of the File menu (**Figure 2.3**).
- To simultaneously open multiple files from the same folder, Ctrl-click each one in the File Browser before you click Open.
- To insert an additional image using the Common Tasks list, choose Add something > Picture from my computer.

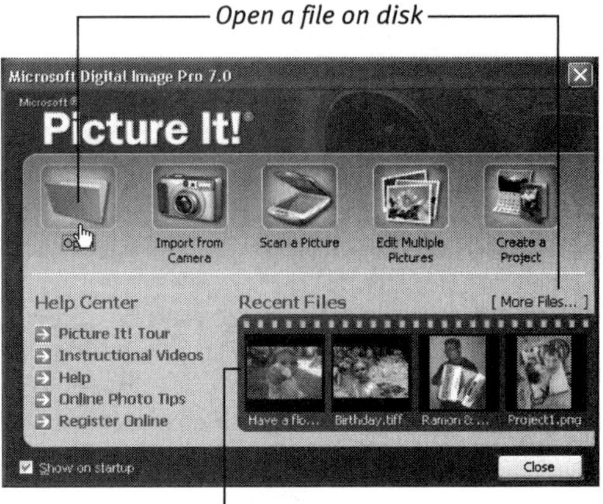

Figure 2.1 You can open files from the Startup Window.

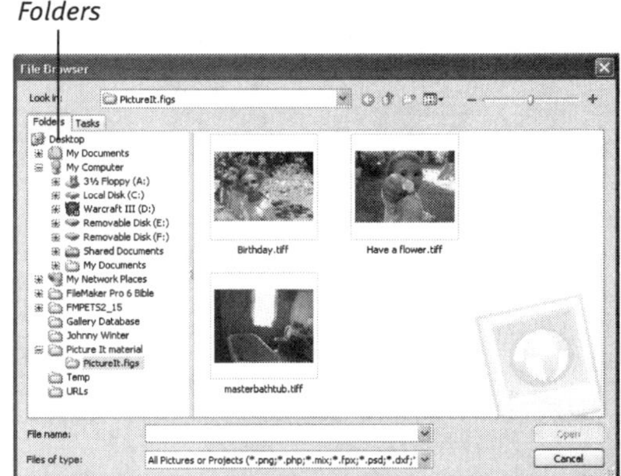

Figure 2.2 During a session, the most common way to open files is to use the File Browser.

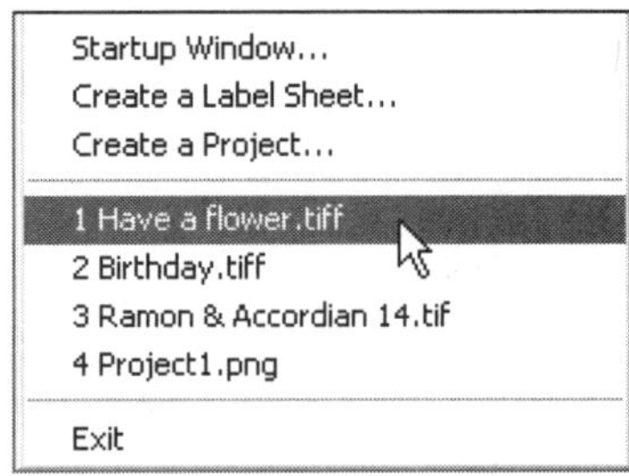

Figure 2.3 Recently opened files are listed at the bottom of the File menu.

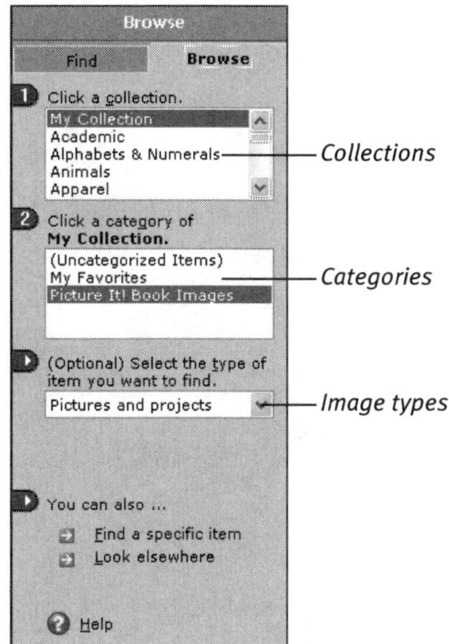

Figure 2.4 Use the Browse tab to visually browse through Gallery images.

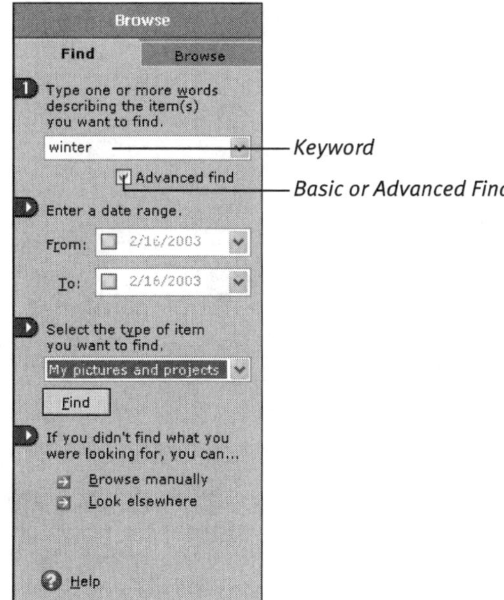

Figure 2.5 Use the Find tab to search for a specific image.

From the Gallery

The Gallery is a Picture It! feature for organizing your images, as well as the bundled photos and clip art. When you add an image to the Gallery, its location on disk is noted—as well as the categories and keywords you've assigned to it—in order to help you find the image later.

For instructions on adding images to the Gallery and creating new categories, see Chapter 3.

To open items from the Gallery:

1. Choose File > Get Picture From > Gallery.
   The Browse pane appears (**Figure 2.4**).
2. Select a collection and a category.
   Items that have not been assigned a category are listed as *(Uncategorized Items).*
3. *Optional:* Select the type of image you wish to find from the drop-down menu.
   Matching images are displayed in the right side of the window.
4. *Do one of the following:*
   - Select the image you want to open, and click the Open button at the bottom of the pane. (To select multiple images, Ctrl-click them.)
   - To browse through images stored on disk or CD-ROM, click Look elsewhere.
   - If you don't know the collection or category in which an image was stored, you can perform a Find or Advanced Find. Click Find a specific item or click the Find tab. Enter criteria (**Figure 2.5**), click Find, select the item(s) you want to open, and click the Open button at the bottom of the pane.

✔ Tip

- To change the size of the thumbnails, choose an option from the View drop-down menu (in the upper-right corner of the window).

From a Digital Camera or Card Reader

If you have a digital camera, you're probably familiar with the process of downloading your photos to your PC. As is the case with most image-editing programs, you can download photos directly into Picture It! The means of accomplishing this varies according to the type of digital camera you have. If your camera has TWAIN or WIA support or operates as a virtual disk drive, photos can be downloaded into Picture It! If your camera can only download photos using its own software, you can use Picture It! to save the photos to disk and then open them as you would any other file.

Note that in this discussion, card readers are treated the same as cameras. Most work as virtual disk drives, presenting a new mounted volume that contains your photos. Be sure your camera or card reader is connected and on before issuing the Digital Camera command.

To open photos from a digital camera or a card reader:

1. Choose File > Get Picture From > Digital Camera, or click Import from Camera in the Startup Window.

   The Digital Camera pane appears (**Figure 2.6**).

2. Select your camera, card reader, or virtual drive from the list.

   A dialog box may appear (**Figure 2.7**), asking what you want Windows to do.

3. Choose the option to Open and edit the pictures with Picture It!, and then click OK.

   If Picture It! isn't running, it launches.

4. In the Digital Camera pane, select one of the following options:

   ▲ To open the downloaded photos for normal editing, click the No radio button.

   ▲ To open the photos in the Mini Lab for batch editing, click Yes. (Note that Picture It! Express does not have a Mini Lab.)

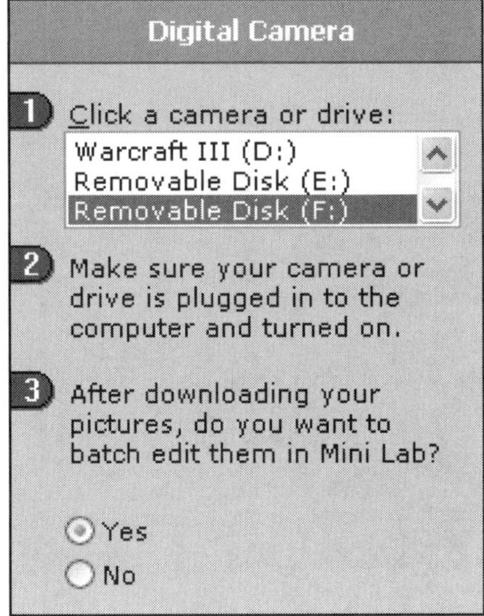

Figure 2.6 Set photo download options in the Digital Camera pane.

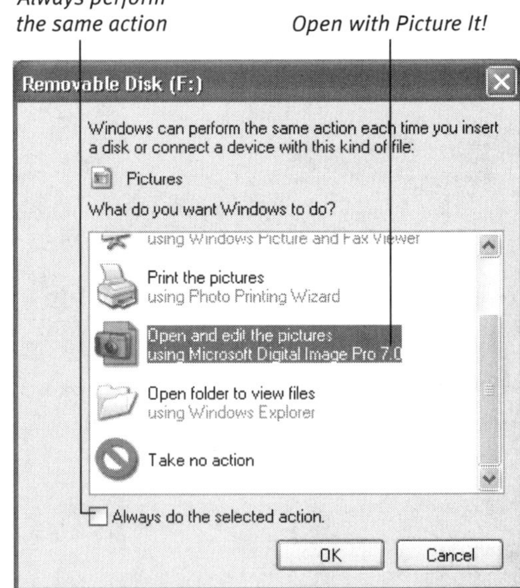

Figure 2.7 Elect to open the photos in Picture It! To always perform this operation when a connected camera or card reader is detected by Windows, click the check box at the bottom of the dialog box.

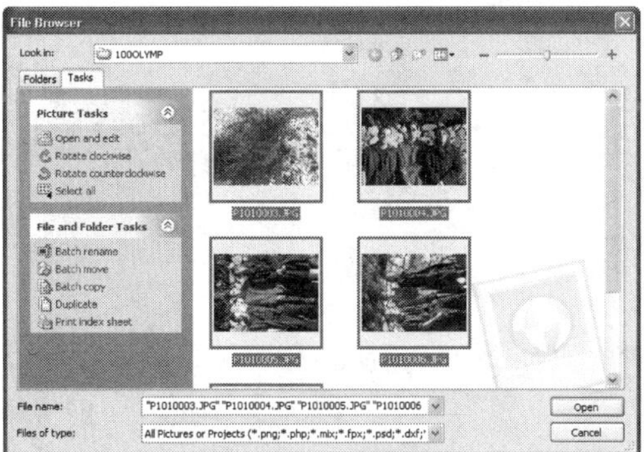

Figure 2.8 Select the photos to download and click the Open button.

5. Click the Download button at the bottom of the pane.

   The File Browser appears, displaying the stored photos (**Figure 2.8**).

6. Select the photos to download. To select multiple photos, press Ctrl A (to select all photos) or Ctrl-click the individual photos.

7. Click the Open button.

   The photos are downloaded to your PC.

To open photos from a WIA- or TWAIN-compliant camera:

1. Perform Steps 1–4 of the previous step list.

2. Click the Automatic Download button.

3. Click the Download button.

   The stored photos are displayed in the workspace.

4. *Do one of the following:*

   ▲ To download all photos in the camera, click Download all pictures.

   ▲ To download only selected photos, drag them from the workspace into the Tray.

5. Click the Done button.

To open photos from other cameras:

1. Perform Steps 1–4 of the first step list.

2. Click My camera software.

3. Click the Download button.

   The camera software launches.

4. Use the camera software to download all or selected photos to your hard disk. Close the camera software when you're done.

5. Choose File > Open, select the downloaded photos that you want to work with, and click Open.

   The selected photos are added to the Tray.

Older Cameras and Picture It!

Older cameras often rely on a serial cable to transfer pictures to your computer. But serial transfers of large digital images can take forever!

If you have a computer that has USB 1.0 or 2.0 ports, you can buy an inexpensive 6-in-1 card reader that connects to a USB port. Such readers support most of the common digital camera memory cards, enabling an inserted card to appear to Windows (or a Mac) as a temporary disk drive. As a bonus, a card reader will also enable you to load your photos *directly* into Picture It!

From a Scanner

Regardless of whether you have a TWAIN- or WIA-compatible scanner or you must use your scanner's included software, you can scan images directly into Picture It! by following the steps below.

To scan an image into Picture It!:

1. Turn on the scanner and place the image to be scanned on the scanner's bed.
2. Choose File > Get Picture From > Scanner or click the Scan a Picture icon in the Startup Window (**Figure 2.9**).
3. Select your scanner from the list.
4. *Do one of the following:*
   - ▲ If you have a TWAIN/WIA-compatible scanner, select Automatic Scan.
   - ▲ For other types of scanners, select My scanner software.
5. Click the Scan button.
6. When the scan has finished, click Done.

✔ Tip

- If you prefer, you can use the software that came with your scanner to perform the scans. Regardless of whether you scan from within Picture It! or using another program, after a scanned image has been saved to disk, it can be opened in Picture It! using the File > Open command.

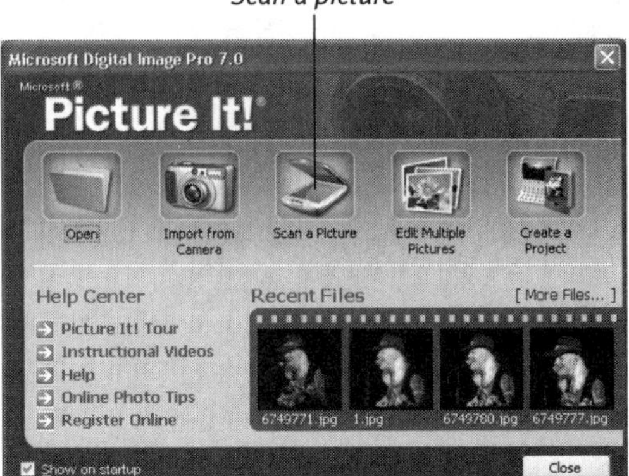

Figure 2.9 If the Startup Window is open, you can initiate a scan by clicking the Scan a Picture icon.

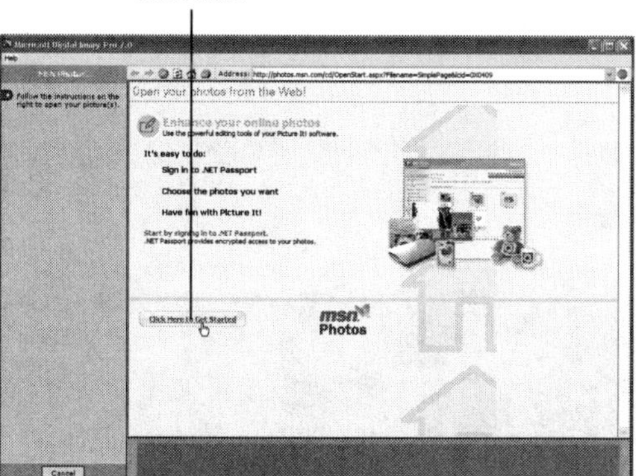

Figure 2.10 In the MSN Photos wizard, click the button to begin the process.

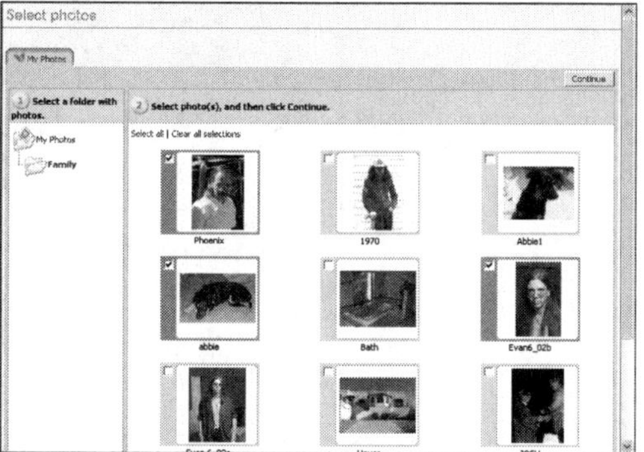

Figure 2.11 To select photos for downloading to your computer, click each one's check box.

From MSN Photos

Photos that you've stored at the MSN Photos Web site can be downloaded to your computer and opened for viewing, editing, or printing in Picture It!

For instructions on saving photos to MSN Photos, see Chapter 3.

To open pictures from MSN Photos:

1. Choose File > Get Picture From > MSN Photos.

   Using your active Internet connection, you are automatically connected to the MSN Photos site.

2. Click the button labeled Click Here to Get Started (**Figure 2.10**).

   You may also be asked to log into your Hotmail or .NET Passport account.

3. If it isn't already selected, click to select the folder that contains the pictures you want to open.

   The pictures contained in the folder are displayed.

4. Click the check box for each photo you want to open (**Figure 2.11**), and then click Continue.

   The selected photos are downloaded to your computer and added as new items to the Tray.

From the Web or Newsgroups

The World Wide Web and Internet newsgroups are both plentiful sources of images. You can save such images using appropriate commands in your browser or newsgroup reader, respectively. After downloading images from either source, you can open, view, edit, and print them with Picture It! (Note that many—if not *most*—of the images on the Internet are protected by copyright laws.)

The specific commands and procedures for saving images may vary somewhat, depending on your particular browser and newsgroup reader. As examples, I'll show you how to save files using Internet Explorer (browser) and Microsoft Outlook Express (newsgroup reader).

To save images from Web pages:

1. In Internet Explorer, open the Web page that contains the image you want to save.
2. *Do one of the following:*
   - ▲ Left-click the image and drag it onto the Desktop.

     A copy of the image is automatically saved on the Desktop using the original file name.
   - ▲ Right-click the image and choose Save Picture As from the pop-up menu that appears (**Figure 2.12**). In the Save Picture dialog box (**Figure 2.13**), select a drive and folder in which to save the image, change or accept the current file name and/or file type, and click the Save button.

   The saved image can now be opened in Picture It! with the File > Open command.

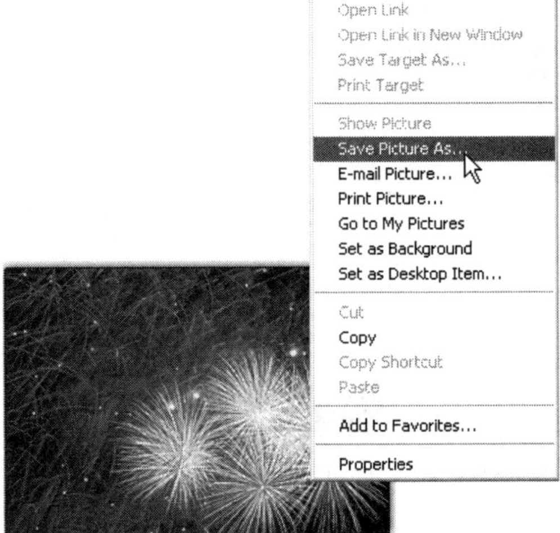

Figure 2.12 To save a Web image on your PC, right-click the image and choose Save Picture As.

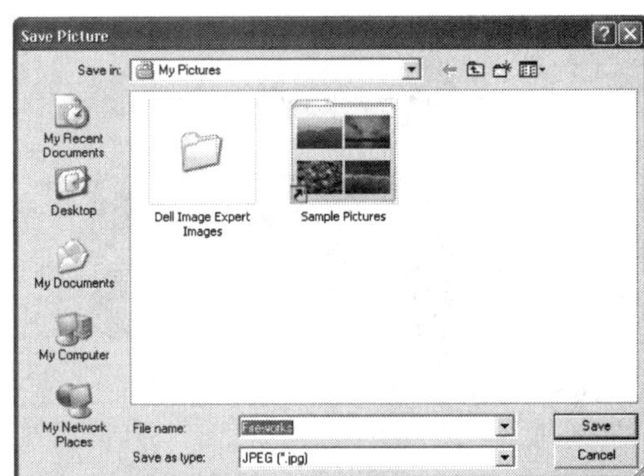

Figure 2.13 Select a location for the picture, change its name and/or file type (if you like), and click Save.

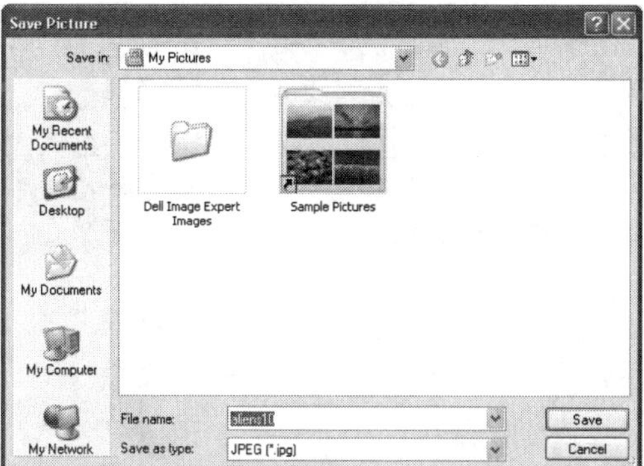

Figure 2.14 Select a folder, edit the file name and/or change the file type, and click the Save button.

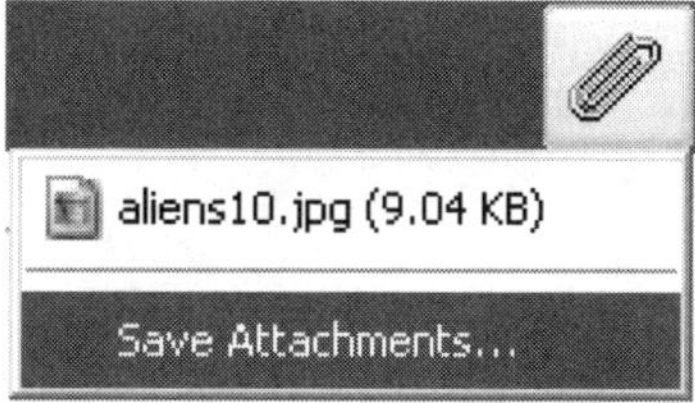

Figure 2.15 Click the paper clip icon in the Preview pane and choose Save Attachments.

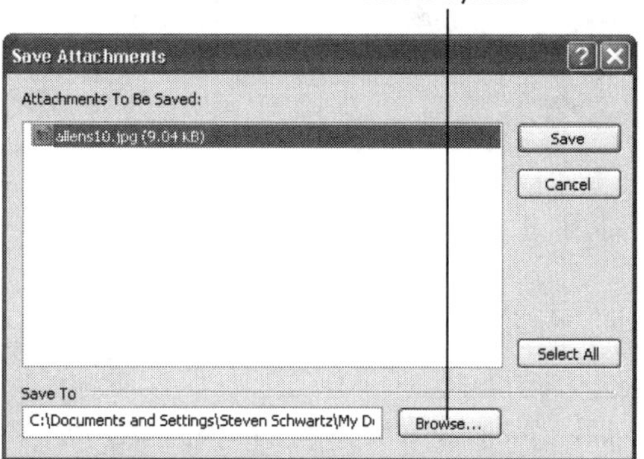

Figure 2.16 Select the attachment (or attachments) that you want to save, select a folder in which to save, and click the Save button.

To save images from newsgroups:

1. In the message pane of Outlook Express, select a message header that contains an attached image. (Attachments are denoted by a paper clip icon.)
2. *Do one of the following:*
   - ▲ If the image is displayed in the message window, right-click it and choose Save Picture As from the pop-up menu that appears.

     The Save Picture dialog box appears (**Figure 2.14**). Select a destination drive and folder for the image, edit the file name (if desired), and click the Save button.
   - ▲ Click the paper clip icon at the top of the *Preview pane* (the bottom half of the window) and choose Save Attachments from the pop-up menu that appears (**Figure 2.15**). Alternatively, you can choose File > Save Attachments.

     The Save Attachments dialog box appears (**Figure 2.16**). Highlight the attachments you wish to save, click the Browse button to select a destination folder, and then click Save.
   - ▲ Open the message in its own window. Drag the attachment from the Attach box onto the Desktop.

   The saved image can now be opened in Picture It! with the File > Open command.

From Email

Most of us receive loads of pictures via email. Those pictures can be saved to disk and then opened, edited, and printed in Picture It! The process of saving an email attachment to disk depends on which email program you use. As an example, here's how to do it in Microsoft Outlook, the Microsoft Office email client.

To save an attachment from email:

1. Double-click an email message header to open the message in its own window.

   Outlook displays a paper clip icon in the header of any message that contains an attachment.

2. *Do one of the following:*

   ▲ If the image is displayed in the message, right-click it (**Figure 2.17**) and choose Save Picture As from the pop-up menu.

   ▲ In the Attachments line at the bottom of the message header (**Figure 2.18**), right-click the attachment and choose Save As from the pop-up menu that appears.

   ▲ Choose File > Save Attachments. If the message contains multiple attachments, the Save All Attachments dialog box appears. Highlight the attachments you wish to save and then click OK.

   ▲ Click and drag the attachment onto the Desktop.

   In all but the last case, the Save Attachment dialog box appears (**Figure 2.19**).

3. Navigate to the drive and folder in which you want to save the file, edit the file name and/or type (if desired), and click Save.

   The saved image can now be opened in Picture It! with the File > Open command.

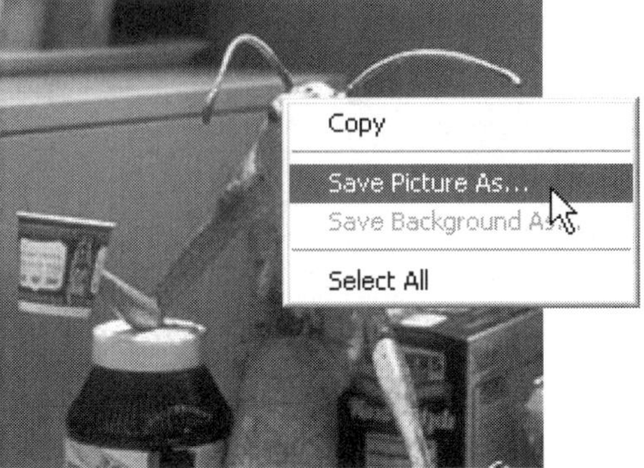

Figure 2.17 To save an image that's displayed in an email message, right-click it and choose Save Picture As.

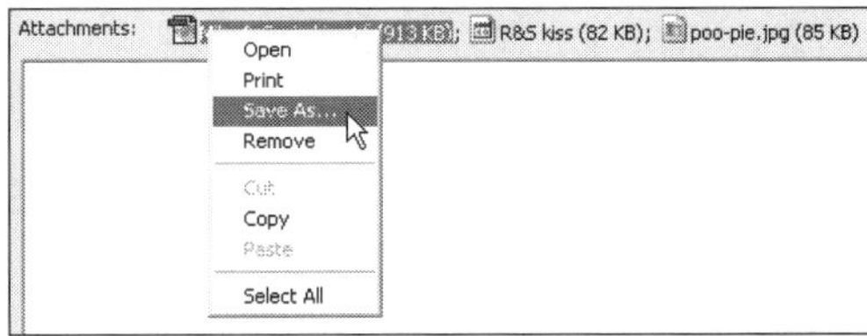

Figure 2.18 You can right-click an attachment and choose Save As.

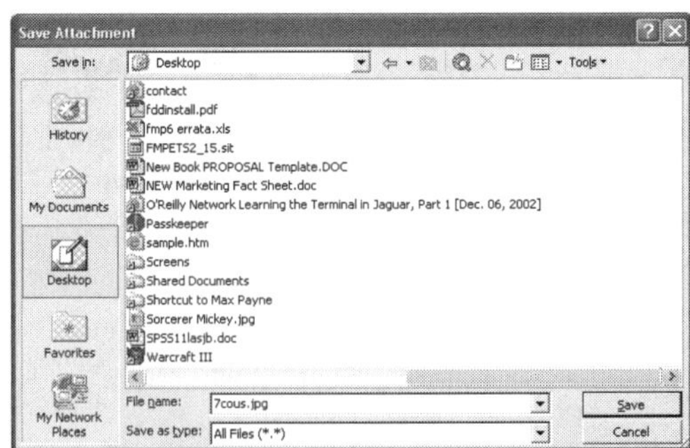

Figure 2.19 Select a folder, edit the file name and/or change the file type, and click the Save button.

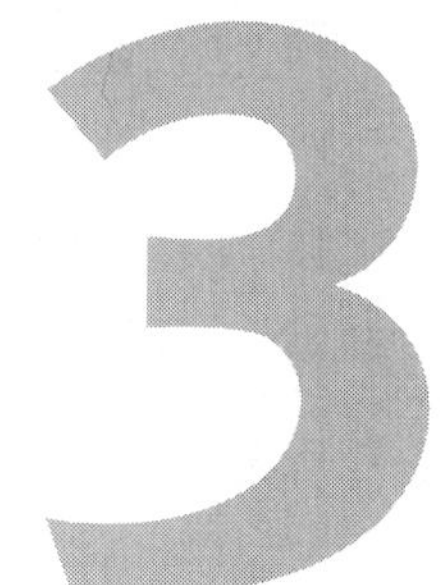

File Handling

File handling is a major concern when working with image files. In addition to archiving files so you can find them later, you'll have to choose the *right* file type for each project. For example, in desktop publishing, TIFF is a common format. But when preparing pictures for emailing to friends or posting on the Web, JPEG is the usual format. When saving images and projects in Picture It!, you can freely change the file format and set other useful options, such as compression.

In this chapter, you'll learn about the following:

- The different types of graphic file formats
- How compression affects file size and image quality
- Saving files and how you can change a file's name, type, location, and other options
- The various methods of creating backup copies of your image files
- Using the MSN Photos Web site to store copies of your important photos
- Creating Windows wallpaper from your favorite photos
- Moving and renaming files
- Using Picture It!'s Gallery to help organize your images and projects

About File Formats

Every computer data file—whether it's a text, word processing, spreadsheet, or graphics file—has its own format. A *format* is an encoding method that allows the data to be read and interpreted by a program. Some formats are *proprietary* (created for a particular program). Others, such as many of the popular graphics formats, were designed as general-purpose formats rather than being specific to one program.

There are dozens of graphic file formats in use today. Luckily, programs such as Picture It! can open most types of graphic files. You can view and edit images without being overly concerned about the programs (or even the computing platform) in which they originated. Picture It! can also save files in a variety of formats—should you decide that the original format doesn't meet your needs. See **Table 3.1** for a list of the file types that Picture It! can open and the formats in which it can save.

Table 3.1

Supported File Formats

File Format	File Extension	Open	Save
Adobe Photoshop	.psd	◆	
AutoCAD	.dxf	◆	
CorelDRAW	.cdr	◆	
Enhanced Metafile	.emf	◆	◆
Flashpix Format	.fpx	◆	
GIF (Graphics Interchange Format)	.gif	◆	◆
Home Publishing (Microsoft Graphics Studio Home Publishing)	.php	◆	
JPEG (Joint Photographic Experts Group)	.jpg	◆	◆
Kodak Photo CD	.pcd	◆	
Micrografx Designer	.drw	◆	
MIX	.mix	◆	
PC Paintbrush	.pcx	◆	◆
PICT (an old Macintosh graphics format)	.pct	◆	
PNG (Portable Network Graphics)	.png	◆	◆
PNG Plus (Portable Network Graphics with layer support)	.png	◆	◆
Targa	.tga	◆	◆
TIFF (Tagged Image File Format)	.tif	◆	◆
Windows bitmap	.bmp	◆	◆
Windows Metafile	.wmf	◆	

Macintosh Files and Extensions

The Windows and Macintosh operating systems use two very different methods of identifying file types. On Windows, files must have a file extension appended to the file name, such as .doc or .jpg. Unless a file has an appropriate extension, Windows has no idea what kind of data the file contains. On a Mac, information about the file type and creating program are embedded in the file itself; no extension is necessary.

In order to maintain cross-platform compatibility, some Mac users (and some Mac programs) make an effort to add the appropriate Windows extension when creating or saving files. However, it's likely that you will occasionally receive a Mac file without an extension. To open it in Picture It!, you must rename the file by adding the correct extension. To rename a file, right-click it and choose Rename. Then add the extension, such as .jpg.

About File Compression

Some Picture It! supported file formats allow you to compress files, making them smaller. Compressed files take less room on disk, print quicker, appear sooner when placed on a Web page, and transmit faster when sent as email attachments.

There are two types of file compression: lossless and lossy. *Lossless compression* reduces file size without losing any of the data. When working with images (especially ones that you want to print), lost data often results in reduced sharpness and detail. LZW compression—available as an option for TIFF (Tagged Image File Format) files—is a popular lossless compression.

A *lossy compression* method, on the other hand, is the best choice when you want to dramatically reduce file size and can accept a reduction in image quality. JPEG files, for example, use this type of compression. This is why JPEG is such a popular format for Web page images and emailed photos.

When working on an image that began its life in a lossy format (such as the JPEG files that most digital cameras create), you may wish to start by immediately saving it in a lossless format, such as compressed TIFF. You can freely edit and resave the image in TIFF format as many times as necessary without incurring any image degradation.

Repeatedly saving a file in a lossy format (such as JPEG), on the other hand, introduces additional compression with every save. While it might not be noticeable on a small image that's designed for the Web, it's very likely to be noticed in printed output.

✔ Tip

- Choose your file format and compression method carefully. When the output will be printed, opt for a lossless format. When it will only be viewed onscreen, a lossy format will often be fine.

Saving Files

As explained in Chapter 1, to preserve any changes you've made to an image or project, you must save them. While saving, you can also change the file's name, type, location, and other options.

To save a file to disk:

- To save a file by *overwriting* (replacing) the original file on disk, choose File > Save, press Ctrl S, or click the Save toolbar icon.

  Use this option when you've edited a file and want to replace the original with the edited version. A Save of this kind records all changes made to the file, while keeping the original file name, type, and location.

  No dialog box appears when performing a File > Save; it happens without your intervention.

- To save a file using another name, as a different file type, or to a new location on disk, choose File > Save As.

  The Save As dialog box appears (**Figure 3.1**). By default, the original file name is proposed. Use the Folders section of the dialog box or the drop-down Save in list of folders to choose a location on disk in which to save the file. You can optionally change the file name, type, and type-related settings.

✔ Tip

- To simultaneously save all open, changed files, choose File > Save All.

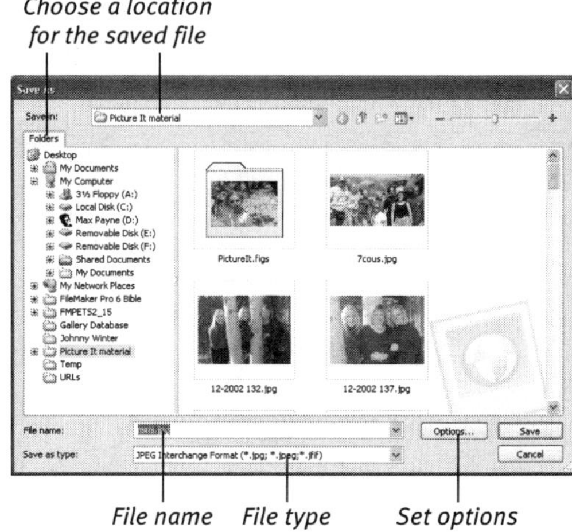

Figure 3.1 When you save a new or modified project or image, the Save As dialog box appears.

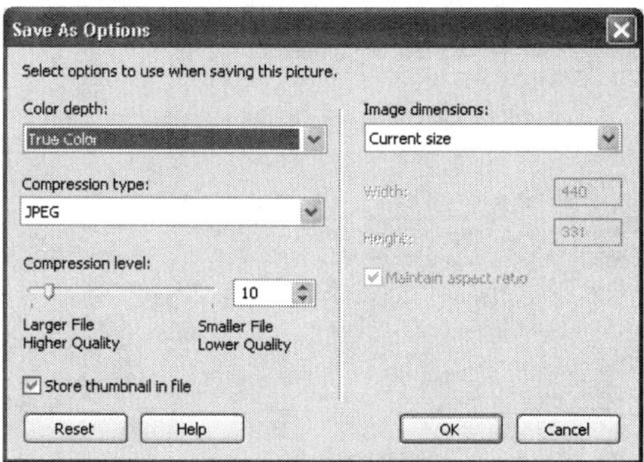

Figure 3.2 Save As options that you can set or change vary with the file type.

To view or set Save As options:

1. Click the Options button in the Save As dialog box (see Figure 3.1).

   The Save As Options dialog box appears (**Figure 3.2**). The options that you can set or change depend on the chosen file type.

2. *Do any of the following:*
   - ▲ Choose a color depth.
   - ▲ Choose a compression method and set a compression level. (The higher the compression level, the smaller the file size and the lower the quality will be.)
   - ▲ Decide whether a thumbnail image will be stored in the file. (When this option is not checked, the operating system will be required to create the thumbnail each time it's needed.)
   - ▲ Change the size of the image by choosing an option from the Image dimensions drop-down list.

3. Click OK to return to the Save As dialog box, and then click Save.

✔ Tips

- You can always make an image smaller, but it's generally not wise to enlarge one without also reducing the resolution. To see how this works, issue the Format > Resize Image command, choose different resolutions, and watch how the image size changes.
- When resizing an image to a custom size, it's usually a good idea to check the option to Maintain aspect ratio. Otherwise, you'll end up with an image that is stretched disproportionately in one direction.

Making Backup Copies

Even if you don't want to save a particular photo for posterity, it's smart to make backup copies of your originals. After editing and resaving a photo, the changes generally can't be undone. But as long as you have a backup copy of the original, you can always start over. Both Picture It! and Windows provide ways for you to create backup copies of your files.

To make a backup copy of a file using Picture It!:

1. Open the image file in Picture It!. Make it the active image (if it isn't already) by clicking its thumbnail in the Tray.
2. Choose File > Save a Copy As.

   The Save As dialog box appears (see Figure 3.1).
3. From the Folders list or the Save in drop-down list, choose a drive and folder in which to save the copy.
4. Edit the proposed file name, if desired.
5. Click the Save button.

✔ Tip

- You can also reach the Save As dialog box to make a backup copy by choosing File > Save As. Be sure to change the file's name or location. Otherwise, the copy will merely replace the original.

To make a backup copy of a file using Windows:

1. Hold down the right mouse button and drag the file's icon to a new location.

   A pop-up menu appears when you release the mouse button (**Figure 3.3**).
2. Choose Copy Here to create the copy.

   If you dragged the icon to a different folder or disk, the copy will have the same name as the original file. If you dragged it within the same folder, it will be named Copy of *original file name*.

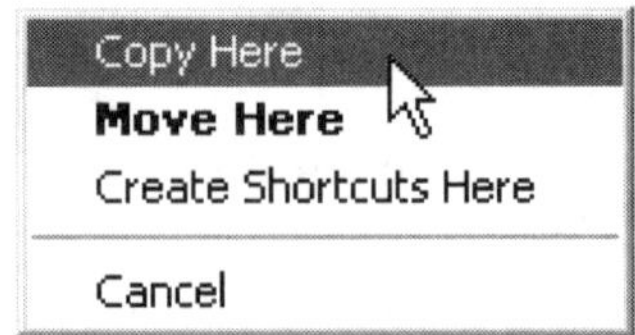

Figure 3.3 To make a copy using Windows, right-click the file icon, drag, and choose Copy Here.

Do You Remember Floppies?

As time passes, computer backup media tends to wither and die. Over the past 15 or so years, I've seen SyQuest cartridges, proprietary tapes, optical disks, and even floppies fade as viable choices for backup media. Even if the media holds up over time, what are you going to do when your backup device fails? Ever try locating a replacement for a 10-year-old tape drive?

The moral is a simple one—technology marches on and so should you. As you buy newer backup devices, you should consider restoring your old backups and making copies of them onto the new media.

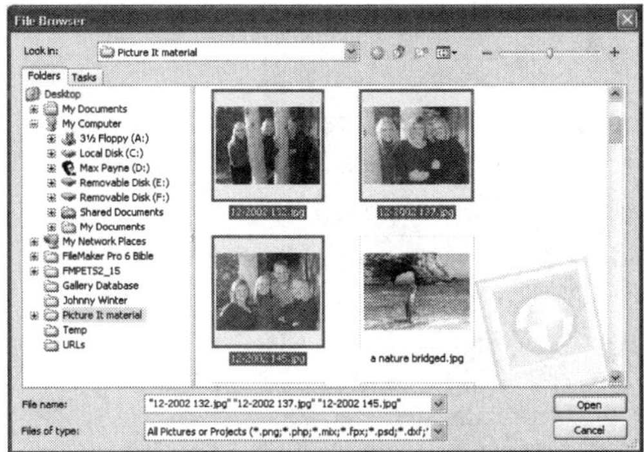

Figure 3.4 To select multiple files, Ctrl-click icons in the File Browser. (In this case, three files are selected.)

Select a destination folder

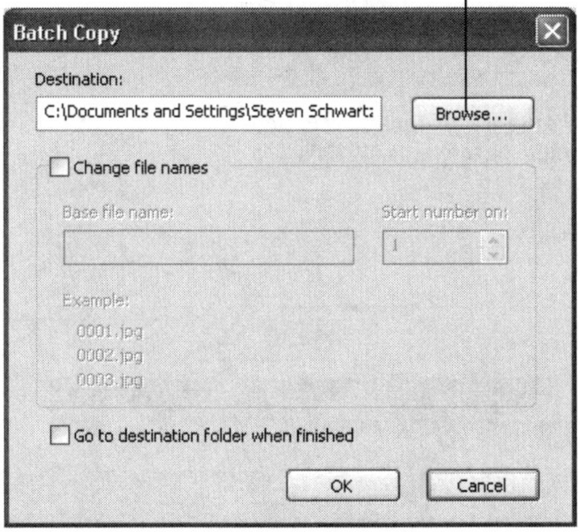

Figure 3.5 Select a destination folder for the copies.

To make backup copies of multiple files using Picture It!:

1. Choose File > Open or press Ctrl O.

   The File Browser appears.

2. From the Folders tab or the Look in drop-down list, select the folder from which you wish to copy files.

3. Hold down Ctrl and select the files you want to copy (**Figure 3.4**). To simultaneously select all files, press Ctrl A.

4. Click the Tasks tab and then click Batch copy in the File and Folder Tasks area.

   The Batch Copy dialog box appears (**Figure 3.5**).

5. Click the Browse button, select a destination folder, and then click OK.

6. In the Batch Copy dialog box, click OK.

7. Click Cancel to close the File Browser.

✔ Tip

- You can make backup copies within the same folder by selecting the files in the File Browser and then clicking Duplicate on the Tasks tab.

To make backup copies of multiple files using Windows:

1. Select the files by dragging a selection rectangle around them or by Ctrl-clicking each one.

2. Press the right mouse button and drag the file icons to a new location.

   A pop-up menu appears when you release the mouse button (see Figure 3.3).

3. Choose Copy Here to create the copies.

   If you dragged to a different folder or disk, the copies will have the same names as the originals. If you dragged within the same folder, each file will be named Copy of *original file name*.

Storing Files at MSN Photos

Although not as secure as keeping backups on your own hard disk, floppy, or CD, any Hotmail user or MSN member can store up to 30 MB worth of photos at the MSN Photos Web site. Once posted, you can allow others to view your photos.

If you aren't an MSN member and don't have a Hotmail account, go to *www.hotmail.com* to create a free Hotmail email account.

To save images to MSN Photos:

1. Open the pictures that you want to save.
2. Choose File > Save to the Web > Save to MSN Photos.

   The Save to MSN Photos pane appears in the left side of the window (**Figure 3.6**).
3. If you want to save multiple pictures, but the correct ones aren't in the Tray, click the Add or remove pictures icon.

   You can either save the current image or all pictures that are in the Tray.
4. *Do one of the following:*
   - ▲ If you only want to save a single picture to MSN Photos, click its thumbnail in the Tray to make it active. Then click The current picture radio button.
   - ▲ To save all open pictures, click the All open pictures in the Tray radio button.
5. Be sure that you have an active Internet connection, and then click the Next button at the bottom of the pane.
6. Click the Click Here to Get Started button.
7. If you aren't signed in to your MSN or Hotmail account, the Sign in to .NET Passport page appears. Enter your Hotmail email address and password, and click the Sign In button (**Figure 3.7**). To upload your photos, follow the instructions on the Web site.
8. Click Done to return to Picture It!

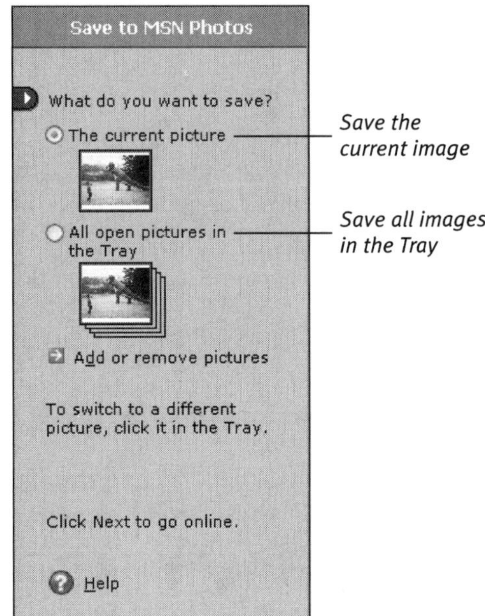

Figure 3.6 Use this pane to store your image files at MSN Photos.

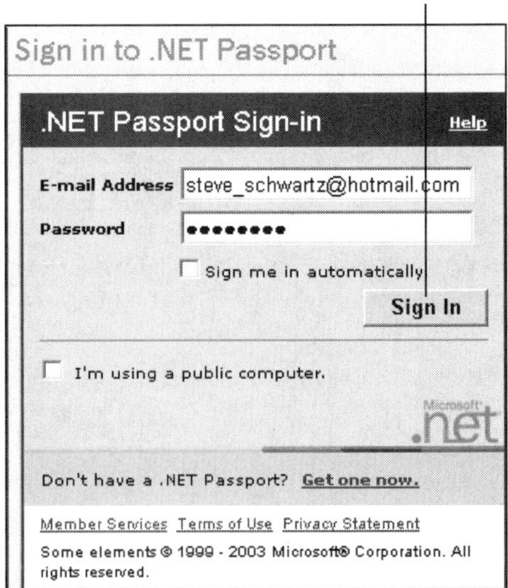

Figure 3.7 If you aren't signed in, enter your Hotmail address (.NET Passport) and password.

Saving Files as Wallpaper

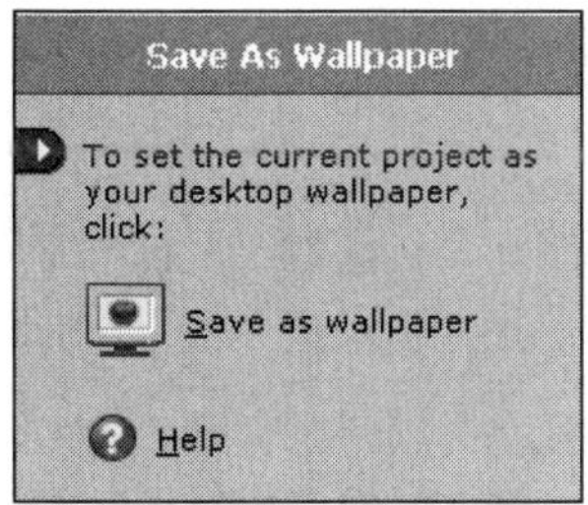

Figure 3.8 You can use Picture It! to make the current image into your Desktop wallpaper.

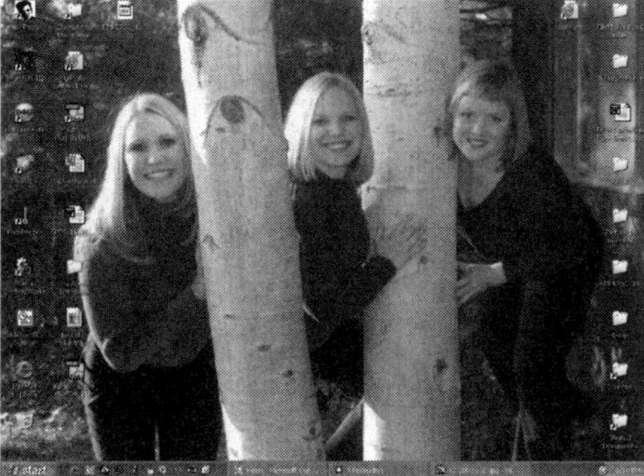

Figure 3.9 A family photo can become an attractive Desktop image.

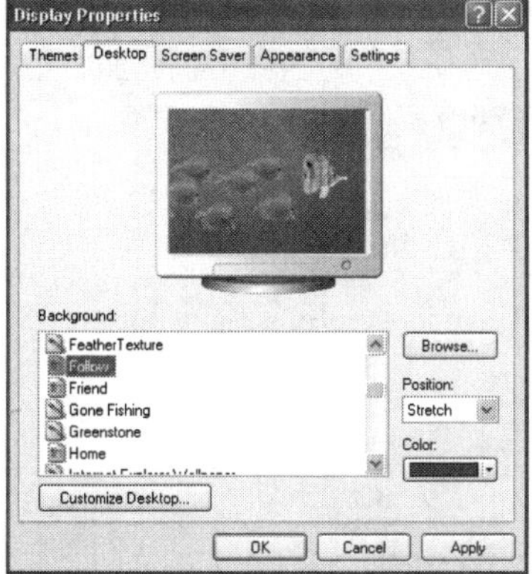

Figure 3.10 To choose another wallpaper image or texture, open the Display Properties control panel and click the Desktop tab.

As you probably know, you can decorate your PC's Desktop with a photo or pattern. This decorative background is known as *wallpaper.* Using Picture It!, you can create new wallpaper from any of your favorite photos.

To create new wallpaper:

1. Open the picture that you want to use as your new wallpaper.
2. Choose File > Save Special > Save as Wallpaper.

   The Save As Wallpaper pane (**Figure 3.8**) appears in the left side of the window.
3. Click the Save as wallpaper icon.

   The picture is saved with the name Picture It! Wallpaper and becomes your current wallpaper (**Figure 3.9**).

✔ Tips

- When creating a wallpaper file, choose a an image with a horizontal orientation. It's more likely to fill the screen and avoid blank space around it.
- To change your wallpaper, right-click the Desktop and choose Properties. In the Display Properties control panel, click the Desktop tab (**Figure 3.10**), choose a different wallpaper image, and then click OK.
- Another way to choose an image to use as wallpaper is to click the Browse button in the Display Properties control panel, select an image file from disk, and click Apply.
- Each time you issue the Save as Wallpaper command, the new Picture It! Wallpaper file replaces the old one in the Display Properties control panel.

Moving and Renaming Files

Using the File Browser, you can move selected files to a new location on disk. You can also rename files as a batch, creating a numbered series (such as scene0001.jpg, scene0002.jpg, and so on).

To move files to a new location:

1. Open the File Browser by choosing File > Open or Tools > Manage Files in File Browser.
2. Select the file or files that you want to move.

   To select multiple files, Ctrl-click them. To select all files in the folder, press Ctrl A.
3. Click the Tasks tab (**Figure 3.11**), if it isn't already selected.
4. In the File and Folder Tasks area, click Batch move.

   The Batch Move dialog box appears (**Figure 3.12**).
5. Click the Browse button.

   The Browse for Folder dialog box appears.
6. Select a folder and then click OK.
7. To complete the move, click OK in the Batch Move dialog box.

To perform a batch rename:

1. Perform Steps 1–3 of the previous step list.
2. In the File and Folder Tasks area, click Batch rename.

   The Batch Rename dialog box appears.
3. *Optional:* To place the renamed files in a different folder, click the Browse button and select a folder.
4. In the Base file name text box (**Figure 3.13**), enter the name that will precede the image number.
5. Enter a starting number for the series in the Start number on box.
6. Click OK.

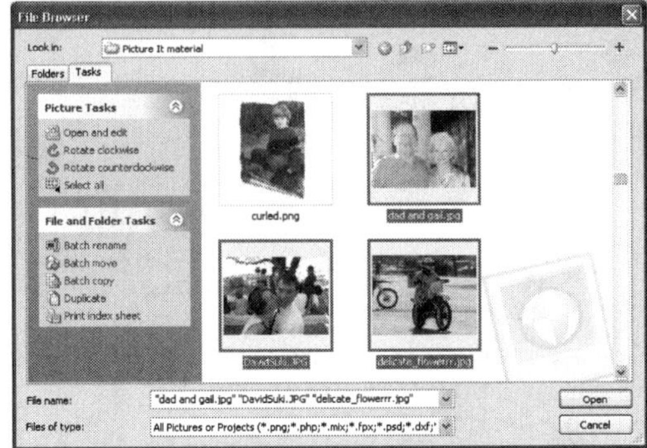

Figure 3.11 Select the files that you want to move, and then click Batch move (on the Tasks tab).

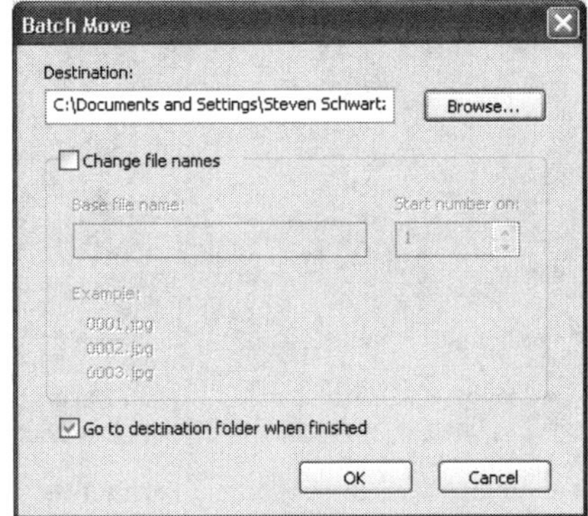

Figure 3.12 Specify a destination folder in the Batch Move dialog box.

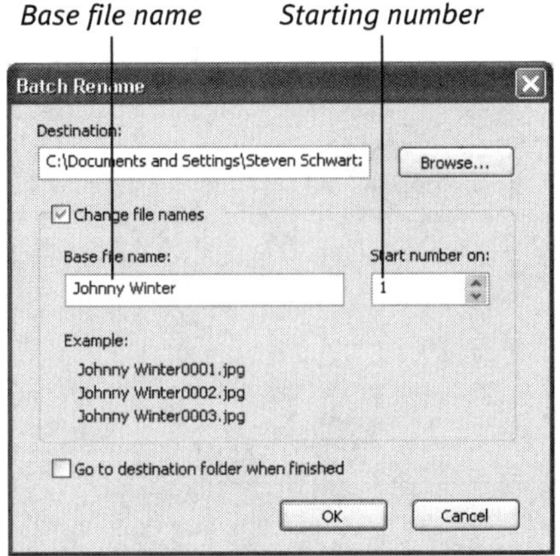

Figure 3.13 You can rename a set of related files in the Batch Rename dialog box.

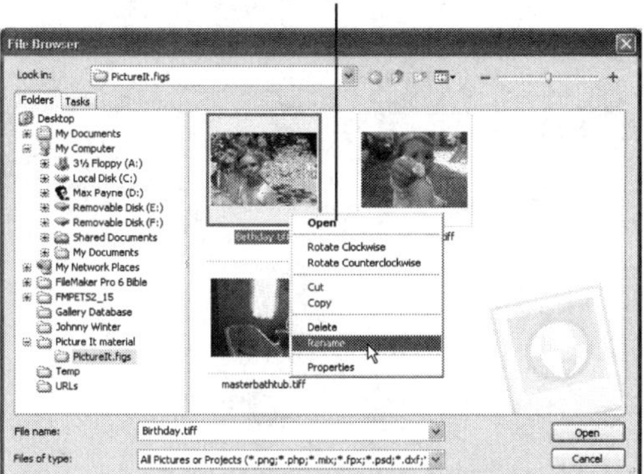

Figure 3.14 You can rename, copy, or delete a file by right-clicking its icon in the File Browser.

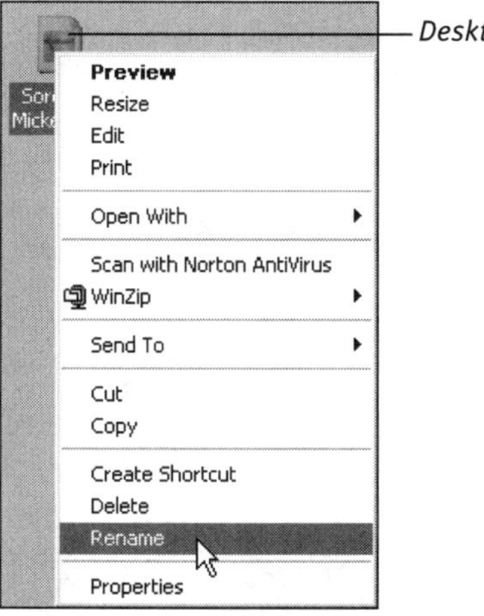

Figure 3.15 You can rename, copy, or delete a file by right-clicking its Desktop icon.

To rename an individual file:

1. Open the File Browser by choosing File > Open or Tools > Manage Files in File Browser.
2. Navigate to the drive and folder that contains the file you wish to rename.
3. Right-click the file and choose Rename from the pop-up menu that appears (**Figure 3.14**).
4. Edit the file name as desired. Be sure to keep the same file extension (such as .jpg) so Windows will still know the file's type.
5. To complete the renaming process, press Enter or click a blank spot in the File Browser.

✔ Tips

- You can also use Windows to rename files. Right-click a file icon on the Desktop or in a folder, choose Rename from the pop-up menu that appears (**Figure 3.15**), edit the file name, and then press Enter or click away from the file icon.
- To delete files from within the File Browser or using Windows, select one or more file icons, right-click any one of them, and choose Delete from the pop-up menu that appears.

Organizing Your Files in the Gallery

Picture It! has a feature called the Gallery that can help you organize your clip art, photos, and scans. The Gallery doesn't store the actual images; it merely records a reference to each one's location on disk, as well as categories and keywords that you've assigned to the item. When you need to find a particular image to use in a project or email to a friend (whether it's one of your own or part of an image collection supplied with Picture It!), having it in the Gallery simplifies the task.

See Chapter 2 for instructions for opening files from the Gallery.

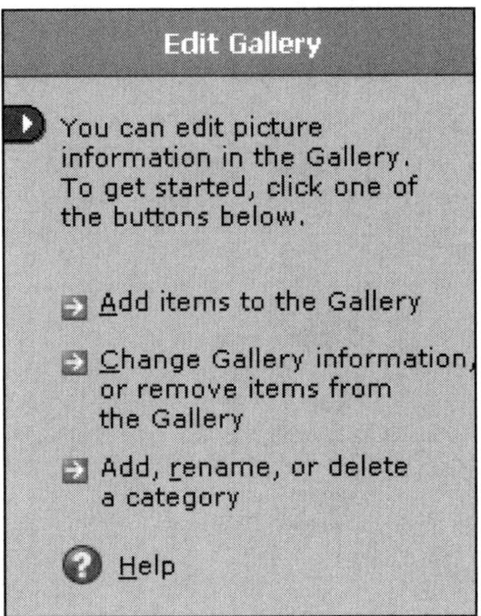

Figure 3.16 Click Add items to the Gallery.

To add an image to the Gallery:

1. Choose Tools > Edit Items in the Gallery.
   The Edit Gallery pane appears (**Figure 3.16**).
2. Click Add items to the Gallery.
   The File Browser opens (**Figure 3.17**). Using the Folders tab or the Look in drop-down list, navigate to the drive and folder that contains the image(s) you want to add to the Gallery.
3. Select the image you want to add to the Gallery. (To select multiple images, Ctrl-click each one.)
4. Click the Open button.
   A thumbnail of each image is added to the Gallery window.

Selected image

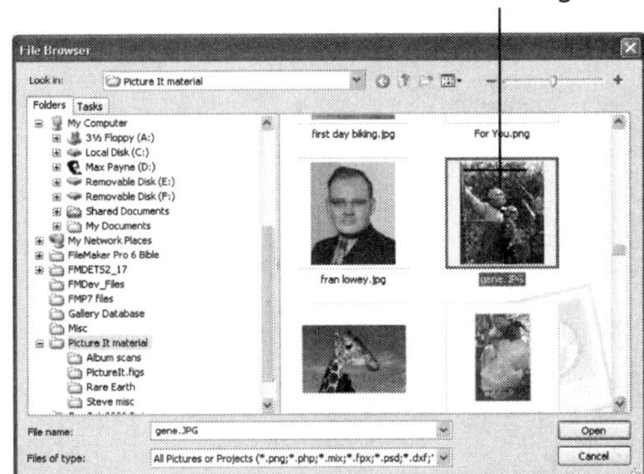

Figure 3.17 In the File Browser, select the image or images that you want to add to the Gallery.

To classify Gallery images:

1. Select the image in the Gallery window.
2. To assign one or more categories to the image (to help you classify and later find it), click each relevant category check box.
   To create additional categories, click the Add/rename/delete category icon.

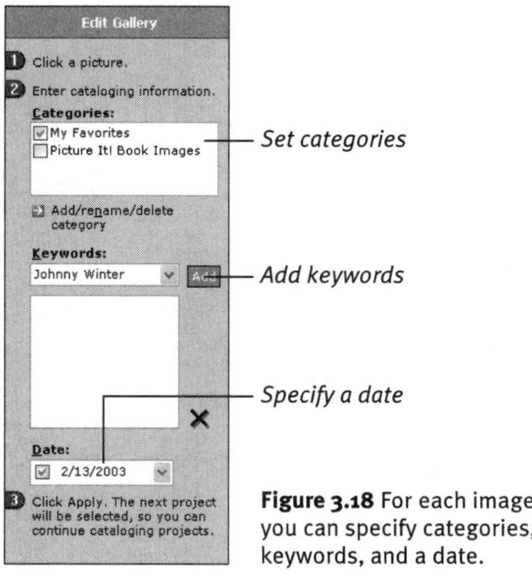

Figure 3.18 For each image, you can specify categories, keywords, and a date.

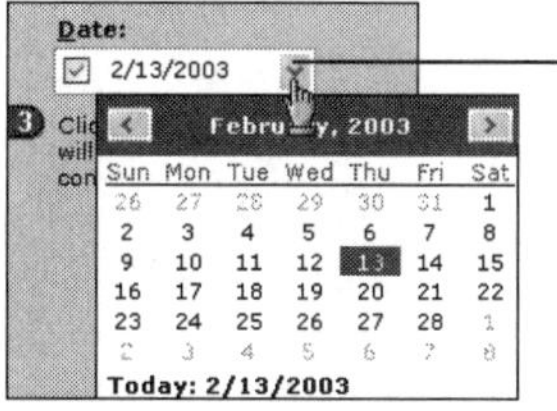

Figure 3.19 Rather than edit the date, you can pick one from this pop-up calendar.

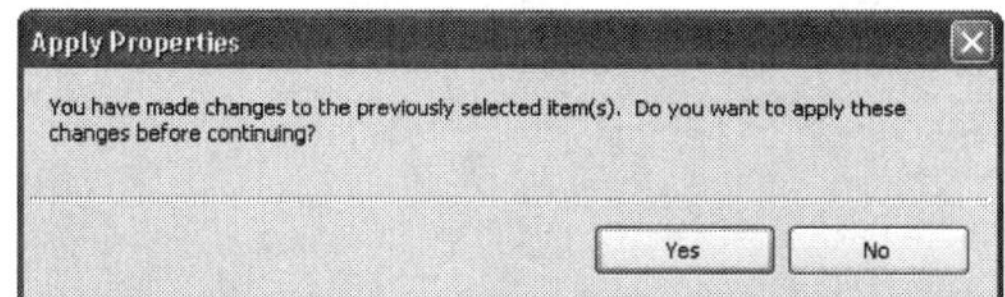

Figure 3.20 If you don't click Apply to record your changes, you'll still get an opportunity to do so.

3. To add a keyword to help you identify the picture, type it in the Keywords text box (**Figure 3.18**) or select it from the drop-down list of previously assigned keywords.

   You'll note that several keywords are automatically assigned (the full file name, the file type, and the part of the file name that precedes the extension). To remove an assigned keyword, select it and click the X.

4. To set a date for the picture (to show the date it was created or added to the Gallery), edit the date or select a new one from the calendar that appears when you click the icon to the right of the date (**Figure 3.19**).

   If you don't wish to associate a date with the image, remove the checkmark.

5. *Do one of the following:*
   - ▲ To record your changes and go to the next picture, click the Apply button.
   - ▲ To record your changes and close the Gallery window, click Apply and then click Done.
   - ▲ To close the Gallery window without saving your changes for the current image, click Done.

   If you try to switch pictures or close the Gallery window without saving the changes made for the current picture, a dialog box appears (**Figure 3.20**), giving you another chance to save the changes.

✔ Tips

- Items that you add to the Gallery are stored in the collection named My Collection.
- To edit the info for one or more pictures or to remove items from the Gallery, choose Tools > Edit Items in the Gallery. In the Gallery pane (see Figure 3.16), click Change Gallery information, or remove items from the Gallery. To edit the categories, click Add, rename, or delete a category.

4

Adjusting Whole Images

No matter how carefully you scan a picture or shoot a photo, it can often benefit from some corrections. Image correction can be done selectively (such as removing red eye) or for an entire image (such as adjusting the contrast). Chapter 5 covers the former topic. In this chapter, you'll learn how to make the following whole image adjustments:

- Setting brightness, contrast, and levels
- Adjusting the tint, hue, and saturation
- Sharpening and blurring
- Improving the lighting
- Restoring old pictures
- Manipulating objects: resizing, cropping, centering, aligning, rotating, flipping, and replacing pictures
- Embellishing objects by applying a fill, adding a shadow, and adding emphasis

If you need to touch up multiple pictures, you can use the Mini Lab (see Chapter 9) to adjust the brightness and contrast, levels, tint, rotation, and cropping. (Note that the Mini Lab and many of the image correction tools in this chapter are not available in Picture It! Express.)

Several of the tools discussed in Chapters 4, 5, and 8 are illustrated in the book's color insert.

Image Tweaking Advice

Here's an important bit of unsolicited advice before you begin correcting your images: think *moderation*. While Picture It! is a capable image-editing application and provides a respectable set of tools for correcting flaws, not every image is salvageable. If major adjustments are needed, knowing when to give up can be an admirable trait.

Adjusting Brightness and Contrast

Digital photos and scans are seldom perfect. They're often too bright or dark, for example. To correct this, you can alter the brightness and contrast. Since brightness and contrast are closely related to one another, if you alter one, it's usually necessary to alter the other. Brightness and contrast can be changed for a selected object or for an entire project.

To alter the brightness and contrast:

1. To alter the brightness/contrast for a specific image within a project, select the image.

   If you want to adjust these settings for the entire project, it isn't necessary to preselect an image.

2. Choose Touchup > Brightness and Contrast, or choose Touchup > Brightness and contrast from the Common Tasks list.

   The Brightness and Contrast pane appears (**Figure 4.1**).

3. *Optional:* If you've preselected an image but decide to adjust the brightness/contrast for the entire project, click the Whole Picture tab.

4. *Do one of the following:*
   - ▲ To allow Picture It! to adjust the contrast, click Contrast auto fix.
   - ▲ Drag the Brightness and Contrast sliders to new positions. (After adjusting one setting, you'll usually want to modify the other setting, too.)

5. When the settings are satisfactory, click the Done button.

✔ Tip

- If you have Digital Image Pro, you can use the Dodge and Burn Brush (see Chapter 5) to change the brightness or contrast of selected areas.

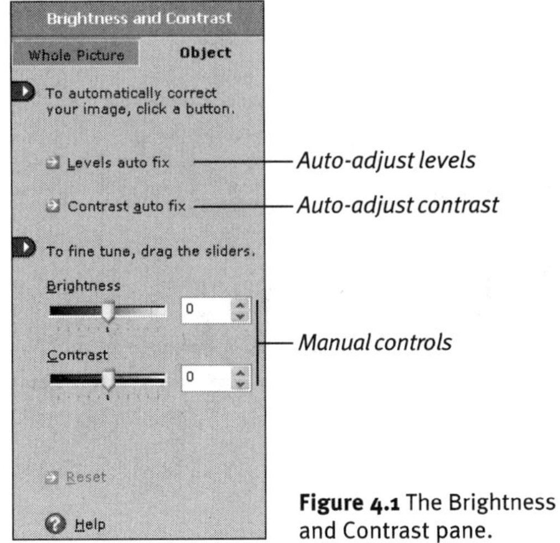

Figure 4.1 The Brightness and Contrast pane.

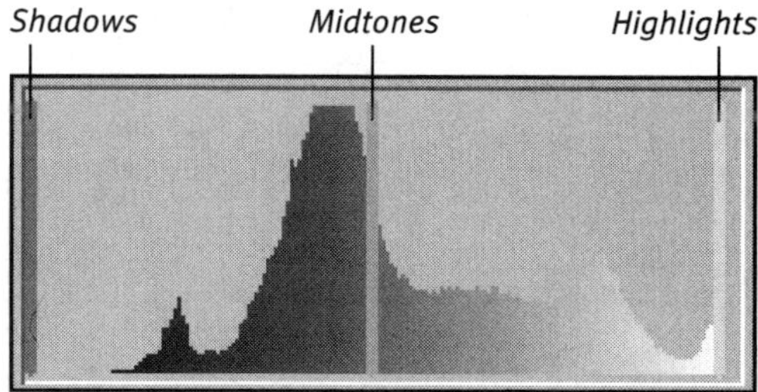

Figure 4.2 This is an example of a Levels histogram in the Adjust Levels pane.

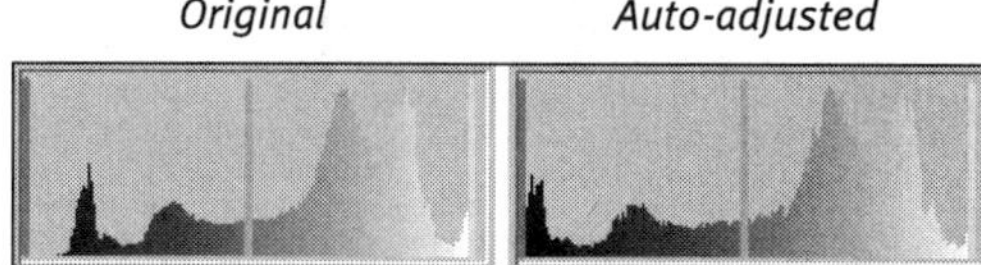

Figure 4.3 After auto-adjusting, the levels are distributed across the image.

Manually Adjusting Levels

The object of adjusting levels is to distribute the brightness values across the image. As you move the Shadows slider to the right or the Highlights slider to the left, any points outside of the slider are discarded. The remaining points are redistributed within the bounds of the new endpoints.

Images that can benefit from adjusting often have a blank area at one or both ends. Since these areas represent zero pixels in the image, you can safely discard them. Drag the Shadows or Highlights slider to the outer edge of the data points. (You'll note that as you drag, the Midtones slider also moves.) If the effect isn't sufficiently pronounced, you can drag farther until you reach the outer edge of the first significant *block* of data points.

To complete a levels adjustment, you may also want to adjust the midtones. Drag the Midtones slider to the left to darken the image or to the right to brighten it.

Adjusting Levels

Another way to simultaneously alter an image's brightness and contrast is to adjust levels. Every image is composed of areas of dark, light, and midtones. The various brightness levels in any image can be displayed as a histogram (**Figure 4.2**), where the horizontal axis represents the range of brightness values in the image and the vertical axis shows the number of pixels at each brightness level. Picture It! lets you automatically or manually adjust levels for any image or project.

To automatically adjust levels:

1. Select an image to adjust.
2. *Do one of the following:*
   - ▲ Choose Touchup > Levels Auto Fix or click the Levels Auto Fix toolbar icon.
   - ▲ In the Common Tasks list, choose Touchup > Levels auto fix.
   - ▲ In the Brightness and Contrast pane (see Figure 4.1), click Levels Auto Fix.

   Picture It! adjusts the selected image. The histogram redraws to show the new distribution of brightness values (**Figure 4.3**).
3. If you aren't pleased with the result, do one of the following:
   - ▲ If you initially chose the Levels Auto Fix command, choose Edit > Undo, press Ctrl Z, or click the Undo toolbar icon.
   - ▲ If you initially clicked Levels auto fix in the Brightness and Contrast pane, click the Reset icon.

✔ Tip

- When performing a Levels Auto Fix from the Brightness and Contrast pane, you can simultaneously adjust levels for *all* images in the project. To accomplish this, select the Whole Picture tab rather than the Object(s) tab.

To manually adjust levels:

1. To adjust levels for a specific image or object within a project, select that item.

   To adjust levels for an entire project, it isn't necessary to preselect anything.

2. Choose Touchup > Adjust Levels.

   The Adjust Levels pane appears (**Figure 4.4**).

3. Ensure that the correct tab is selected: Whole Picture (for all images in the project) or Object (for a selected object).

4. Adjust the levels by dragging the sliders (**Figure 4.5**).

   As you drag, the picture changes to reflect the new settings.

5. Click Done to accept the new settings or click Cancel to discard the changes.

   The Adjust Levels pane closes (**Figure 4.6**).

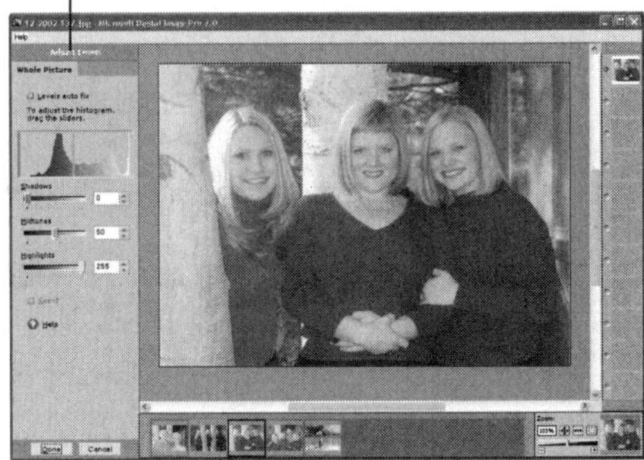

Figure 4.4 To manually adjust levels, you can drag any or all of the sliders in the Adjust Levels pane.

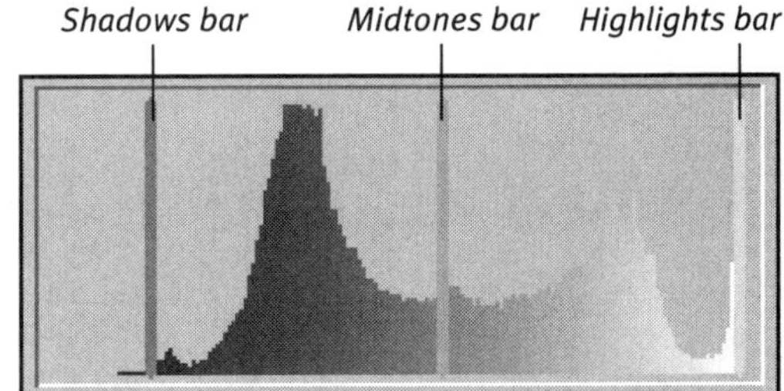

Figure 4.5 To adjust this image, the Shadows slider was moved to the left edge of the first significant block of dark pixels.

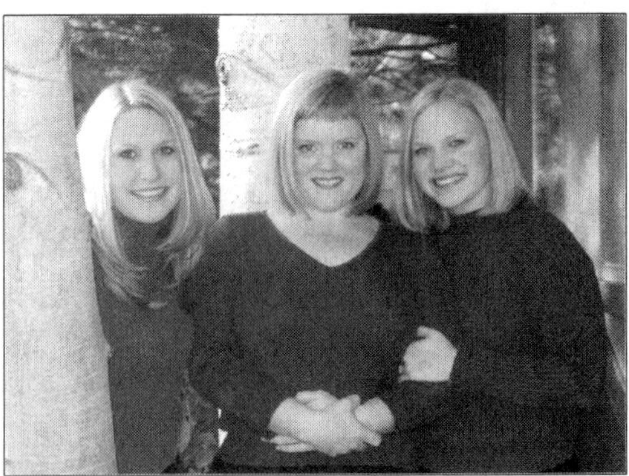

Figure 4.6 Note how the corrected image is darker and sharper. It's no longer muddy or cloudy.

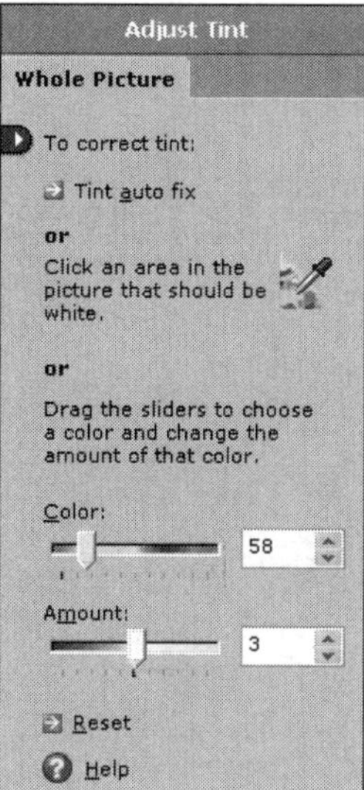

Figure 4.7 Move the sliders to adjust the tint.

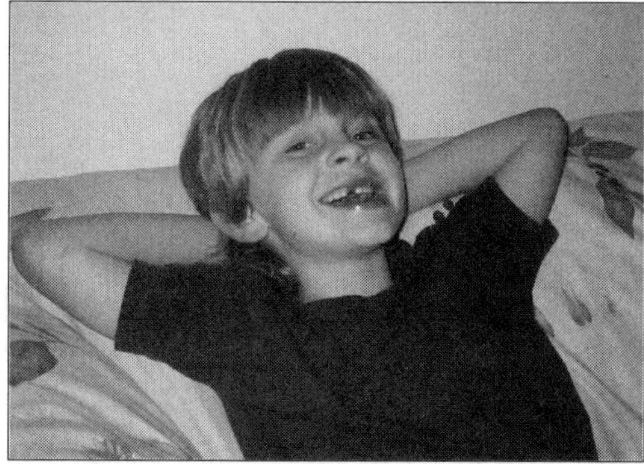

Figure 4.8 After correcting the tint, the wall and sofa have lost their pinkish cast, while the subject retains his natural skin tones. (See color insert.)

Correcting Tint

Due to lighting conditions, some photos may have an unusual color tint. Many types of indoor lighting will lend a nonwhite tint to your shots, as can shooting indoors after dark with normal room lighting. If one color is predominant in a scene, such as a brightly colored bed sheet, other objects in the shot may also appear tinged with that color.

Picture It! provides three methods for you to correct the tint in an image or an entire project: automatic, manual, and selective. The latter method uses the Tint Brush (see Chapter 5).

To correct the tint:

1. To adjust the tint for a specific image or object, select that item.

   To adjust the tint for an entire project, it isn't necessary to preselect anything.

2. Choose Touchup > Adjust Tint, click the Adjust Tint toolbar icon, or choose Touchup > Adjust tint from the Common Tasks list.

   The Adjust Tint pane appears (**Figure 4.7**).

3. Make sure that the correct tab is selected: Whole Picture or Object.

4. *Do one of the following:*
   - ▲ Click Tint auto fix.
   - ▲ Using the Eyedropper, click a spot in the picture that should be white. Picture It! adjusts all other colors as necessary.
   - ▲ Using the Color slider, select a color to be altered. To specify the amount of the selected color that is added or reduced, drag the Amount slider to the right or left, respectively. As you drag, the picture changes to reflect the new settings.

5. Click Done to accept the new settings (**Figure 4.8**) or Cancel to discard the changes.

Adjusting Hue and Saturation

You can use the Hue and Saturation pane to modify a color/shade and its intensity for an object, multiple objects, or an entire project.

To adjust the hue and saturation:

1. Select one or more objects to adjust.
   To apply the modifications to an entire project, either select them all or select nothing.
2. Choose Touchup > Hue and Saturation.
   The Hue and Saturation pane appears (**Figure 4.9**).
3. Using the Eyedropper, click the color within the image that you wish to change.
4. *Do any of the following:*
   - ▲ To change the hue, move the yellow ball around the outer circle.
   - ▲ To change the saturation, move the smaller ball around the inner circle.
   - ▲ To change the color's brightness, move the smaller ball closer to or farther away from the center circle.
   - ▲ To fine tune the hue, saturation, or brightness, enter new values in the three Fine tune text boxes.
5. Click Done to accept the changes (**Figure 4.10**) or Cancel to discard the changes.

✔ Tips

- Adjusting hue and saturation is one of the most difficult image alterations to make. You may find it easier to adjust the tint.
- While you adjust the hue, saturation, and brightness, changes are shown instantly when dragging the balls. However, when entering values in the Fine tune text boxes, you must pause to see the changes.

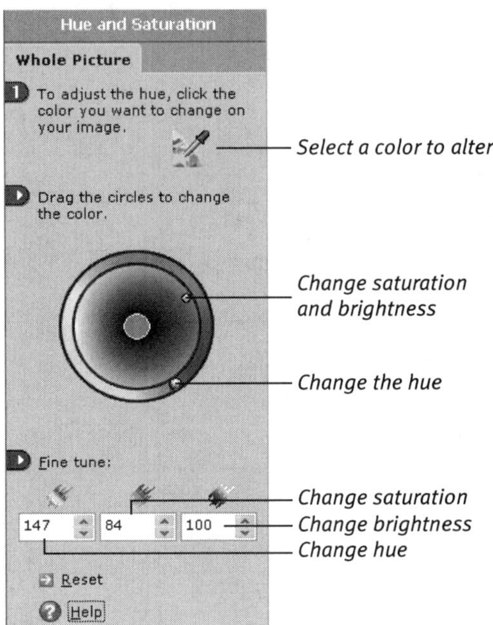

Figure 4.9 The Hue and Saturation pane.

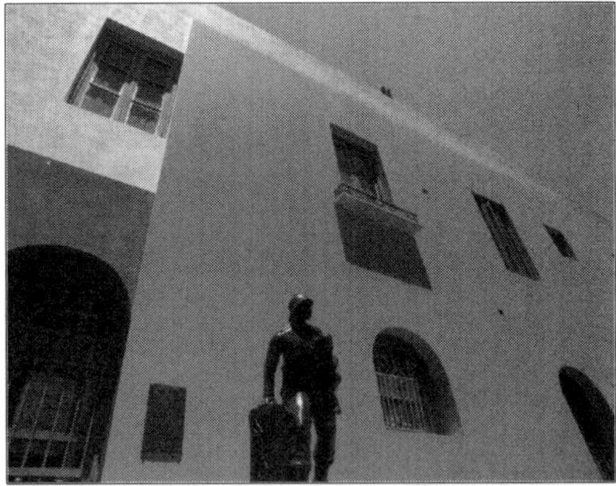

Figure 4.10 Altering the hue and saturation resulted in dramatic new colors in this building's exterior. (See the color section in this book.)

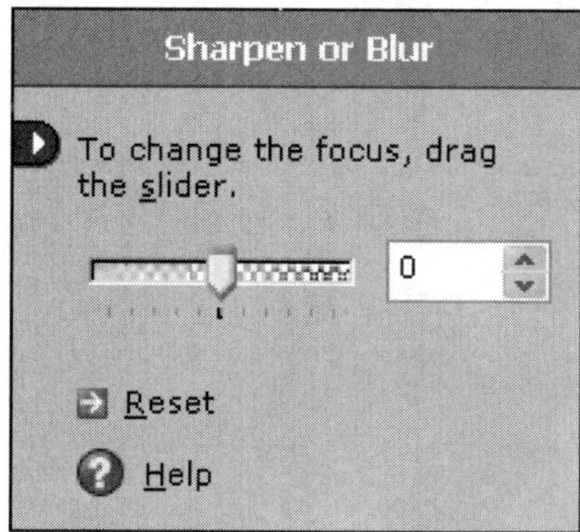

Figure 4.11 Drag the slider to sharpen or blur the image.

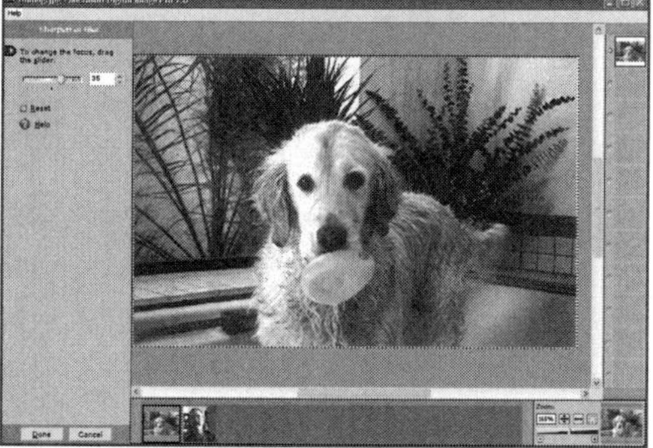

Figure 4.12 It's easier to see the effects of sharpening if you examine the image at a higher zoom level.

Sharpening and Blurring

Scans seldom come out razor sharp. And if your hand isn't steady, digital photos can suffer, too. Using the Sharpen or Blur pane, you may be able to correct this problem, as well as deliberately soften other images for a slightly ethereal effect.

To sharpen or blur an image:

1. *Do one of the following:*
   - ▲ If the project contains multiple images, select the one you want to sharpen or blur. (The command can only be used with a single image at a time.)
   - ▲ If the project contains only one image, it isn't necessary to preselect it.
2. Choose Touchup > Sharpen or Blur, click the Sharpen or Blur toolbar icon, or choose Touchup > Sharpen or blur from the Common Tasks list.

   The Sharpen or Blur pane appears (**Figure 4.11**).
3. Drag the slider to the right to sharpen the image or to the left to soften the focus.
4. Click Done to accept the changes or Cancel to discard the changes.

✔ Tips

- The Sharpen or Blur command is best suited for images that need only minor correction.
- It can be helpful to increase the zoom when sharpening (**Figure 4.12**).
- Grainy and low-resolution images don't sharpen well. Focus problems may be accentuated rather than corrected.

Improving the Lighting

Using the Adjust Lighting command, you can add foreground lighting (*flash*) or reduce the background lighting of selected images or an entire project.

To alter the lighting:

1. Select one or more objects to adjust.

   To apply the adjustments to the entire project, it isn't necessary to select anything.

2. Choose Touchup > Adjust Lighting.

   The Adjust Lighting pane appears (**Figure 4.13**).

3. Drag the Add Flash and/or the Reduce Backlighting slider to the desired position.

   As you drag, the lighting changes.

4. Click Done to accept the changes (**Figure 4.14**) or Cancel to discard the changes.

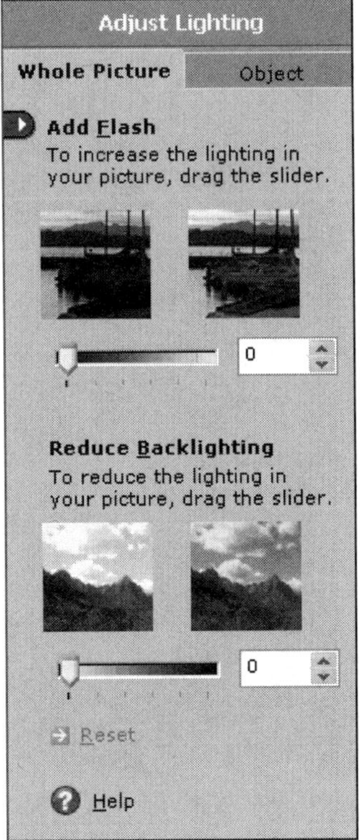

Figure 4.13 Drag the sliders to add flash or reduce the background lighting.

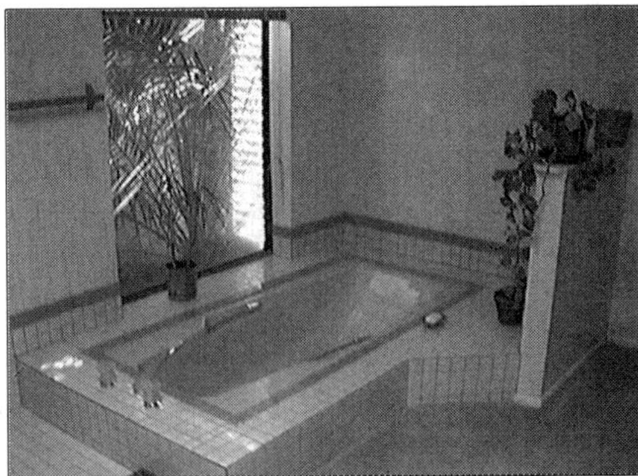

Figure 4.14 This previously dark picture—taken without benefit of flash—was improved by increasing the foreground lighting.

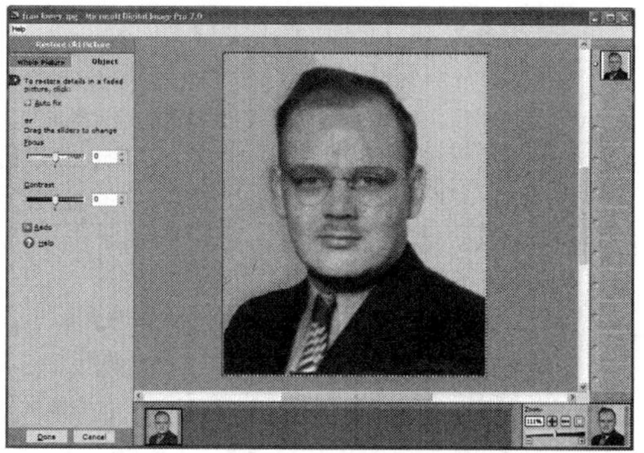

Figure 4.15 Using the controls in this pane, you can automatically or manually restore an old photo.

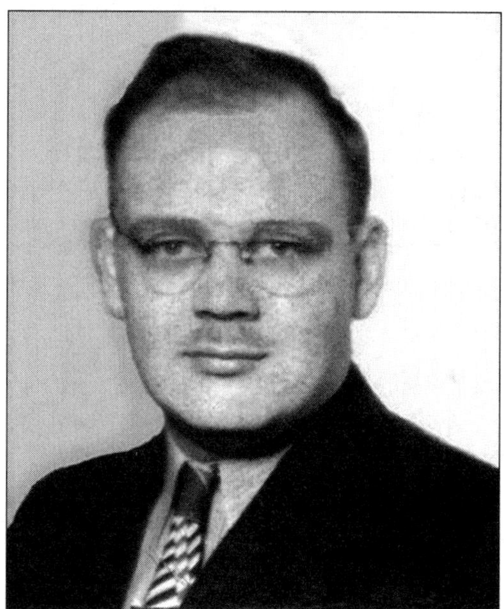

Figure 4.16 The corrected picture is brighter and clearer than the original.

Restoring Old Pictures

Old photographs often show signs of fading. Using the Restore Old Picture command, you can improve the picture's focus and contrast.

To restore an old picture:

1. If the project contains multiple items, select one or more images to adjust.
2. Choose Touchup > Other Photo Repair > Restore Old Picture.

   The Restore Old Picture pane appears (**Figure 4.15**).
3. Make sure that the correct tab is selected: Object(s) or Whole Picture.
4. *Do one of the following:*
   - ▲ To allow Picture It! to correct the image(s), click the Auto fix icon.
   - ▲ To manually correct the image(s), drag the Focus and/or Contrast sliders to new positions.
5. Click Done to accept the changes (**Figure 4.16**) or Cancel to discard the changes.

Manipulating Objects

While the first part of this chapter covered the ways in which you can alter image quality, the remainder focuses on procedures you can use to change the size, placement, rotation, and similar image options.

Changing canvas and object size

You can resize objects manually by dragging handles, but Picture It! provides several more precise methods for resizing objects or the canvas. You can do any of the following:

- Resize the canvas
- Resize a specific object to fit the canvas
- Crop the canvas or an image, hiding or discarding the unwanted portions

To resize the canvas (setting a new page size):

1. Choose Format > Resize Image.
   The Resize pane appears (**Figure 4.17**). The current canvas size and resolution are displayed in the text boxes.
2. Select a canvas orientation by clicking the Portrait or Landscape radio button.
3. *Do one of the following:*
   - ▲ To change the canvas size without altering the resolution, select a page size from the drop-down list or enter a new height or width.
   - ▲ To change the resolution while allowing Picture It! to specify the appropriate canvas size, select a resolution from the drop-down list.
4. Click Done to accept the changes or Cancel to discard the changes.

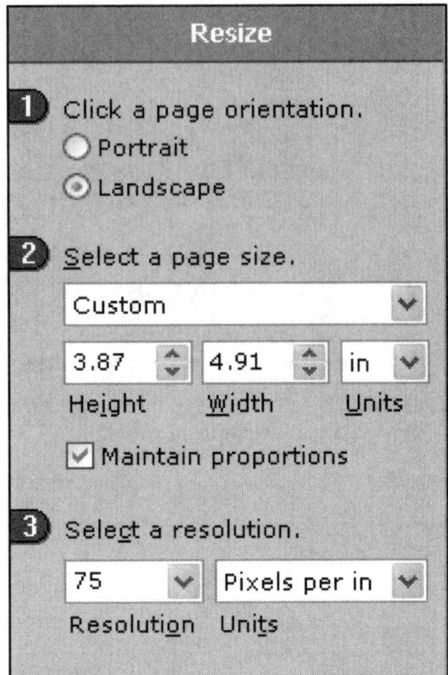

Figure 4.17 Use the Resize pane to set a new page/paper size for the current project.

✔ Tips

- Unless you want your image to be stretched nonproportionately, be sure that Maintain proportions is checked.
- If an image fills the canvas (or is the full width or height of the canvas), the Resize Image command will cause the image to fill at least one dimension. If no image fills the canvas (or is the full width or height of the canvas), only the canvas will be resized.
- Another way to change the canvas size is to create a new, blank canvas by using the File > New command. Then place your images and objects by dragging them from the Tray or by issuing Insert commands. When creating a multi-image/object project, this is often the best way to ensure that the canvas matches your paper size.

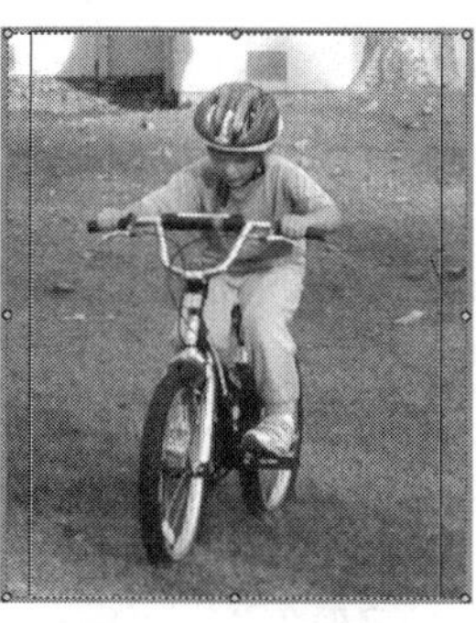

Figure 4.18 Fill causes the excess width to spill over into the workspace.

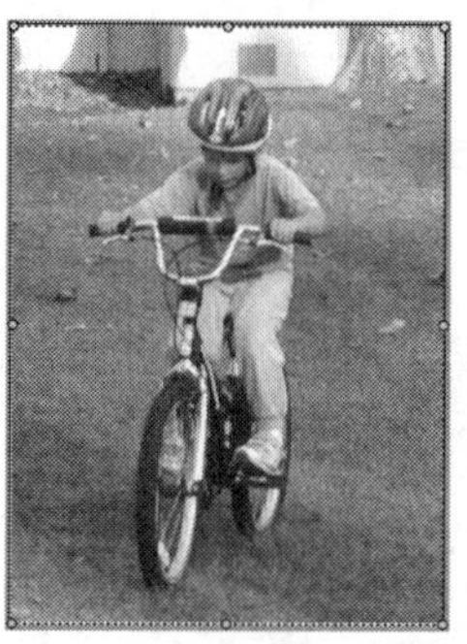

Figure 4.19 Stretch to Fit perfectly fills the canvas, but elongates this subject.

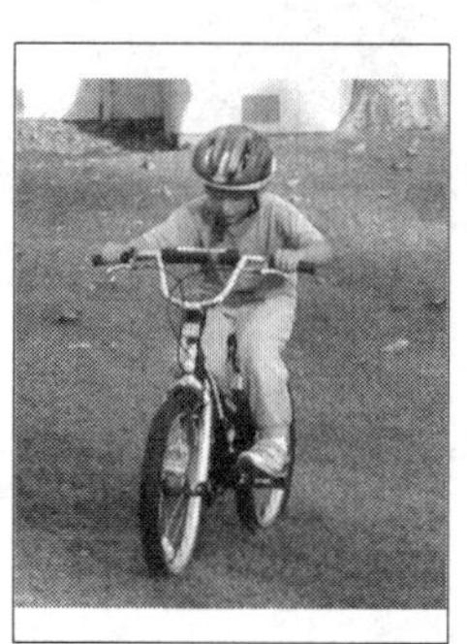

Figure 4.20 Fit Within fills the horizontal dimension, but leaves white space at the top and bottom.

To resize an object to fit the canvas:

1. Select the object that you want to resize.
2. Choose one of the following commands from the Format > Resize Object to Fit Canvas submenu:
   - ▲ *Fill.* Proportionately resize the object so it completely covers the canvas. Parts of the object that do not fit will spill into the workspace (**Figure 4.18**).
   - ▲ *Stretch to Fit.* Precisely fit the object to the canvas, stretching nonproportionately if needed (**Figure 4.19**).
   - ▲ *Fit Within.* Proportionately resize the object so that it fits perfectly in at least one dimension (width or height). Blank areas in the other dimension are allowed to occur, if necessary (**Figure 4.20**).

✔ Tip

- You can also resize an object proportionately by dragging any corner handle. To resize nonproportionately, drag any other handle.

To crop the canvas or an image/object:

1. To crop a specific image, select the image.

   It isn't necessary to preselect an image if you want to crop the canvas.

2. *Do one of the following:*
   - ▲ To crop the canvas and the image(s) it contains, choose Format > Crop > Canvas, choose Crop or rotate > Crop canvas from the Common Tasks list, or click the Crop Canvas toolbar icon.
   - ▲ To crop a selected object or image, choose Format > Crop > Selected Object.

   The Crop pane appears (**Figure 4.21**).

3. Click and drag to select the portion of the image that you want to retain (**Figure 4.22**).

4. *Optional:* You can modify the crop by doing any of the following:
   - ▲ To restrict the cropped proportions to that of a particular paper size, choose a size from the drop-down list or enter numbers in the Height and Width text boxes. Then move the selection rectangle to highlight the part of the image that you want to retain.
   - ▲ To change the crop shape, select a shape icon from the scrolling list.

5. Click Done to complete the process.

   If you cropped the canvas, the crop fills the resized canvas (**Figure 4.23**). If you cropped an image or object, only that item is cropped—leaving the canvas unchanged.

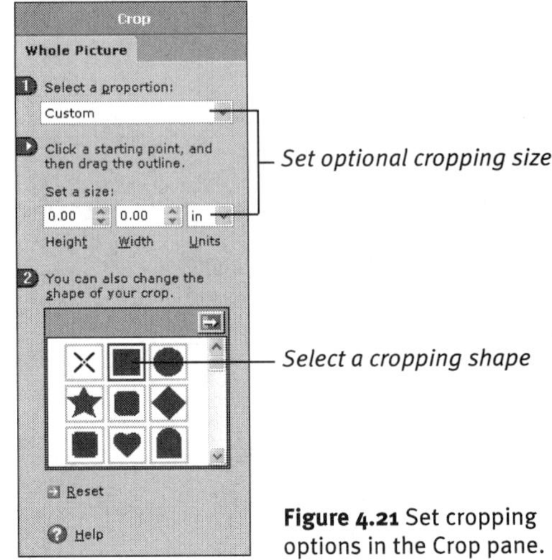

Figure 4.21 Set cropping options in the Crop pane.

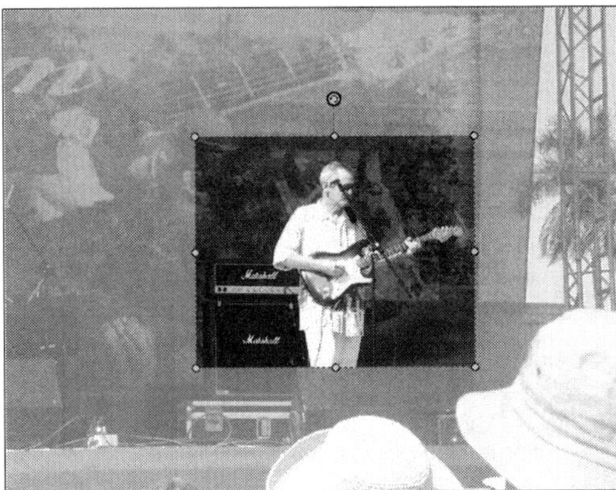

Figure 4.22 The darkened area represents the part of the image that will be retained following the crop.

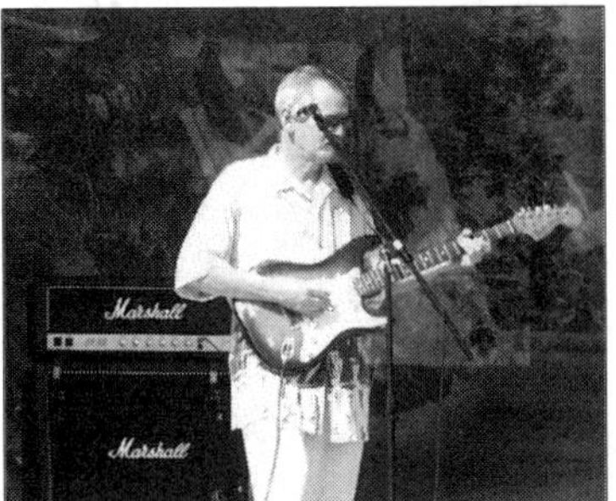

Figure 4.23 After the image is cropped, no distractions remain.

Placing and aligning objects

Although you can position objects manually by dragging, Picture It! has commands to achieve more precise positioning and alignment.

To center an object on the canvas:

1. Select the object.
2. Choose Format > Center Object on Canvas.

To align multiple objects to one another:

1. Select the objects to align (**Figure 4.24**).
2. Choose Format > Align Multiple Objects, and choose one of these commands from the submenu:
   - ▲ *Left, Right, Top, or Bottom.* Align the left, right, top, or bottom edges of the selected objects (**Figure 4.25**). The object farthest to the left, right, top, or bottom, respectively, is treated as the target for purposes of the alignment.
   - ▲ *Center Horizontally.* Align the objects in a vertical stack so that each is centered horizontally in respect to one another (**Figure 4.26**).
   - ▲ *Center Vertically.* Align the objects in a horizontal string so that each is centered vertically in respect to one another (**Figure 4.27**).
   - ▲ *Space Horizontally.* Set the spacing between objects in a vertical stack so it is equidistant between each object pair.
   - ▲ *Space Vertically.* Set the spacing between objects in a horizontal string so it is equidistant between each object pair.

   The selected objects are aligned as directed.

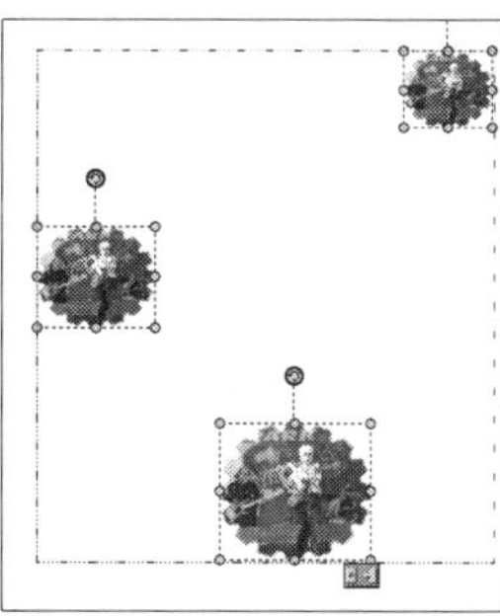

Figure 4.24 These are the three objects to be aligned.

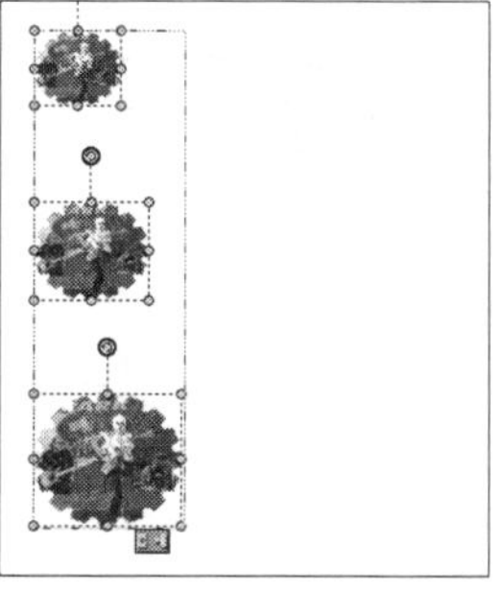

Figure 4.25 These objects are aligned along their left edges.

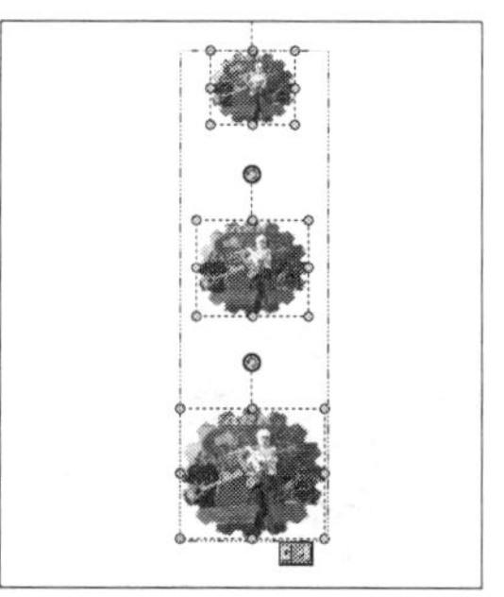

Figure 4.26 These objects are horizontally aligned along their centers.

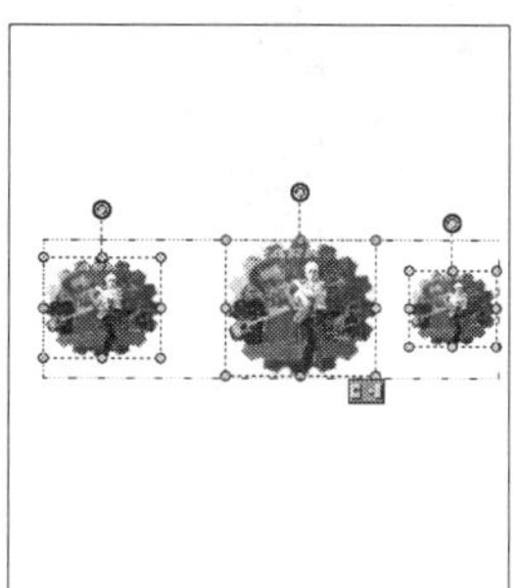

Figure 4.27 These objects are vertically aligned along their centers.

✔ Tip

- ■ You may have to issue multiple commands to get the alignment you want. For example, when aligning several objects in a stack, you might choose Space Vertically *and* Center Horizontally.

Rotating and flipping

Another way to manipulate objects or the canvas is by changing the orientation—either by rotating or flipping. (*Flipping* reverses an object, producing a mirror image.)

To rotate the canvas or an object:

1. To rotate one or more specific objects, select the object(s).

   It isn't necessary to preselect an object if you're rotating the canvas.

2. *Do one of the following:*
   - ▲ Choose Format > Rotate > Canvas or Format > Rotate > Selected Object.
   - ▲ Choose Crop or rotate > Rotate from the Common Tasks list.

   The Rotate pane appears (**Figure 4.28**). Make sure that the correct tab is selected: Whole Picture or Object(s).
3. *Do one of the following:*
   - ▲ Click a radio button for the desired 90-degree rotation increment.
   - ▲ Click the Custom radio button, enter a rotation angle in the text box, and then press Tab or Enter.
4. Click Done to accept the changes or Cancel to discard the changes.

✔ Tips

- If you hold a digital camera sideways while taking some shots, the Rotate command can right them for you.
- You can rotate the canvas or selected objects in 90-degree increments by clicking the Rotate Counterclockwise or Rotate Clockwise toolbar icon (**Figure 4.29**). Note that if the canvas contains multiple items, you *must* preselect one or more items before clicking a Rotate toolbar icon.
- Another way to rotate an object to *any* angle is to select the object and then drag its rotate handle (**Figure 4.30**).

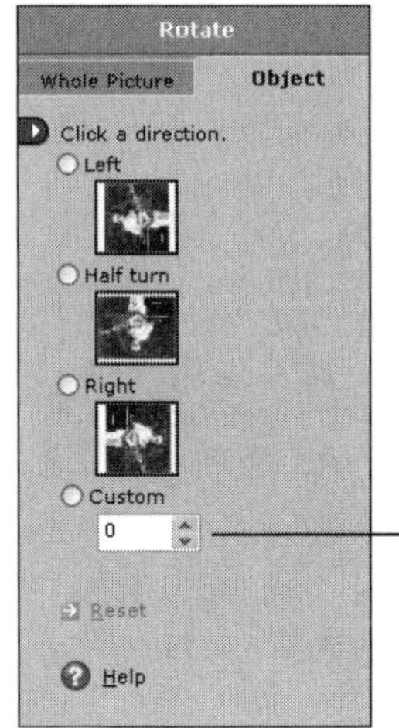

Figure 4.28 You can rotate in 90-degree increments or to an angle.

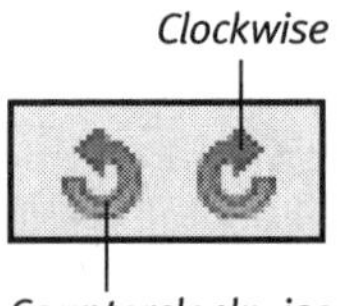

Figure 4.29 The toolbar contains rotation icons.

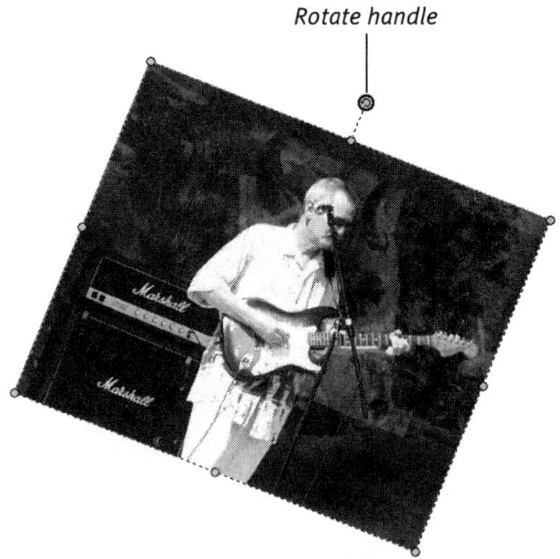

Figure 4.30 You can drag the rotate handle to manually rotate a selected object.

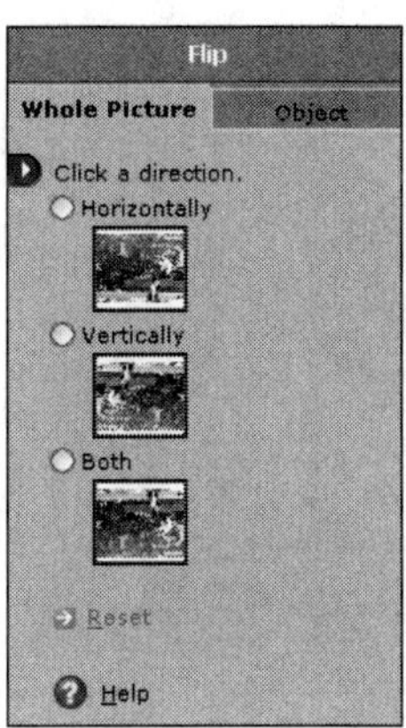

Figure 4.31 Click a radio button for the desired direction of the flip.

To flip the canvas or a selected object:

1. To flip one or more specific objects, select the object(s). (It isn't necessary to preselect an object if you're flipping the canvas.)
2. Choose Format > Flip > Canvas or Format > Flip > Selected Object.

   The Flip pane appears (**Figure 4.31**).
3. Click a radio button for the type of flip desired: Horizontally, Vertically, or Both.
4. Click Done to accept the changes or Cancel to discard the changes.

✔ Tip

- You can also flip the canvas or a selected image by clicking the Flip Horizontally or Flip Vertically toolbar icon.

Replacing a picture

Picture It! allows you to replace one image with another, while retaining the original image's formatting (rather than deleting a picture, replacing it with another image from the Tray, and then resizing and formatting it).

To replace a picture:

1. *Do one of the following:*
   - ▲ Double-click the picture that you want to replace.
   - ▲ Select the picture (**Figure 4.32**) and choose Format > Replace Picture.

   The Replace Picture pane appears (**Figure 4.33**).
2. *Do one of the following:*
   - ▲ If the replacement image is already in the Tray, double-click its thumbnail.
   - ▲ Open, create, or download the replacement image by clicking the appropriate icon. When the image appears in the Tray, double-click its thumbnail.

   If necessary, move and resize the replacement image (**Figure 4.34**).
3. Click Done.

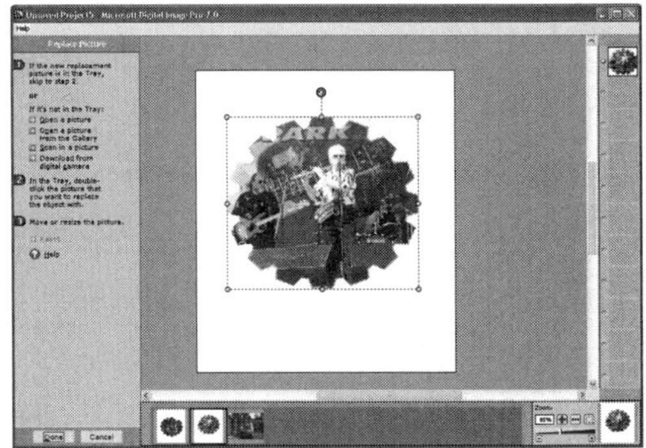

Figure 4.32 The selected picture's formatting will be applied to the replacement picture.

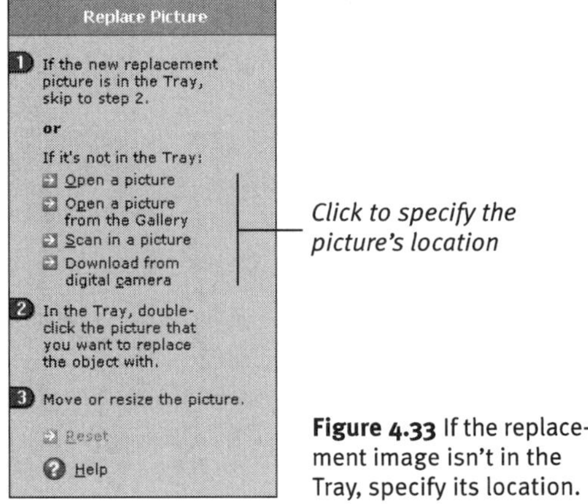

Figure 4.33 If the replacement image isn't in the Tray, specify its location.

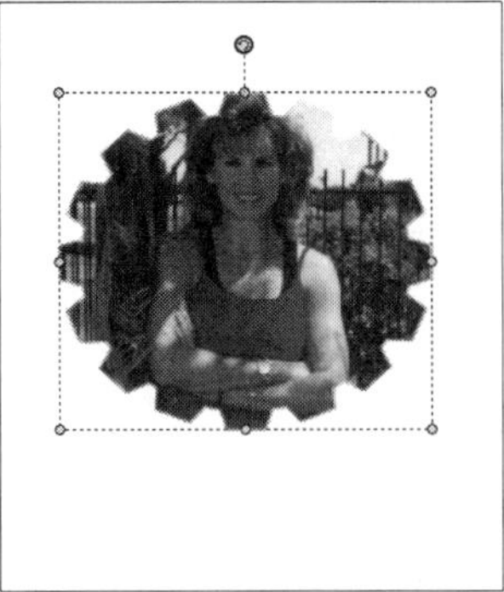

Figure 4.34 The replacement image adopts the original image's cog cropping.

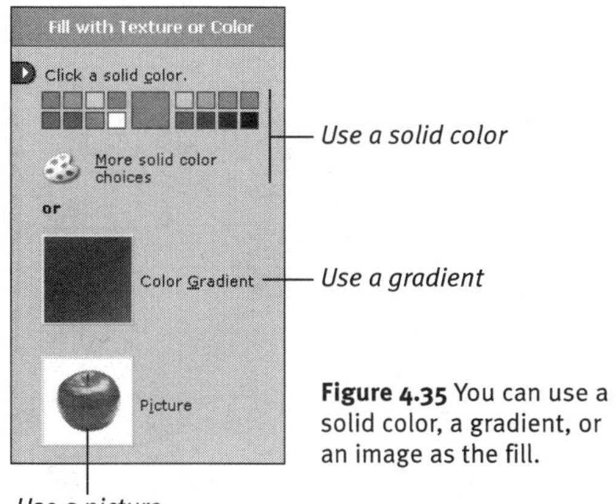

Figure 4.35 You can use a solid color, a gradient, or an image as the fill.

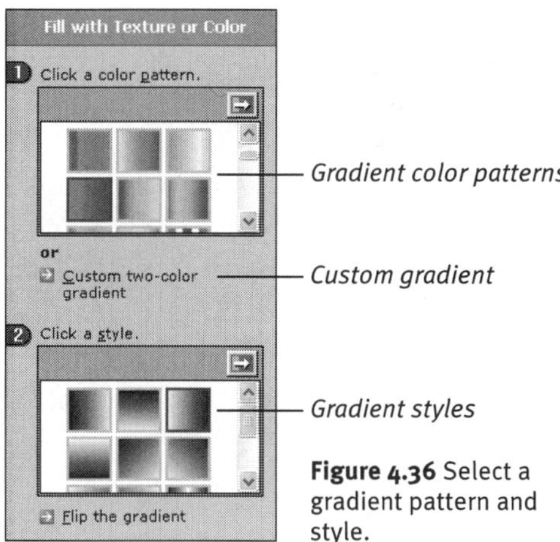

Figure 4.36 Select a gradient pattern and style.

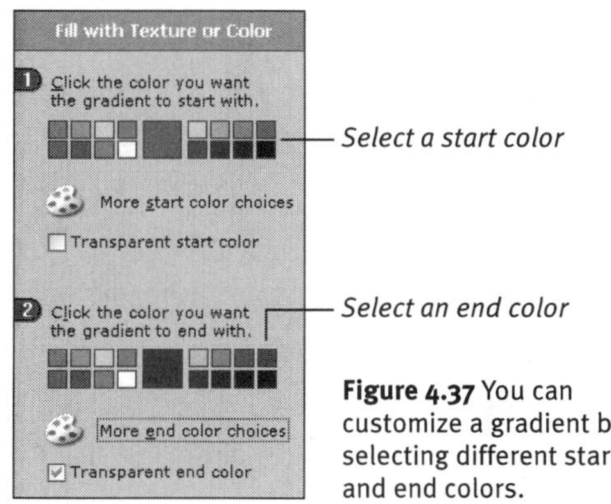

Figure 4.37 You can customize a gradient by selecting different start and end colors.

Embellishing Objects

You can also use Picture It! to fill a selected object with a color, gradient, or picture; add a shadow around an object; or emphasize images to differentiate them from the other images.

To apply a fill to an object:

1. Select one or more objects to fill.
2. Choose Effects > Fill with Texture or Color.

   The Fill with Texture or Color pane appears (**Figure 4.35**).
3. *Do one of the following:*
   - Click a solid color in the left side of the palette. To change the color's shade, click a shade in the right side of the palette.

     To pick a different color, click More solid color choices.
   - To fill the object(s) with a color gradient, click the Color Gradient icon. In the new pane (**Figure 4.36**), select a pattern and style. To reverse the gradient, click Flip the gradient.

     To customize the gradient, click Custom two-color gradient, select start and end colors (**Figure 4.37**), and designate one of the colors as transparent (if desired).
   - To fill the object(s) with a picture, click the Picture icon. If the picture is in the Tray, double-click its thumbnail. Otherwise, click an icon to specify the picture's source, and open or download the picture.
4. When you are satisfied with the results, click the Done button.

✔ Tip

- You can create a fillable background for a collage by adding a rectangular shape that fills the canvas and then moving it to the back.

To place a shadow around an object:

1. Select an object or a set of grouped objects to which you want to apply a shadow.

   The shadow effect can only be applied to a single object or a group (which is considered a single object for formatting purposes). Attempting to apply a shadow to multiple *individual* objects is not allowed.
2. Choose Effects > Shadow.

   The Shadow pane appears (**Figure 4.38**).
3. Select a shadow style from the scrolling list of examples.
4. *Optional:* Click Customize the shadow.

   In the new pane (**Figure 4.39**), you can change the shadow color, its transparency, or the edge softness. Click Done to return to the previous pane.
5. *Optional:* Since the shadow is an object, you can change its position and size by dragging it or its handles, respectively.
6. When you are satisfied with the results, click the Done button.

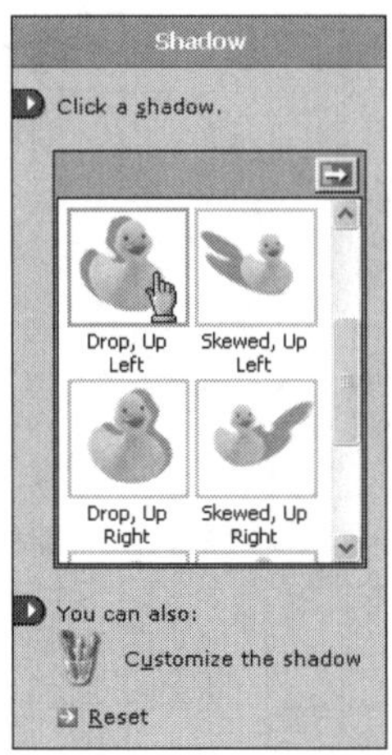

Figure 4.38 Select a shadow style from these examples.

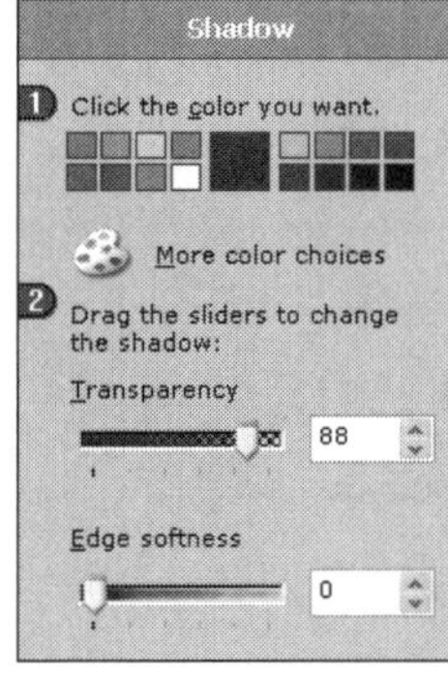

Figure 4.39 You can modify the shadow by selecting options from this pane.

✔ Tips

- To edit an applied shadow effect, select the object or group to which the shadow has been applied, choose Effects > Shadow, and then select new options.
- To remove a previously applied shadow, select the object or group to which the shadow has been applied, choose Effects > Shadow, and then click the No Shadow style in the Shadow pane.
- Projects to which shadows have been applied have layers. To maintain the layers (enabling the shadows to later be edited), you can save the project as a .PNG file.

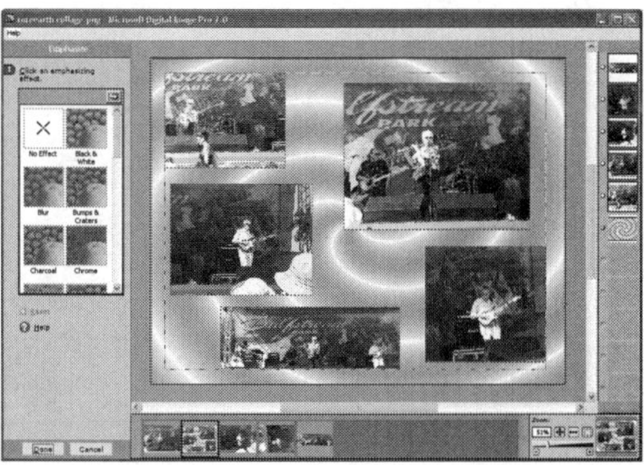

Figure 4.40 To emphasize the pictures in this collage, all of them have been selected. The effect will be applied only to the unselected background.

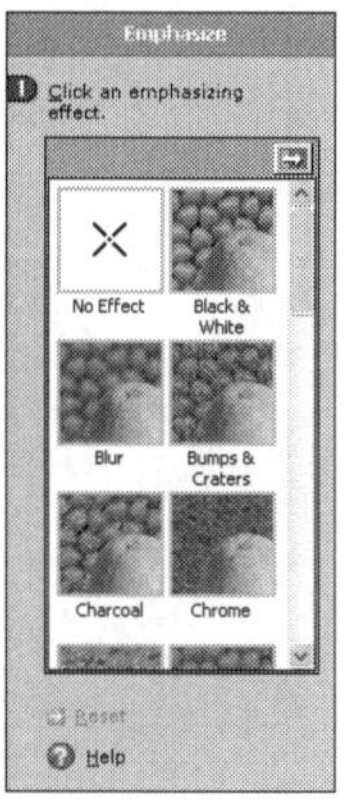

Figure 4.41 Select an emphasis effect from this scrolling list.

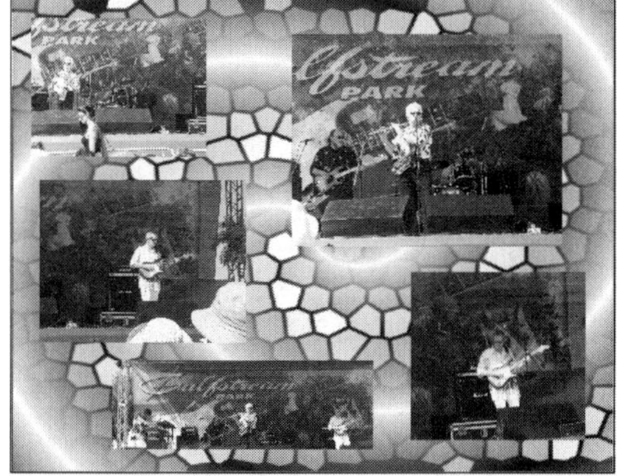

Figure 4.42 In the finished collage, the Stained Glass emphasis effect has been applied to the background.

To emphasize one or more objects:

1. Select the object or objects that you want to emphasize (**Figure 4.40**). At least one object must *not* be selected.

   The unselected objects are the ones to which the effect will be applied—resulting in the selected object(s) being emphasized.

2. Choose Effects > Emphasize.

   The Emphasize pane appears (**Figure 4.41**).

3. Select an emphasis effect from the scrolling list of examples.

   The effect is applied to all unselected objects and images. If you don't like the result, repeat this step.

4. Click Done when you are satisfied with the results (**Figure 4.42**).

✔ Tip

- In order for an emphasis effect to be visible, it must generally be applied to objects that contain some sort of pattern, texture, or image. Gradients often work nicely, as do pictures. Solid colors and blank areas, on the other hand, successfully accept only a few emphasis effects.

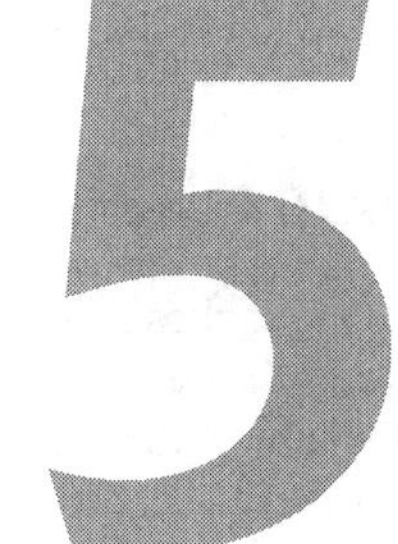

Selective Editing

In Chapter 4, you learned about the kinds of modifications you can make that affect entire images or projects. This chapter focuses on the Picture It! tools you can use to perform *selective editing* (modifications to user-selected areas within images and objects). Most such tools and techniques are for image correction, but I'll cover methods of embellishing images, too.

In this chapter, you'll learn how to make the following selective edits:

- Correcting photos and scans by removing red eye, spots, blemishes, wrinkles, scratches, and dust
- Using an assortment of brushes to make corrections and add artistic touches
- Creating cutouts and trimming selected areas of images

Note that several of the tools discussed in this chapter are illustrated in the color insert in the center of this book.

Fixing Red Eye

A flash makes it possible to take photos in less than optimal lighting. Unfortunately, human eyes sometimes appear red when exposed to a flash. *Red eye* can transform even the most beautiful child into a creature who looks more at home in a horror flick.

To remove red eye:

1. Open the picture that you want to correct.
2. Choose Touchup > Fix Red Eye, choose Touchup > Fix red eye from the Common Tasks list, or click the Fix Red Eye toolbar icon.

   The Fix Red Eye pane appears (**Figure 5.1**).
3. If necessary, adjust the zoom so you can clearly see the red in the eye(s).
4. Click a red area in one of the eyes (**Figure 5.2**), and then click Red-eye auto fix. Repeat for the other eye, if needed.
5. Click Done when you are satisfied with the results.

✔ Tips

- One adjustment doesn't always suffice. You can continue to adjust red eye until all of the redness has been removed.
- Animal eyes often turn white when exposed to a flash. Attempting to correct this using the Fix Red Eye command is liable to make pets look like zombies. A better approach is to use the Airbrush tool (described later in this chapter). If a human photo can't be corrected with Fix Red Eye, it's also worth trying the Airbrush.

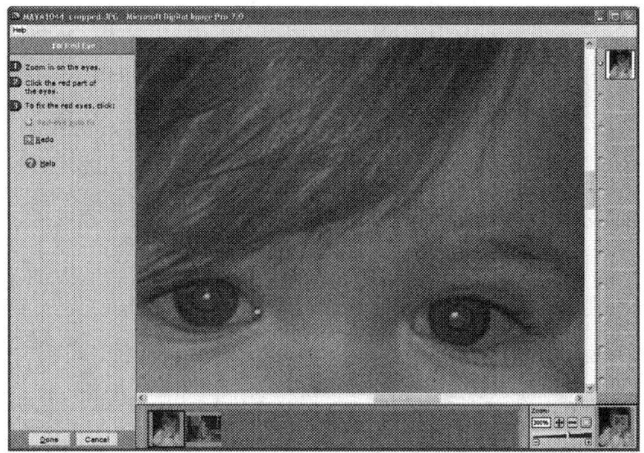

Figure 5.1 Before trying to correct red eye, zoom in so you can clearly see the eyes.

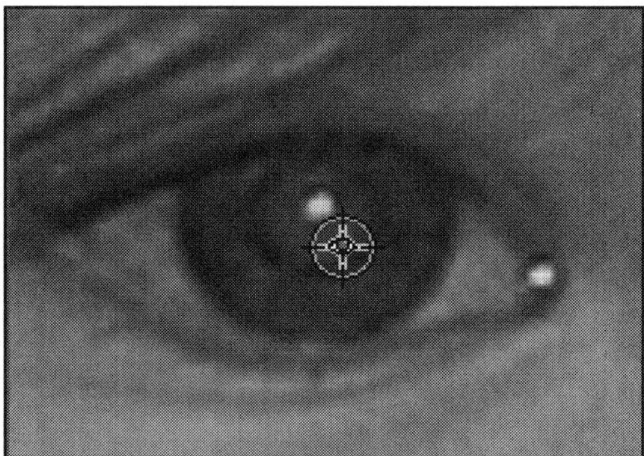

Figure 5.2 Move the cursor over a red area, click to set its position, and click Red-eye auto fix. (See the color section in this book for the resulting image.)

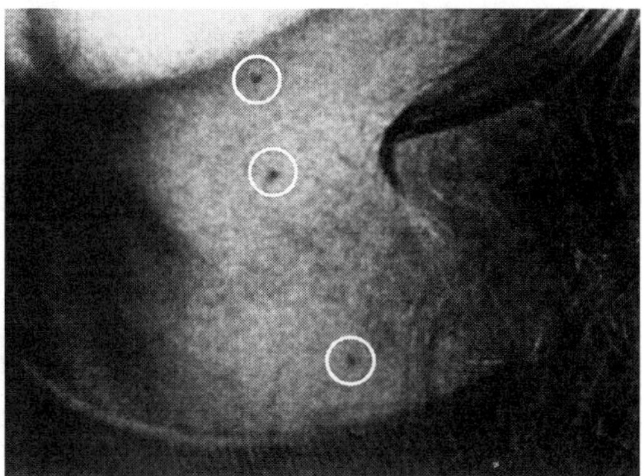

Figure 5.3 The person in this photo has several moles on his neck (marked by white circles) that we can easily remove.

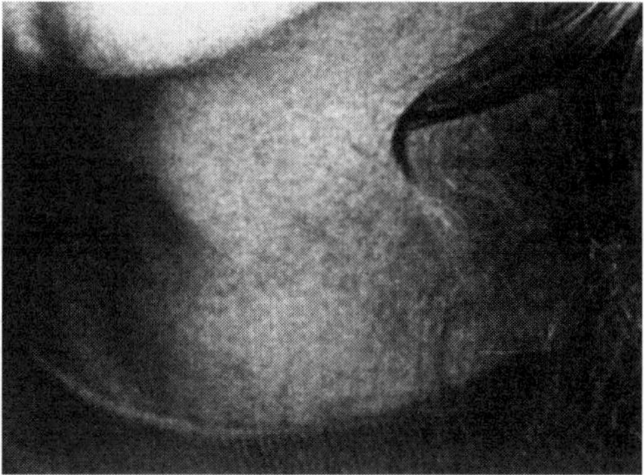

Figure 5.4 This is the same photo *sans* moles.

Removing Spots and Blemishes

Using the Remove Spots or Blemishes tool, you can eliminate minor spots and blemishes from many images. The tool works by painting over the spot/blemish with pixels like the ones surrounding the spot.

To remove a spot or blemish:

1. Open the picture that you want to correct.
2. Choose Touchup > Remove Spots or Blemishes, or choose Touchup > Remove spots or blemishes from the Common Tasks list.

   The Remove Spots or Blemishes pane appears.
3. If necessary, adjust the zoom so you can clearly see the spot or blemish (**Figure 5.3**).
4. Click the spot to remove it.
5. Click Done when you are satisfied with the results (**Figure 5.4**).

✔ Tips

- The Remove Spots or Blemishes tool works best on small spots. For larger spots, you can try clicking several times in different areas of the spot. If that fails, reset or cancel your corrections and then try another tool, such as the Clone Brush or Airbrush.
- The success of spot removal also depends on the complexity of the colors and textures in the surrounding area. Sometimes a correction blends well; sometimes it's hideously apparent.

Removing Wrinkles

Sun exposure and aging eventually take their toll on all of us. Using the Remove Wrinkles tool, you can smudge wrinkles and laugh lines, blending them with the surrounding skin.

To remove wrinkles:

1. Open the picture that you want to correct.
2. Choose Touchup > Other Photo Repair > Remove Wrinkles.

   The Remove Wrinkles pane appears.
3. Adjust the zoom so you can clearly see the wrinkles.
4. Click to select a circle that corresponds to the width of the wrinkles.
5. Click the starting point of the wrinkle, drag to cover a straight segment of the wrinkle, and then click to set the segment's end point (**Figure 5.5**).

   The area indicated by the cursor's selection box is smudged to hide the wrinkle.
6. Repeat Step 5 to select each additional straight segment of the wrinkle.
7. Click Done when you are satisfied with the results (**Figure 5.6**).

✔ Tips

- If attempting to remove a wrinkle with a single selection gives unsatisfactory results, try breaking it into shorter, straight segments and correct it in multiple passes.
- You can also use the Remove Scratches tool (discussed on the next page) to correct wrinkles, if you wish.

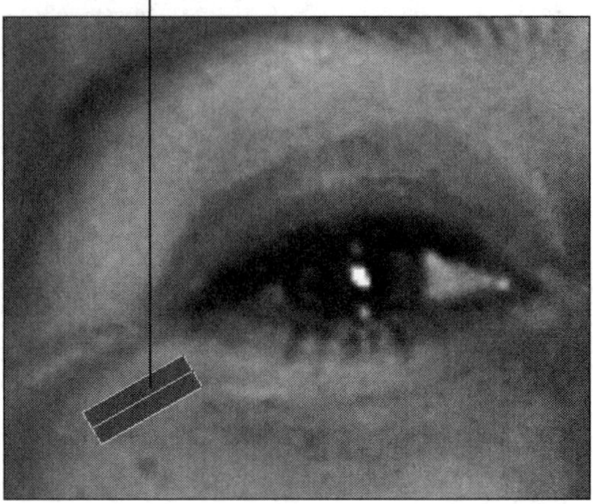

Figure 5.5 Drag to select a straight wrinkle segment.

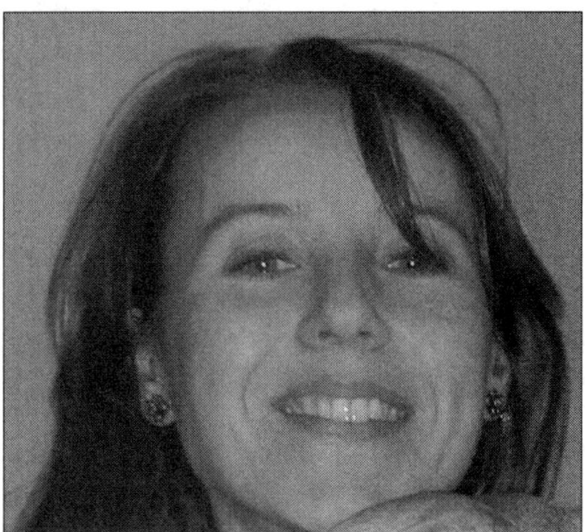

Figure 5.6 The Remove Wrinkles tool can be effective at removing small laugh lines around the eyes.

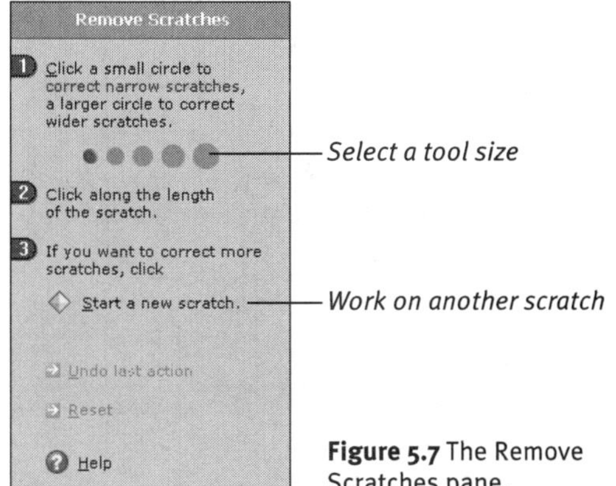

Figure 5.7 The Remove Scratches pane.

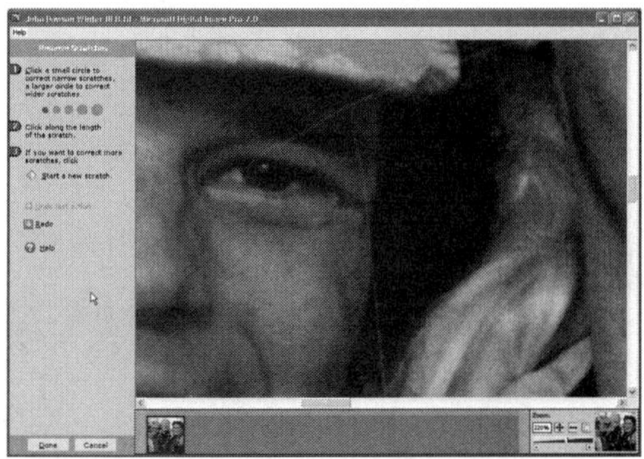

Figure 5.8 Zoom out so you can clearly see the scratches, as well as the effects of your edits.

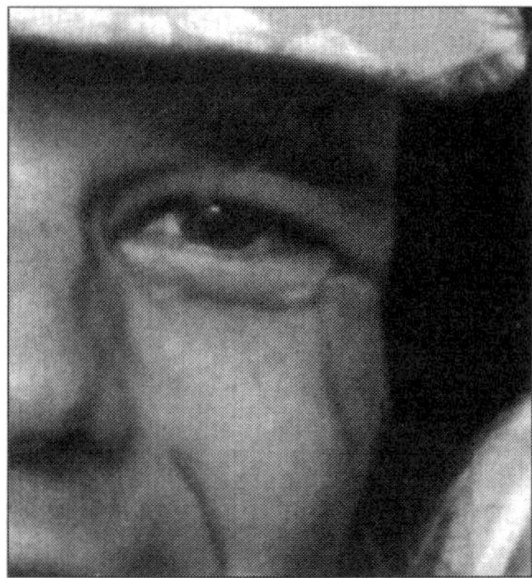

Figure 5.9 You can make a badly scratched scan presentable.

Removing Scratches

Scans—especially ones of old photos and similar materials—can contain scratches. Think of a scratch as just another form of wrinkle. The procedure for using the Remove Scratches tool is virtually identical to that of using the Remove Wrinkles tool.

To remove scratches:

1. Open the picture that you want to correct.
2. Choose Touchup > Other Photo Repair > Remove Scratches.

   The Remove Scratches pane appears (**Figure 5.7**).
3. Adjust the zoom so you can clearly see the scratches (**Figure 5.8**).
4. Click to select a circle that corresponds to the width of the scratches.
5. Click the starting point of the scratch, drag to cover a straight segment of the scratch, and then click to set the segment's end point.

   The area indicated by the cursor's selection box is smudged to hide the scratch.
6. *Do one of the following:*
   - ▲ Select another segment of the same scratch. The end point of the previous segment is used as the starting point of the new segment.
   - ▲ To begin work on a new scratch, click Start a new scratch and then click to select a new starting point.
7. Click Done when you are satisfied with the results (**Figure 5.9**).

✔ Tip

- You can also use the Remove Wrinkles tool (discussed on the previous page) to correct scratches, if you wish.

Removing Dust

When scanning a picture, dust on the image or the scanner bed can become a visible part of the scan (as tiny specks). You can use the Remove Dust command to attempt to eliminate the effects of the dust. (The Remove Dust correction is applied to an entire picture. You don't click to select individual dust specks.)

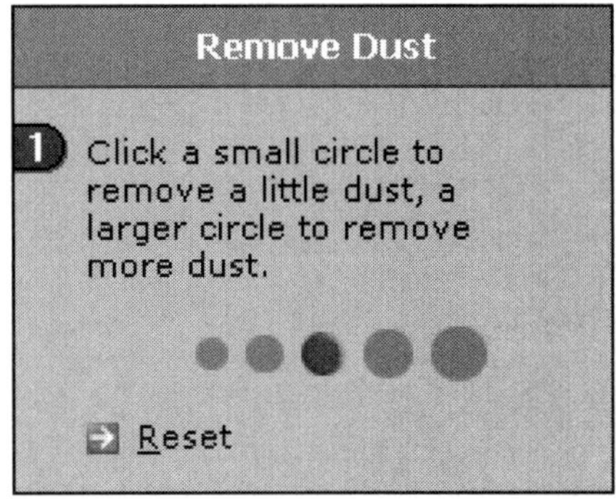

Figure 5.10 To allow Picture It! to correct a dusty scan, simply click a circle.

To remove dust from an image:

1. Open the picture that you want to correct.
2. Choose Touchup > Other Photo Repair > Remove Dust.

   The Remove Dust pane appears (**Figure 5.10**).
3. Click the circle that represents the approximate amount of dust to be removed. (Select a smaller circle for a little dust or a larger one to remove a lot of dust.)

   Picture It! adjusts the picture.
4. *Do one of the following:*
   - ▲ Click a different-sized circle to change the amount of the dust removal effect.
   - ▲ To restore the image to its previous state, click Reset.
   - ▲ To return to the Workspace with the image unchanged, click Cancel.
   - ▲ If you're satisfied with the results, click Done.

✔ Tips

- Since the effects of using the Remove Dust tool aren't cumulative, you may want to start with the smallest circle (representing the smallest dusting effect) and then work your way up. The more dusting you allow Picture It! to do, the greater the sacrificed image clarity.
- If the scan you're correcting is one of your own, forget the Remove Dust procedure. Instead, clean your scanner and the item you're scanning, and then scan it again.

Using Image Correction Brushes

Picture It! also provides a variety of special brushes for touchup work that enable you to modify or enhance specific areas of any image. The brushes can roughly be classified as one of two types: image correction and artistic. The *image correction brushes* are used mainly for editing and correcting defects, much like the tools described in the previous sections of this chapter. You use the *artistic brushes* to embellish images by adding artistic effects.

The image correction brushes include the Clone Brush, Dodge and Burn Brush, Airbrush, and Tint Brush.

- **Clone Brush.** Help suggests that the function of the Clone Brush is to duplicate objects within an image. However, its more common purpose is cleaning up images by duplicating an area to cover up smudges, scratches, and unnecessary objects.
- **Dodge and Burn Brush.** You use the Dodge and Burn Brush to make spot corrections of brightness and contrast—without affecting the entire image.
- **Airbrush.** You use the Airbrush to do touchup work by painting over areas with solid colors. The Airbrush paints in a new layer, rather than directly modifying images. As a result, there's no need to pre-select an image before issuing the command.
- **Tint Brush.** Because of unusual lighting conditions, some photos can have areas where the colors are slightly off. Although you can adjust the tint for an entire image with the Adjust Tint command (see Chapter 4), you can use the Tint Brush to correct selected parts of an image.

To use the Clone Brush:

1. If the current project contains multiple images or objects, select one to edit.
2. Choose Touchup > Clone Brush.
   The Clone Brush pane appears (**Figure 5.11**).
3. *Optional:* Click Customize settings to select a different brush shape, set the brush transparency, and/or paint with a texture.
4. Select a brush size by clicking a circle.
5. Click within the image to set the start position (the crosshair cursor).
6. Paint by clicking and dragging.
   As you drag, Picture It! maintains the distance and direction between the start position and the brush.
7. When you are satisfied with the results, click Done (**Figure 5.12**).

✔ Tips

- To avoid unnatural-looking repetition in the painted area, vary the start point, brush size, direction, and distance.
- The Clone Brush is also very useful for correcting blemishes that are too large for the Remove Spots or Blemishes tool to fix.

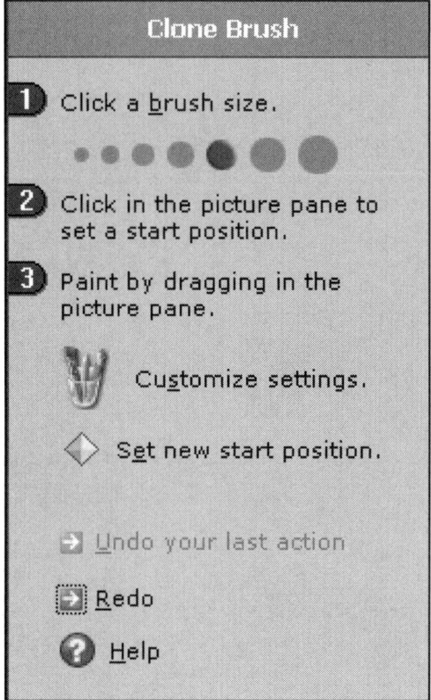

Figure 5.11 Select brush settings from the Clone Brush pane.

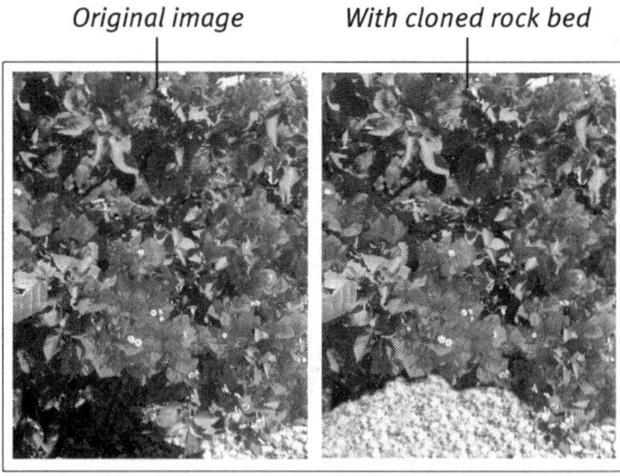

Figure 5.12 By cloning the tiny section of rocks in the original image (left), the revised image (right) has been given a rock bed to border the plant.

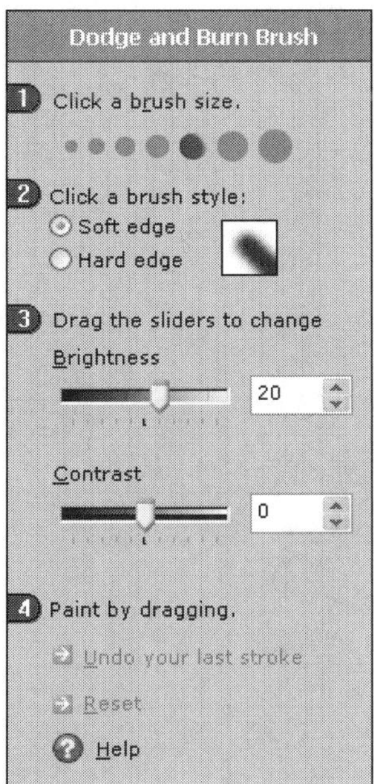

Figure 5.13 Whether you're dodging (lightening) or burning (darkening) depends on these control settings.

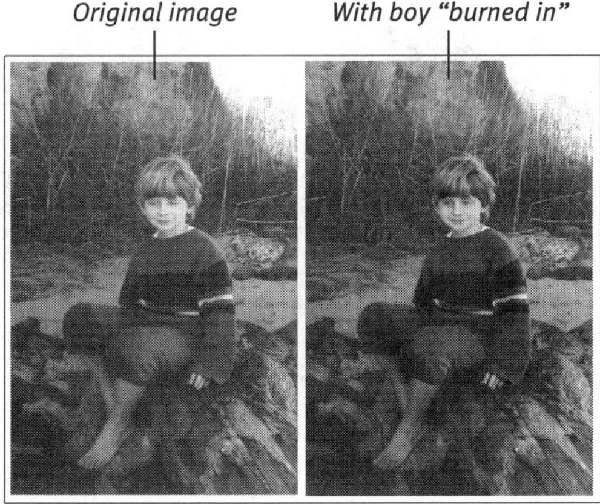

Figure 5.14 By burning in only this photo's subject, we can show more detail in his hair and face without altering the overall brightness/contrast of the image.

To use the Dodge and Burn Brush:

1. If the current project contains multiple images or objects, select one to edit.
2. Choose Touchup > Other Photo Repair > Dodge and Burn Brush.

   The Dodge and Burn Brush pane appears (**Figure 5.13**).
3. Click a circle to select a brush size.
4. Select a soft or hard edge brush style.
5. Adjust the Brightness and Contrast sliders or enter values in their text boxes.
6. Paint by clicking and dragging over areas of the image.
7. Click Done when you're satisfied with the results (**Figure 5.14**).

To use the Airbrush:

1. Choose Touchup > Other Photo Repair > Airbrush.

   The Airbrush pane appears (**Figure 5.15**). Make sure that the Airbrush paint tool is selected.
2. Select a paint color.

   To view additional color choices or to use a color that's in use in the project (by selecting it with the Eyedropper tool), click More color choices.
3. Click a circle to select a brush size.
4. *Optional:* Click Customize paint settings to select a different brush shape, set the brush transparency, and/or paint with a texture.
5. Paint by clicking and dragging over areas of the image.
6. Click Done when you're satisfied with the results (**Figure 5.16**).

   The airbrushed painting is added as a new item in the Stack.

✔ Tips

- Because the airbrush editing is simply another new object, you'll find that you can easily move, resize, or delete it.
- To avoid inadvertently moving an airbrush object, you may wish to group it with the underlying image. Refer to Chapter 6 for information on grouping images and objects.

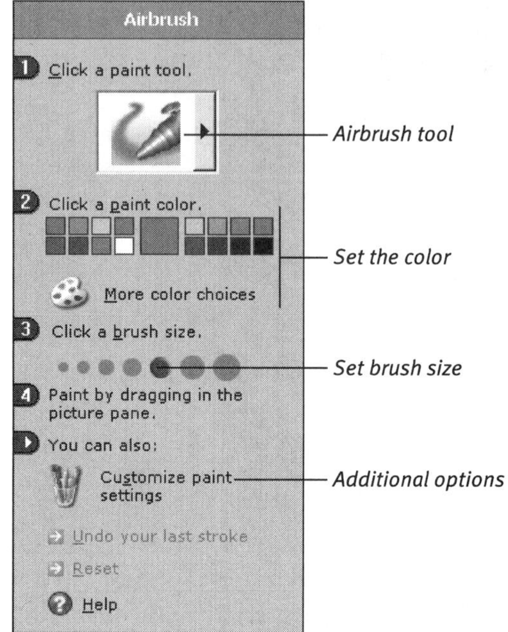

Figure 5.15 Before painting, set options in the Airbrush pane.

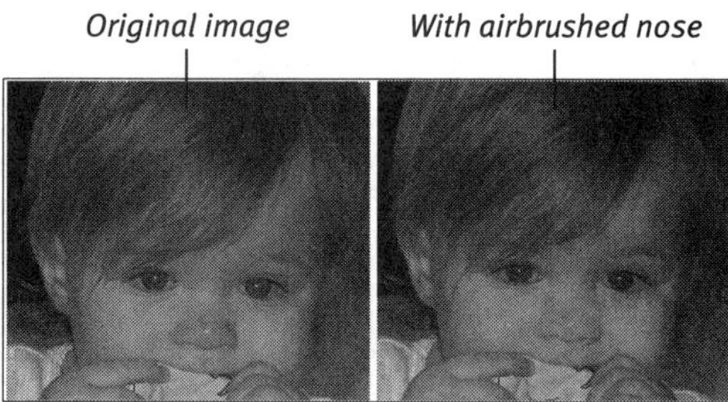

Figure 5.16 By painting over the baby's nose with a flesh-colored brush (sampled from the face), I was able to eliminate much of her nose's redness.

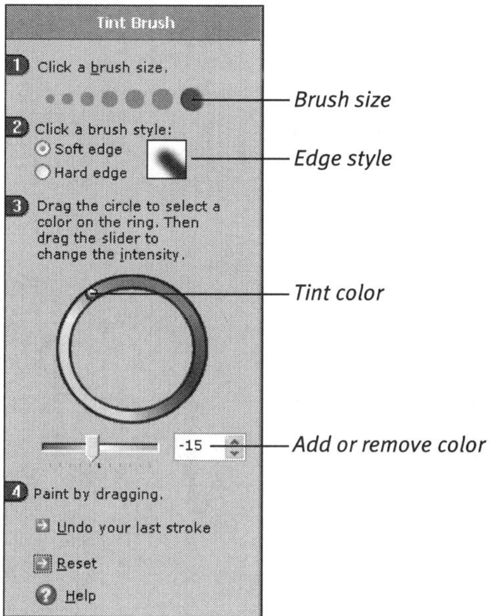

Figure 5.17 The Tint Brush pane.

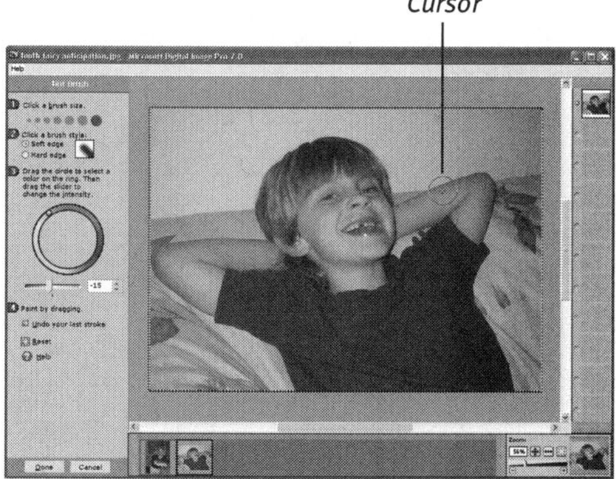

Figure 5.18 Using the Tint Brush, you can selectively reduce the reddish tint in this subject's face and arms without altering the rest of the photo.

To use the Tint Brush:

1. If the current project contains multiple images or objects, select one to edit.
2. Choose Touchup > Other Photo Repair > Tint Brush.

   The Tint Brush pane appears (**Figure 5.17**).
3. Click a circle to select a brush size.
4. Select a soft or hard edge brush style.
5. Select the color that you want to increase or decrease by dragging the ball inside the ring.
6. Adjust the slider or the number in the text box to indicate whether you are adding or removing the selected color.
7. Paint by dragging over areas of the image (**Figure 5.18**).
8. When you're satisfied with the results, click Done.

✔ Tip

- Be careful how you drag the cursor over the image. If you repeatedly drag over the same area, the effect is cumulative. Instead of removing only a little of the reddish tint in Figure 5.18, repeatedly dragging the cursor over the boy's face and arms can result in a zombie-like appearance.

Using Artistic Brushes

Use artistic brushes to create artistic effects in your images and photos. The artistic brushes include the Colorize Brush, Distortion Brush, Transparency Brush, and Paint Brushes.

- **Colorize Brush.** You use the Colorize Brush to selectively add color to images in much the same way as you would use a paint brush.
- **Transparency Brush.** You can use the Transparency Brush to soften parts of an image. Unlike the Transparent Fade commands (Even and Gradual), the Transparency Brush can be applied selectively to an image.
- **Distortion Brush.** The Distortion Brush is a "just for fun" tool. Using it, you can create outlandish distortions by stretching and reshaping images and objects.
- **Paint Brushes.** Picture It! provides two styles of paint brushes. The Freehand Brushes work like real paint brushes and are used to touch up or modify images. The Photo Stroke, Art Stroke, and Stamps Brushes let you add artistic touches (to embellish greeting card projects, for example). All brush styles automatically store their strokes in a new layer.

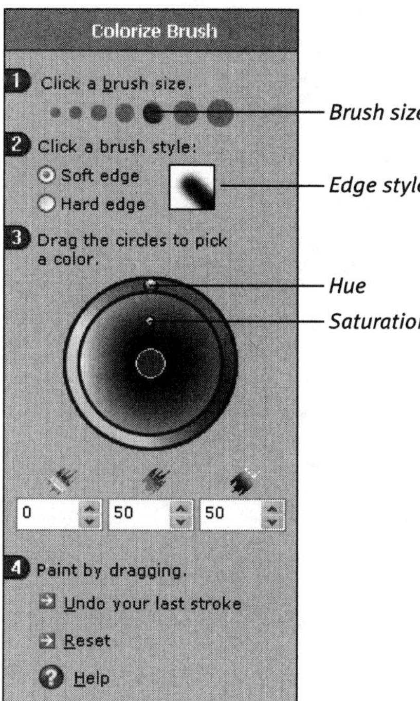

Figure 5.19 Set options for the Colorize Brush in this pane.

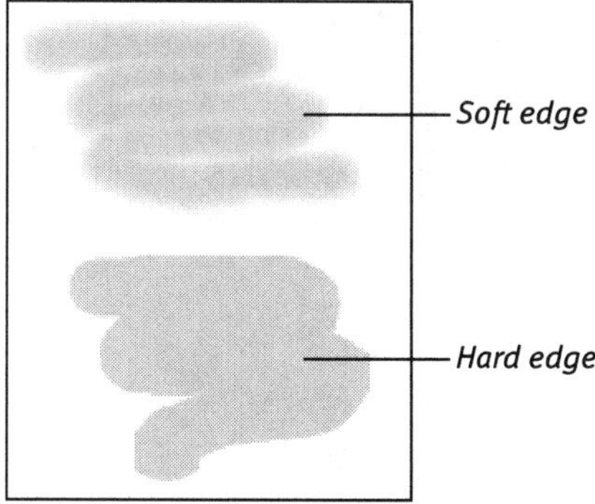

Figure 5.20 Examples of soft- and hard-edged brush styles.

To use the Colorize Brush:

1. Choose Effects > Colorize Brush.

   The Colorize Brush pane appears (**Figure 5.19**).

2. Click a circle to select a brush size.

3. Select a soft- or hard-edge brush style (**Figure 5.20**).

4. Select a drawing color by dragging the balls inside the colored circles or by entering numbers in the text boxes.

   For instructions, see "Adjusting Hue and Saturation" in Chapter 4.

5. Color by clicking and dragging within your picture.

6. When you're satisfied with the results, click Done.

✔ Tips

- Although you can use the Colorize Brush to add extra color to a color image, it works best on grayscale (black-and-white) images. To change a color photo or scan to grayscale, choose Effects > Black and White.

- Colorizing tends to start out faint. To make a colored area more intense, drag the brush over it again.

To use the Transparency Brush:

1. If the current project contains multiple images or objects, select one to edit.
2. Choose Effects > Transparent Fade > Transparency Brush.
   The Transparency Brush pane appears (**Figure 5.21**).
3. Click a circle to select a brush size.
4. Select a soft- or hard-edge brush style (see Figure 5.20).
5. Set the degree of transparency by dragging the slider.
6. Click and drag within the picture to add transparency.
7. When you're satisfied with the results, click Done.

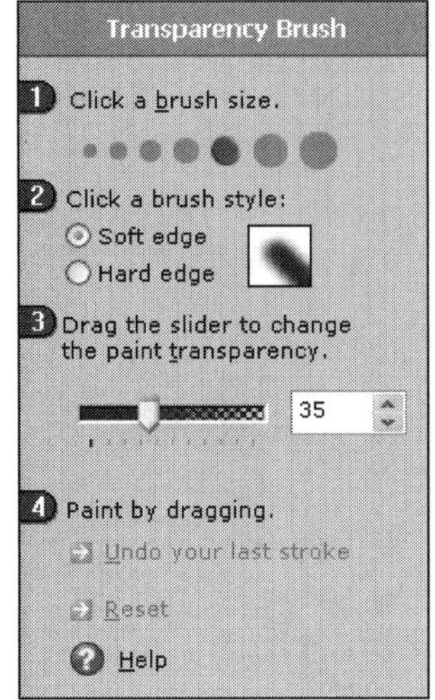

Figure 5.21 Set options for the Transparency Brush in this pane.

✔ Tips

- To increase the transparency/softening effect, run the brush repeatedly over an area.
- Having added transparency to an image, other images and objects placed on a lower layer can now shine through (**Figure 5.22**). See Chapter 6 for more information about layers.

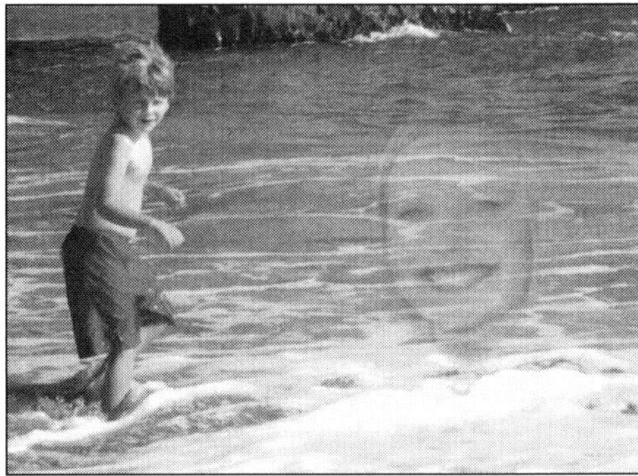

Figure 5.22 Objects and images placed beneath a transparent area can now show through.

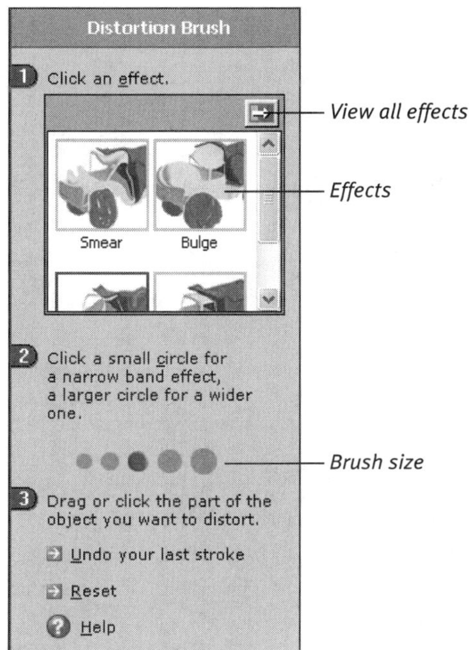

Figure 5.23 Select an effect and a brush size from this pane.

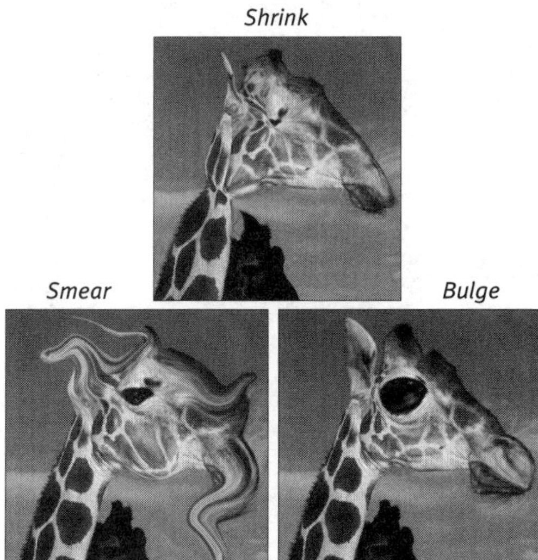

Figure 5.24 The three Distortion Brush effects.

To use the Distortion Brush:

1. If the current project contains multiple images or objects, select one to edit.
2. Choose Effects > Distortion Brush.
   The Distortion Brush pane appears (**Figure 5.23**).
3. Select a distortion effect by clicking its icon.
   To view all effect icons without having to scroll, click the arrow icon above them.
4. Click a circle to select a brush size.
5. Click and drag over the image to distort it.
6. Click Done when you're satisfied with the results (**Figure 5.24**).

✔ Tips

- You can change distortion effects while you're painting. That is, you don't have to restrict your edits to a single effect.
- As with most other brushes, the more times you drag over an area, the greater the resulting distortion.
- To undo all or part of a distortion effect, choose the Erase effect and then paint over the area that you want to undo. To completely restore the image to its original form, click Reset.
- You can remove the effects of your most recent stroke by clicking Undo your last stroke. You can use this to your advantage by making a series of small strokes rather than a single, continuous stroke. (Releasing the mouse button ends a stroke.) Undoing your most recent stroke is usually preferable to using the Reset command to undo *all* of your brush strokes.

To paint with the Freehand Brushes:

1. Choose Effects > Paint Brush > Freehand, or choose Effects > Freehand painting from the Common Tasks list.

   The Freehand Painting pane appears (**Figure 5.25**).
2. Select a paint tool (**Figure 5.26**) and color with which to paint.

   To choose a different color or use the Eyedropper to pick up an existing color from your project, click More color choices.
3. Click a circle to select a brush size.
4. *Optional:* Click Customize paint settings to select a different brush shape, set the brush transparency, and/or paint with a texture.
5. Click and drag to paint.
6. Click Done when you're satisfied with the results (**Figure 5.27**).

   Your painting is saved as a new Stack layer.

✔ Tips

- While painting, you can freely change brush types, sizes, and colors.
- Make additional passes over a painted area to increase the effect's saturation.
- You can use the Eraser brush to selectively remove parts of a painted effect.

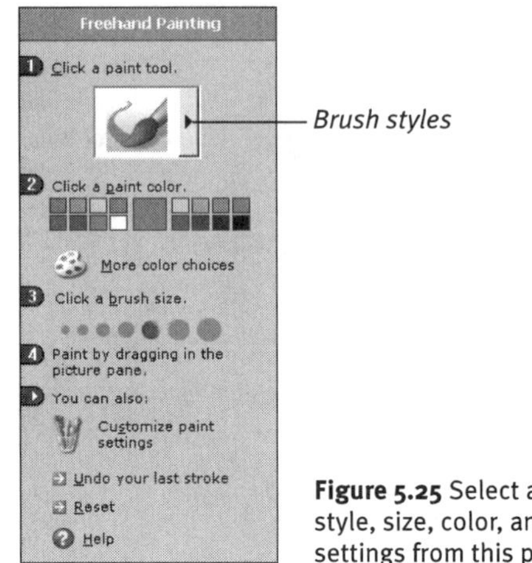

Figure 5.25 Select a brush style, size, color, and other settings from this pane.

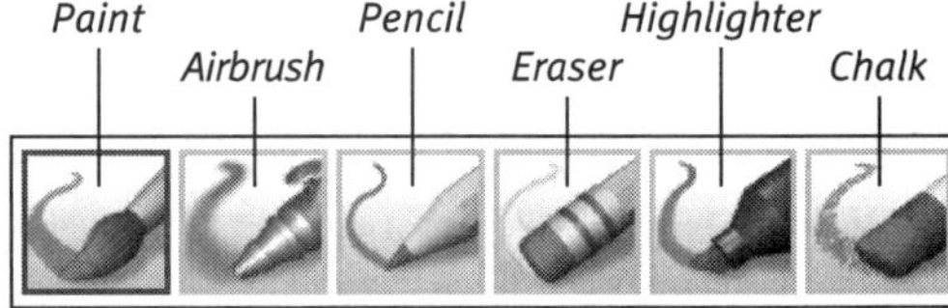

Figure 5.26 Select a Freehand Brush style.

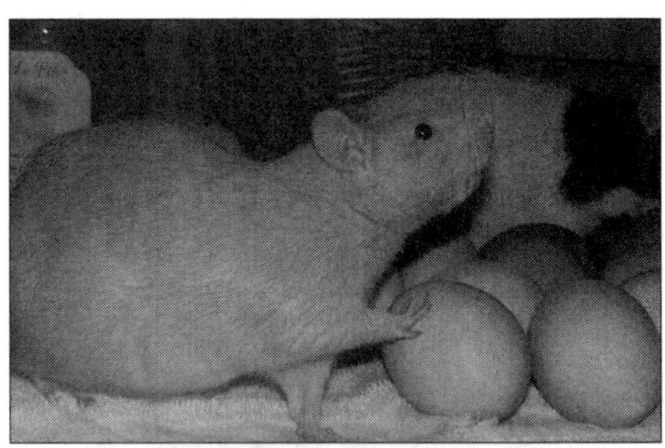

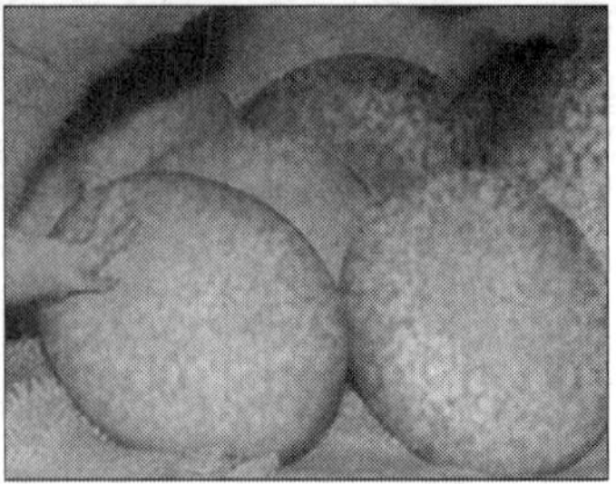

Figure 5.27 I used a white, textured Chalk Brush to add a speckled pattern to the eggs.

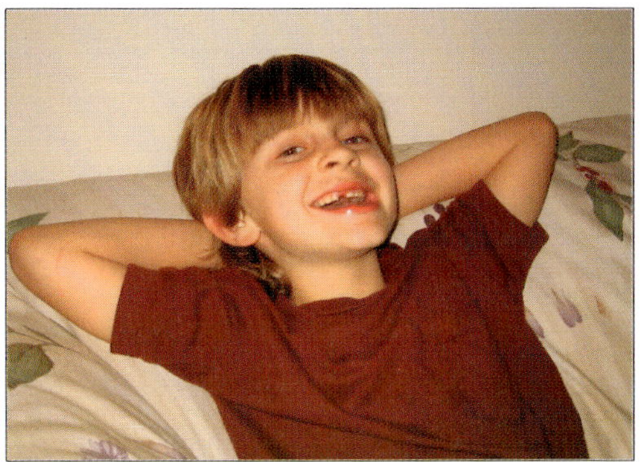

Original image

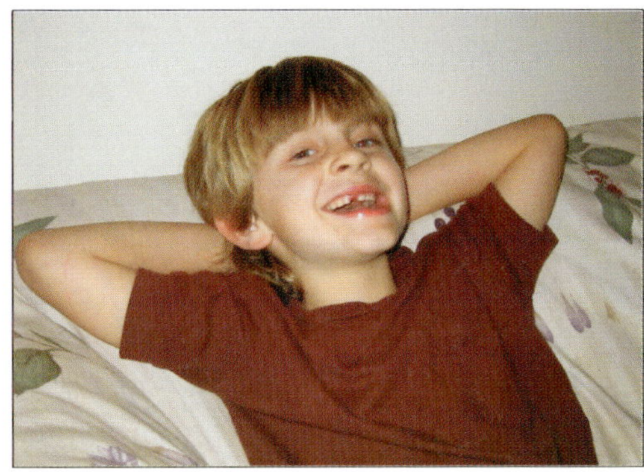

Tint Auto Fix applied

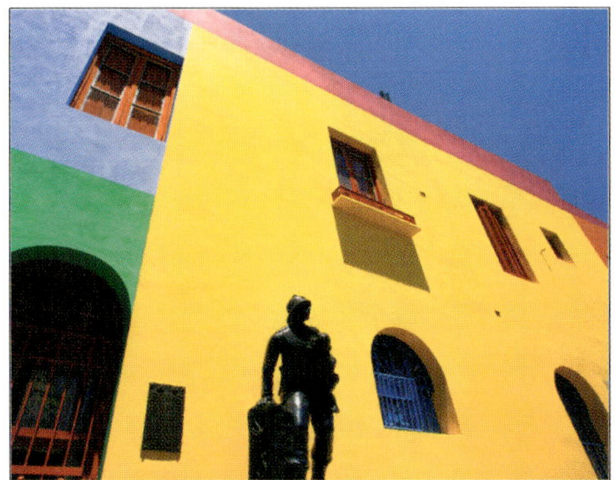

Original image

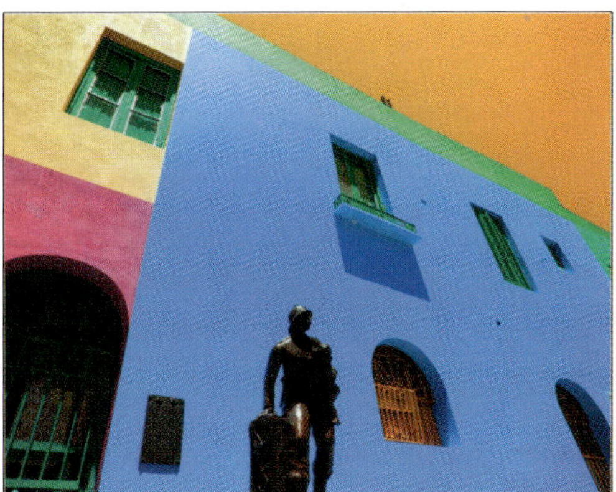

Hue and saturation altered

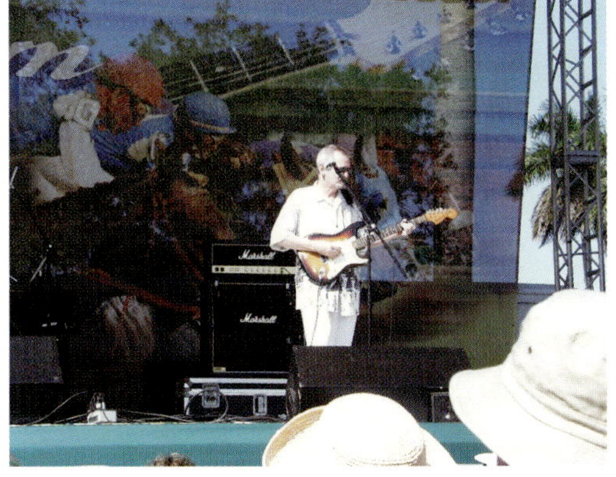

Original image

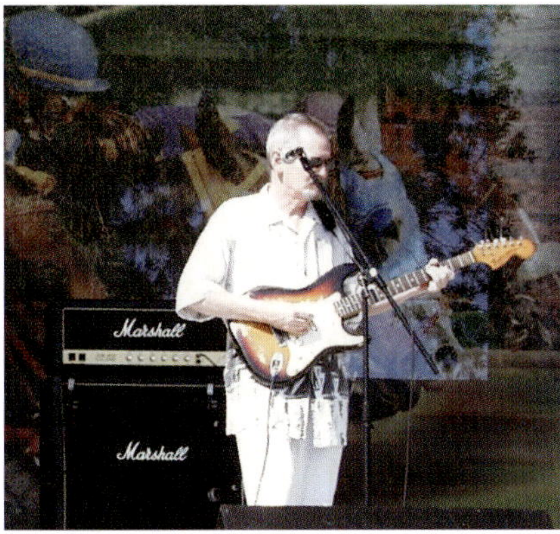

Cropped to remove distractions

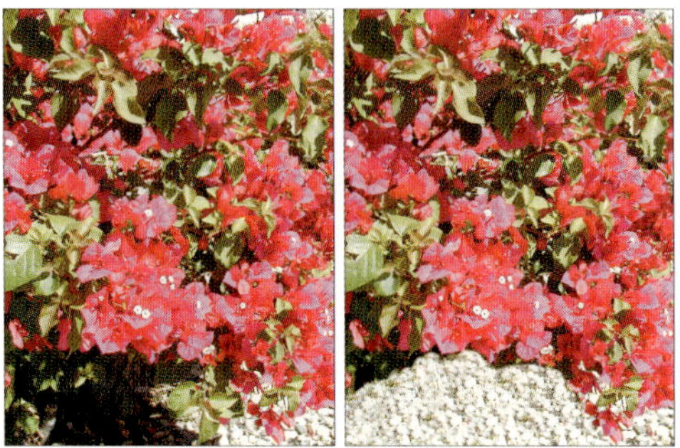

Cloned rock bed

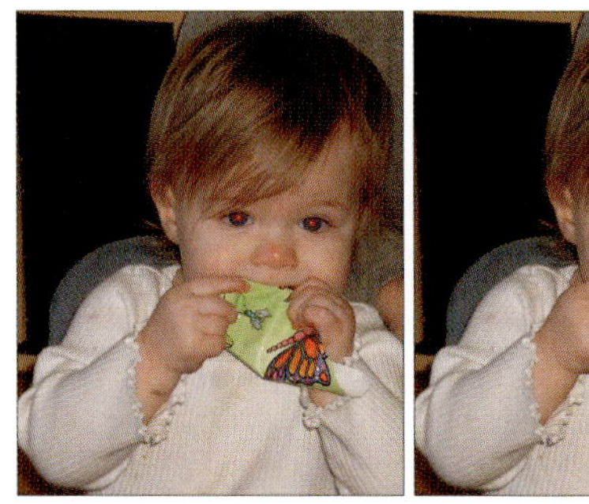

Red eye correction

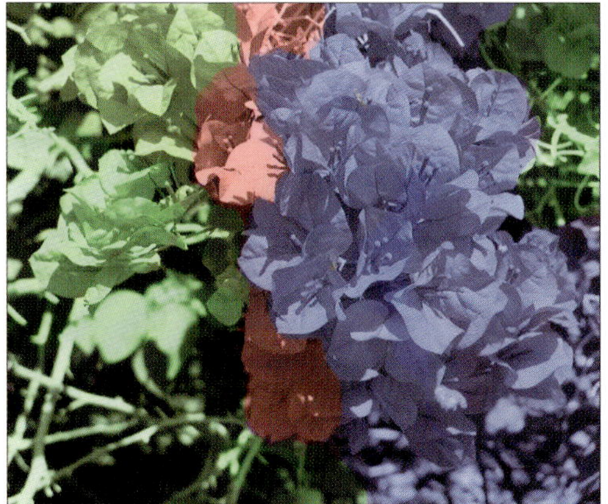

Colorized bougainvillea

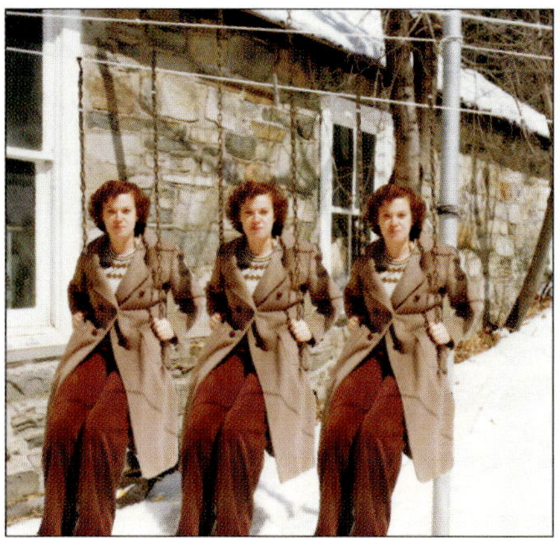

Triplets created by duplicating a cutout

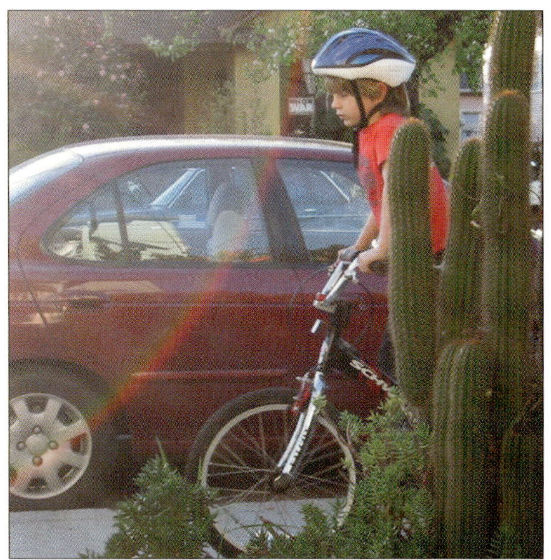

Original photo

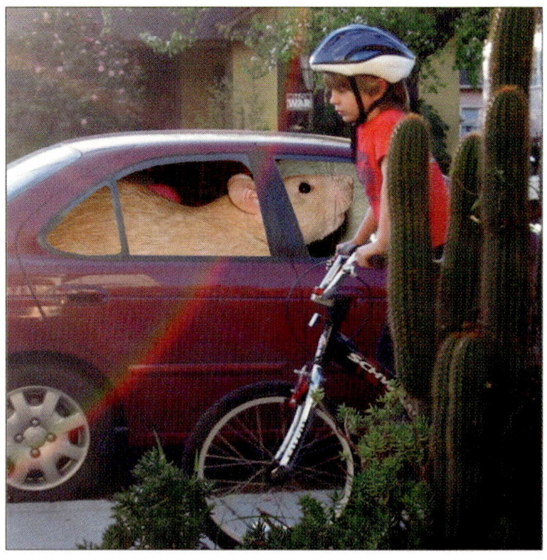

Modified by trimming the car windows

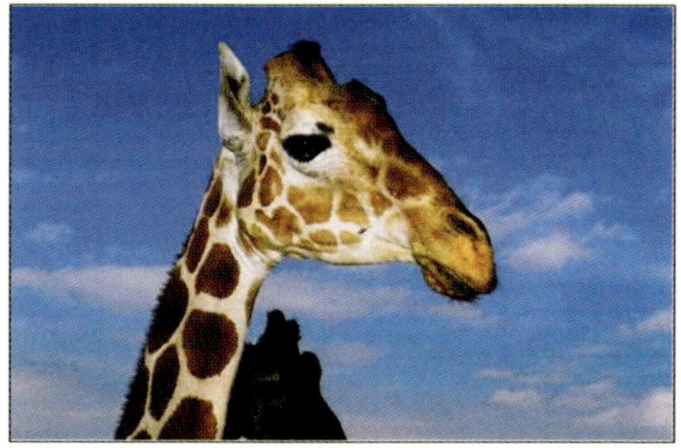

Original image

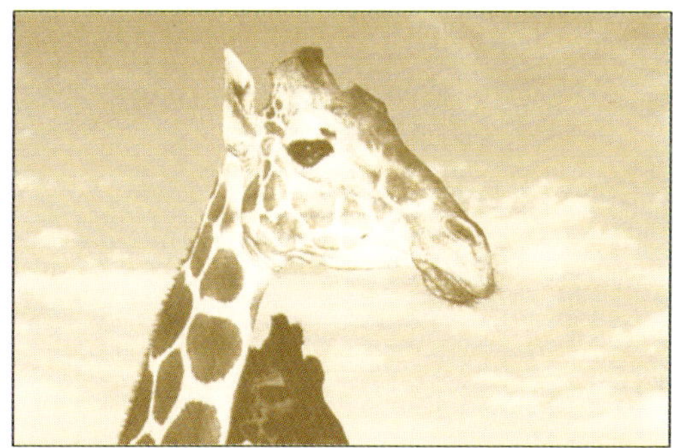

Antique

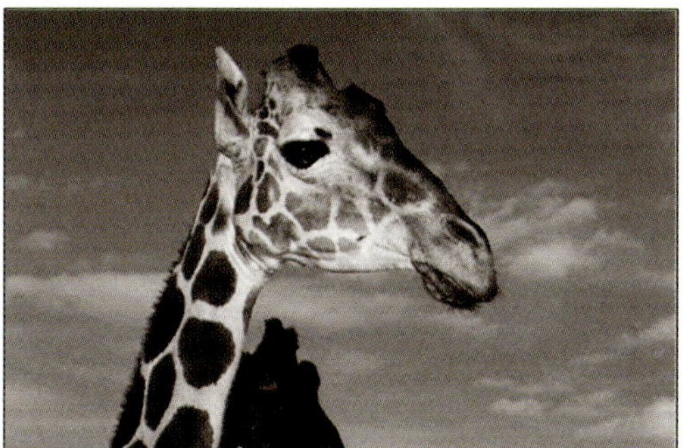

Black and White

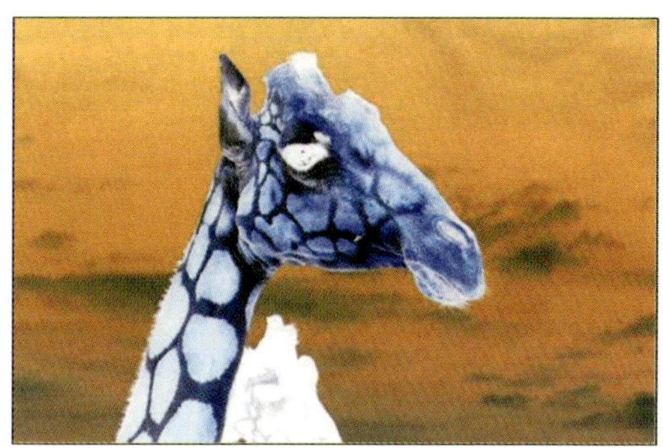

Negative

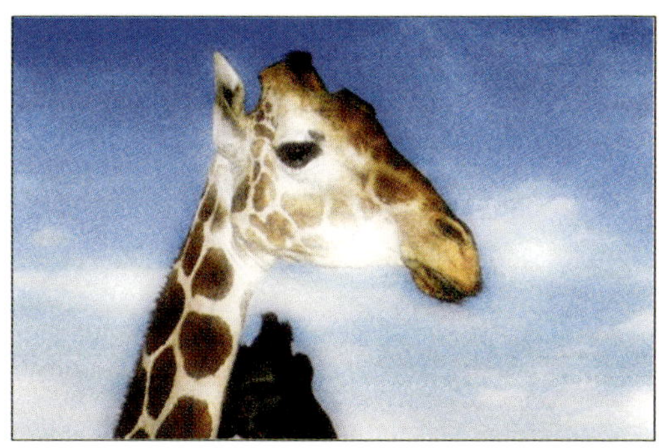

Diffuse Glow

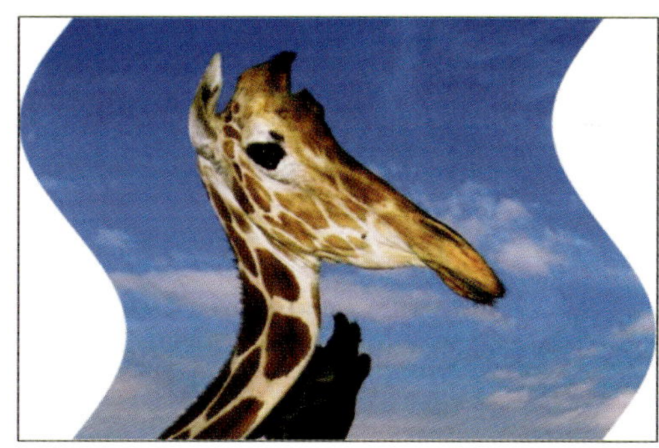

Distort

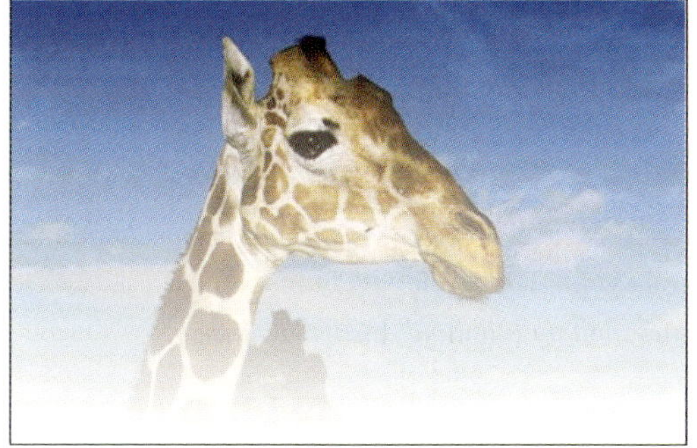

Transparent Fade - Gradual

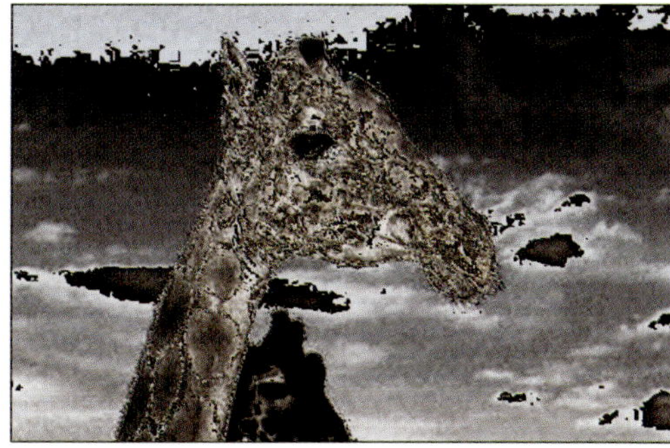

Metallic Onion (Photoshop plug-in)

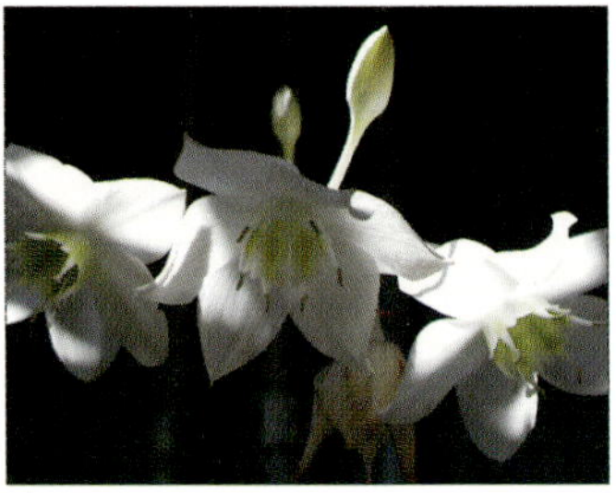

Original image

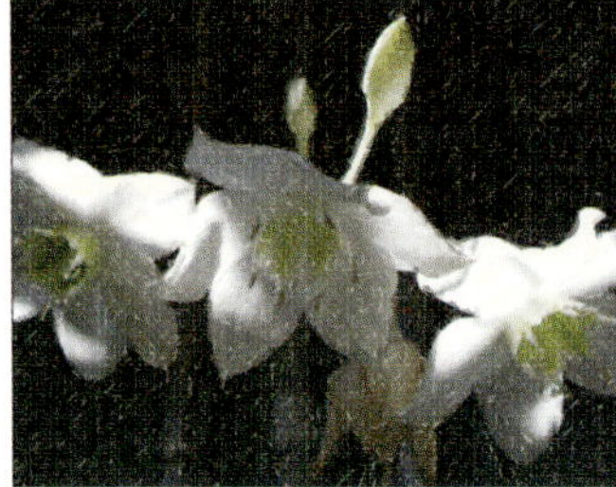

Burlap

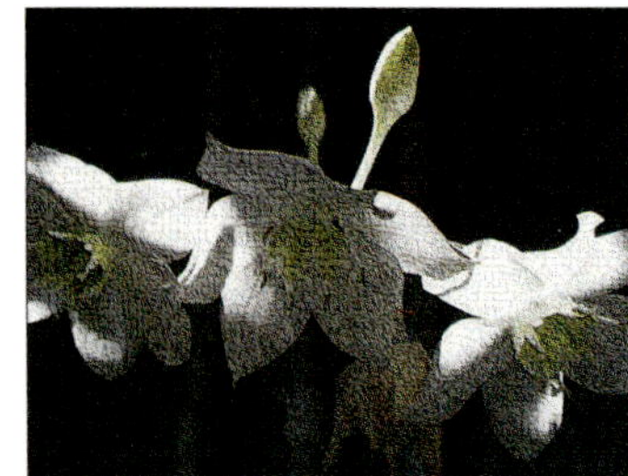

Charcoal: Contrast

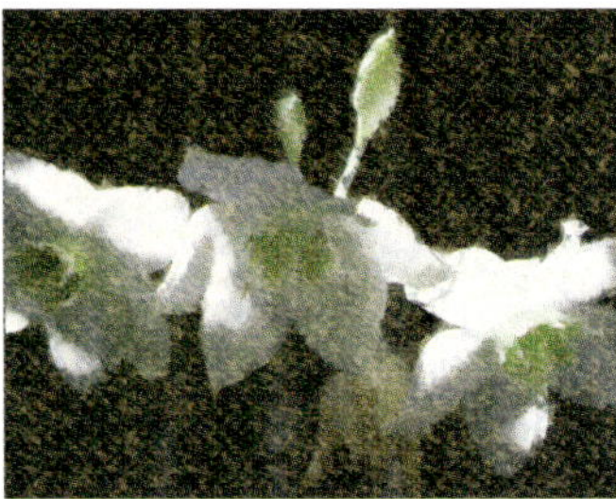

Crayon Rub

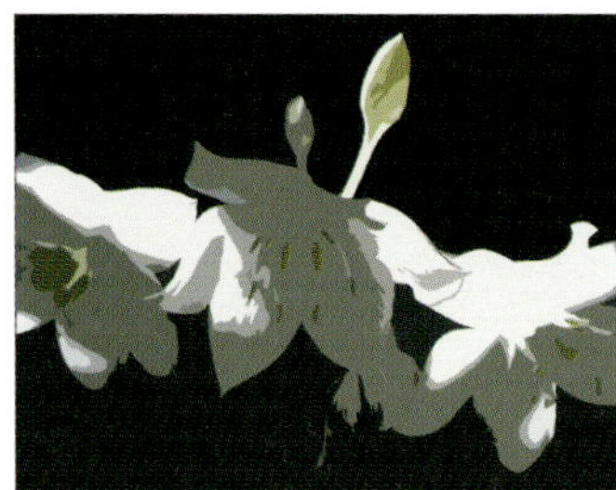

Cutout

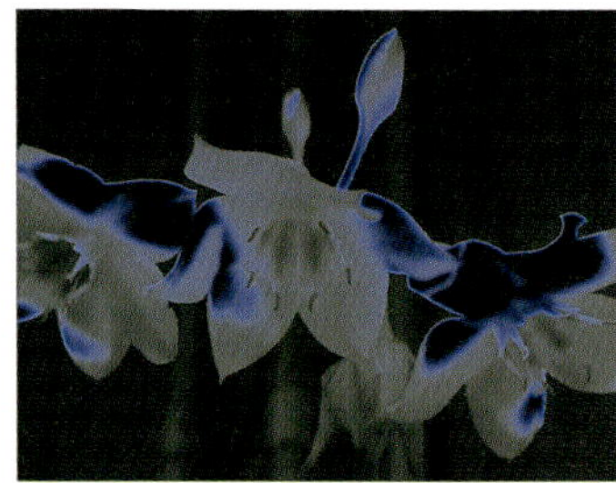

Glow: Neon

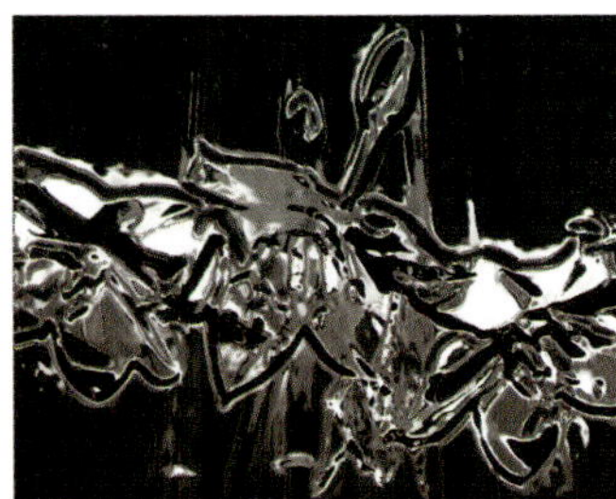

Metal: Chrome Simple

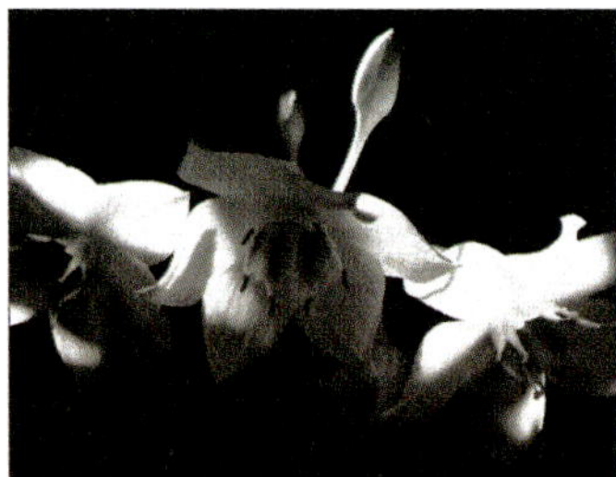

Pencil: Canvas

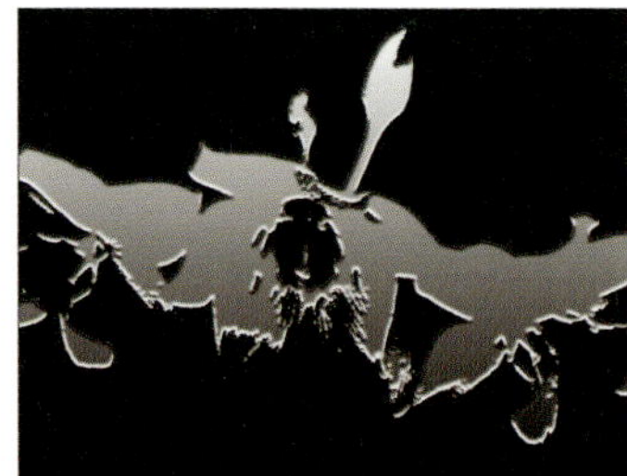

Plaster

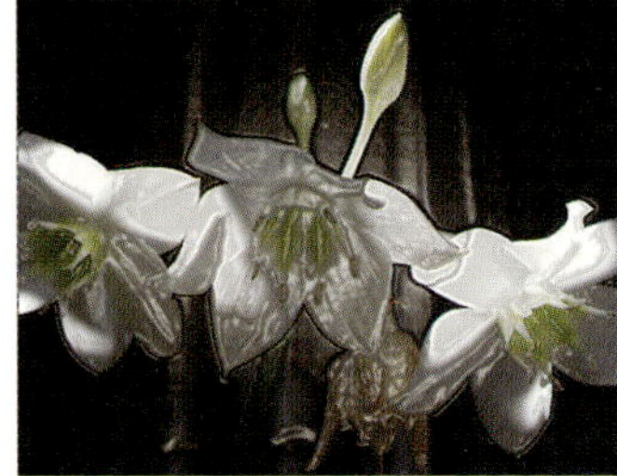

Plastic Wrap

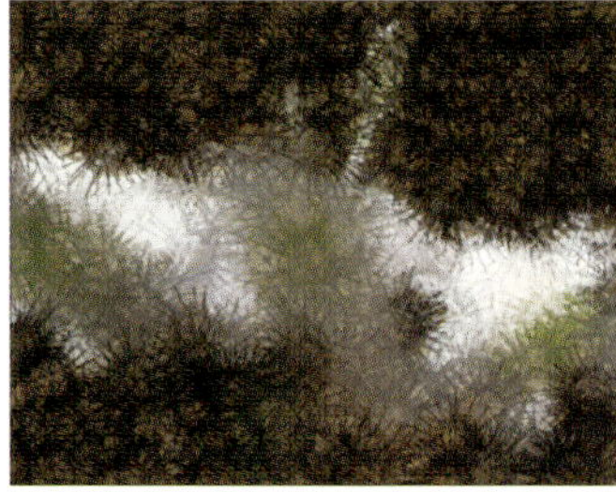

Water Color: Big Splatter

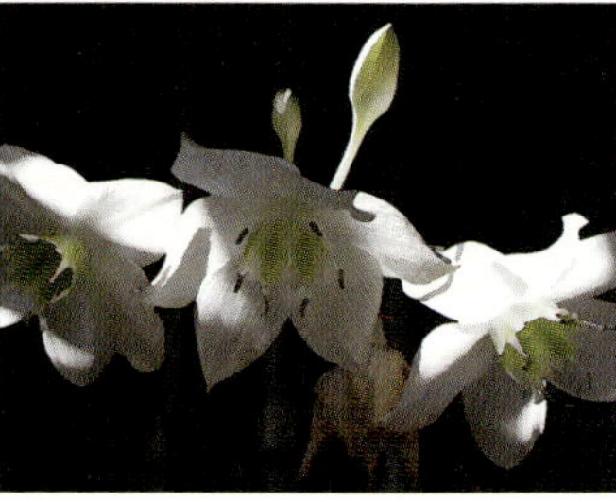

Water Color: Traditional

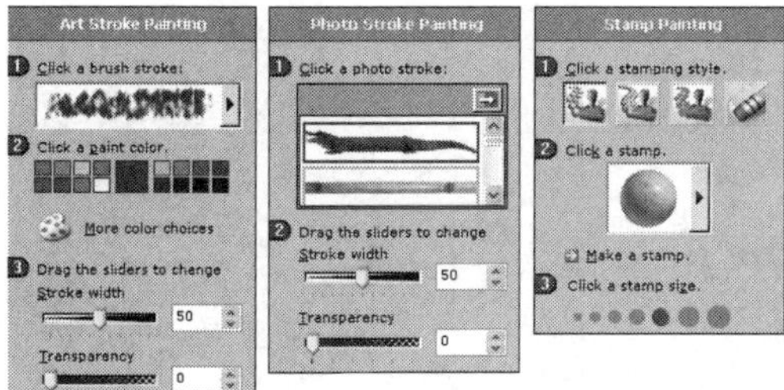

Figure 5.28 Set options in one of these Painting panes.

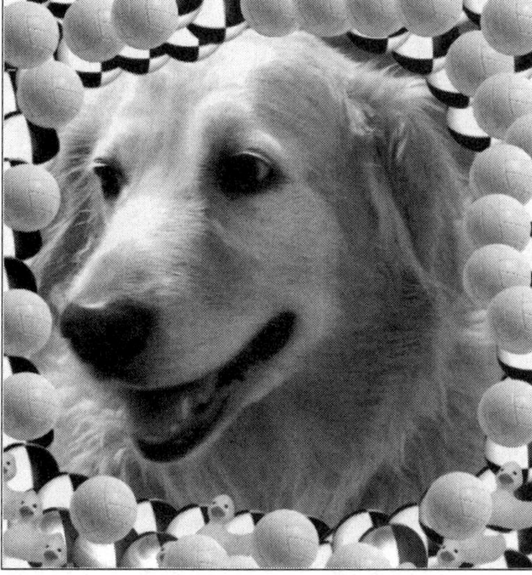

Figure 5.29 Using the Stamps Brush, I framed Murphy with an assortment of her favorite toys.

To paint with the Photo Stroke, Art Stroke, or Stamps Brush:

1. From the Effects > Paint Brush submenu, choose Photo Stroke, Art Stroke, or Stamps.

   A Painting pane appears (**Figure 5.28**).

2. Select a pattern or object with which to paint.

3. Depending on the brush type you chose in Step 1, you can set the following additional options:

   ▲ Set the stroke width (Art Stroke, Photo Stroke) or brush size (Stamps).

   ▲ Set the stamping style (Stamps).

   ▲ Specify a transparency percentage (Art Stroke, Photo Stroke).

   ▲ Set the color (Art Stroke).

4. Click and drag to paint.

5. Click Done when you're satisfied with the results (**Figure 5.29**).

   Your painting is saved as a new Stack layer.

✔ Tips

■ While painting, you can freely change brush options and settings.

■ The Stamps Brush has an Eraser stamp, which you can use to remove stamps by dragging over them.

Creating Cutouts

The Picture It! manual says that a cutout is a special effect. (A *cutout* is a traced part of an image that is automatically copied and made into a new layer.) While a cutout can indeed be used to create interesting visual effects, it's also one of the main tools for selective editing. After creating a cutout of an object or person, you can:

- Apply filters, corrections, and other edits to the cutout without affecting the rest of the image or project.
- Duplicate the cutout (using the Copy command), and then Paste it into the same photo or other Picture It! projects.

To create a cutout:

1. Open the image from which you want to create a cutout.
2. Choose Format > Create a Cutout, or choose Crop or rotate > Create a cutout from the Common Tasks list.

   The Create a Cutout pane appears.
3. Select one of these cutout methods:
   - *With the Edge Finder.* Drag straight line segments around the item and then close the outline. Click Next and adjust the outline by dragging the line segments (**Figure 5.30**).
   - *By tracing an area on my own.* Drag to trace around the item, close the outline, and click Next. (Dragging is done freehand.)
   - *By color selection.* In uncluttered photos, this is the quickest, most accurate method. In the new pane (**Figure 5.31**), you can elect to add or remove clicked colors from the selection, click spots or drag across an area, change the Eyedropper's sensitivity, and select only areas connected to the clicked spot or all similar areas. When you're finished (**Figure 5.32**), click Next.

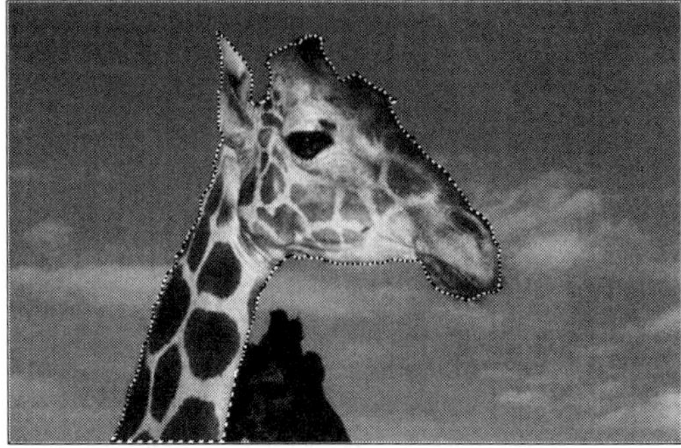

Figure 5.30 Using the Edge Finder method, it's possible to get good outlines of fairly complex objects.

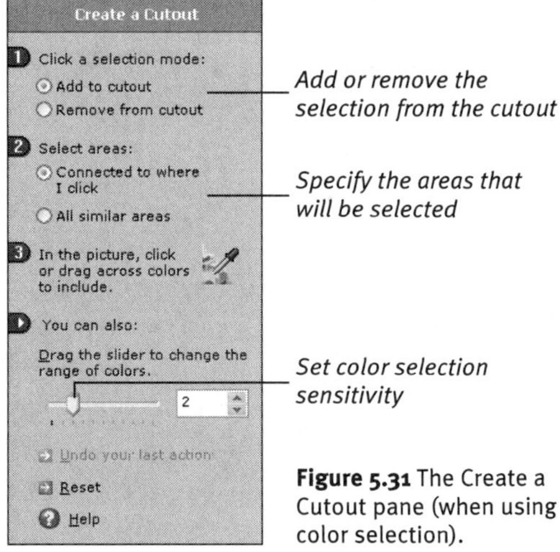

Figure 5.31 The Create a Cutout pane (when using color selection).

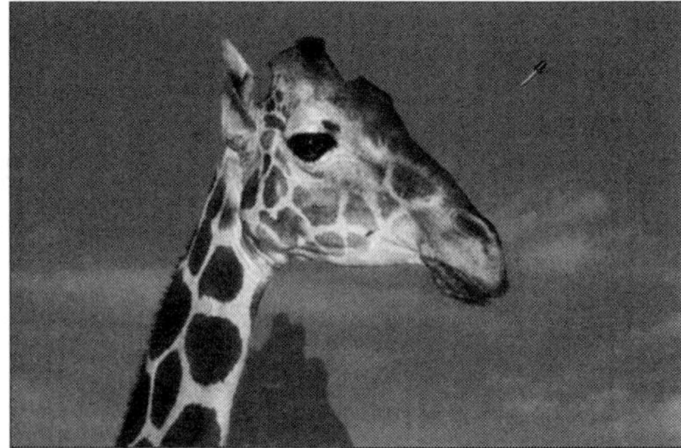

Figure 5.32 Because the background in Figure 5.30 is simple and the giraffe is complex, I used the Eyedropper to select all background components.

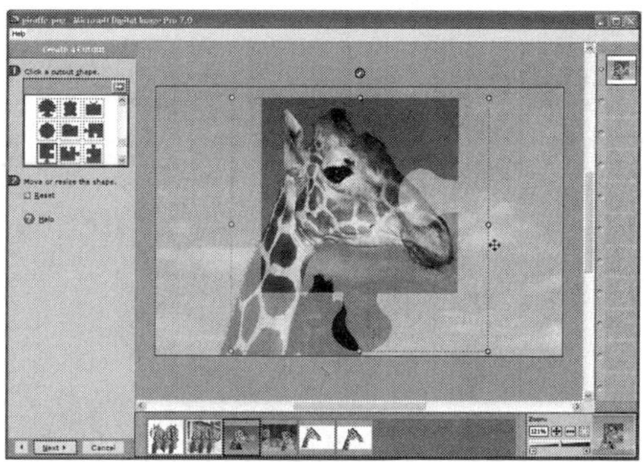

Figure 5.33 Creating a shape-based cutout is similar to cropping to a selected shape.

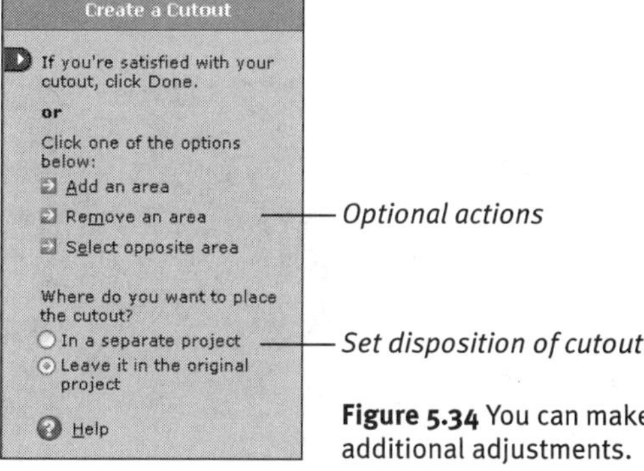

Figure 5.34 You can make additional adjustments.

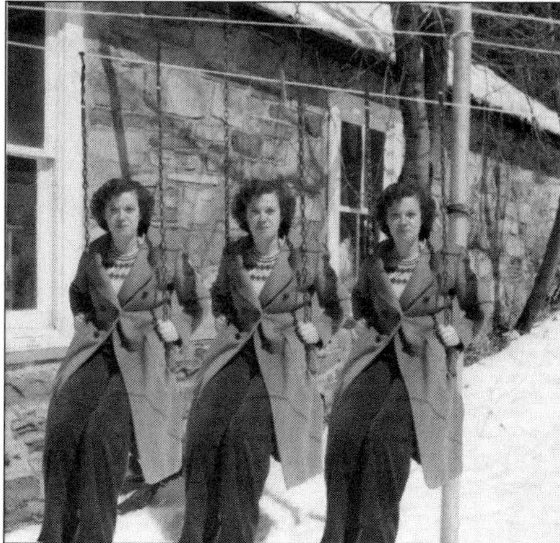

Figure 5.35 By duplicating the woman and the swing set chain, I transformed her into identical triplets.

- ▲ *With a cookie cutter shape.* This method is excellent for creating greeting card images, since it doesn't rely on precise object selection. You just enclose part of the image in a predefined shape.

  Select a shape (**Figure 5.33**), resize it with the adjustment handles, move it over the part of the image to be cut, and click Next.

4. *Optional:* In the new pane that appears, you can choose from these options:
   - ▲ If you used a tracing method, you can instruct Picture It! to Smooth last edge.
   - ▲ To edit the cutout (**Figure 5.34**), click Add an area or Remove an area (to add or remove an area from the cutout).
   - ▲ To swap the removed and selected areas, click Select opposite area (see Figure 5.34).
5. From the same pane (see Figure 5.34), choose one of these cutout disposition options:
   - ▲ To create the cutout as a duplicate object directly over the old object, click Leave it in the original project.
   - ▲ To place the cutout in a new project, click In a separate project.
6. Click Done (**Figure 5.35**).

✔ Tips

- Although it's possible to cut out objects from almost any photo, you'll find it easiest when the object is relatively distinct from the other items in the photo. It also helps if the object is fairly high contrast—making it simpler to distinguish its edges from the surrounding items.
- Using the color selection method, it's sometimes easier to select the parts of the picture to *not* include in the cutout (see Figure 5.32, for example). Then in Step 4, click Select opposite area.
- Cutouts and trimming are not available in Picture It! Express.

Trimming Areas

Trimming an image is similar to creating a cutout. Rather than duplicating a selected area, trimming removes the selection from the image, leaving a transparent hole. A common use for trimming is to remove a scene from a window and place a new scene behind it that shows through the trimmed panes.

To trim an area:

1. Open the image that you want to trim and then select it.
2. Choose Format > Trim.
3. Select one of the following methods from the Trim pane that appears:
   - *With the Edge Finder.* Drag straight line segments around the area and then close the outline. Click Next and adjust the outline by dragging line segments.
   - *Trace it on my own.* Drag to trace around the area, close the outline (**Figure 5.36**), and click Next.
   - *With a cookie cutter shape.* Select an area using a predefined shape. Select a shape, resize it using the adjustment handles, move it over the part of the image to be trimmed, and click Next.
4. *Optional:* In the new pane, you can choose any of these options:
   - To allow Picture It! to try to smooth the selection, click Smooth last edge.
   - To trim an additional area, select a method by clicking With the Edge Finder or By tracing an area on my own.
   - To swap the removed and selected areas, click Select opposite area.
5. Click Done (**Figure 5.37**).

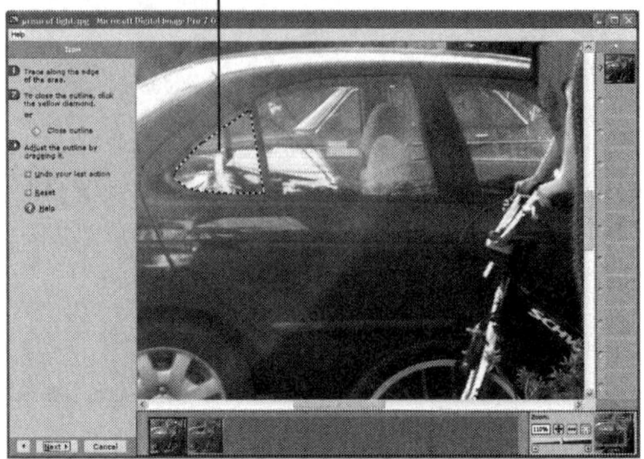

Figure 5.36 The car has three window sections that can be trimmed by manually tracing them.

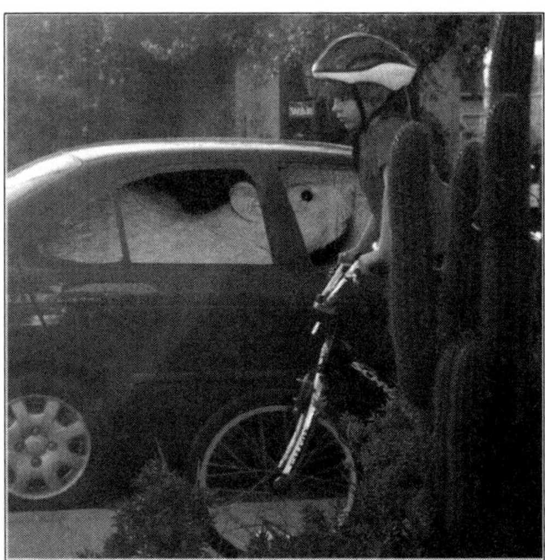

Figure 5.37 By trimming the three car windows and placing a photo of Aura (the rat) behind the original image, I've created a movie poster for *Attack of the Oversized Rats.*

Working with Layers

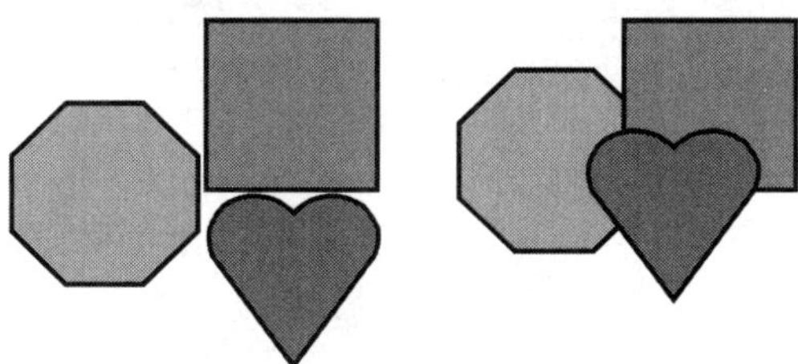

Figure 6.1 When you add objects that don't overlap (left), the layering isn't apparent. Shift their positions slightly (right), and you can see that each object is in a different layer.

As you add objects to a Picture It! project (such as text, shapes, and additional images), each new object is stored in its own layer, one layer higher than the previous object (**Figure 6.1**). This has several important implications for how you will work in Picture It!

First, having objects in separate layers means that you can edit each one individually. For example, an added text title isn't just a mass of dots embedded in your image. It's still ordinary, editable text. If you later find the need to make changes, you can move the text to a different location, edit what it says, or alter its font, size, or color.

Second, because there are layers, the order in which objects are placed determines what you can or can't see. A solid object in a higher layer will obscure any object that it's placed over.

In this chapter, you'll learn to do the following:

- Use the Stack to select objects and change the layering order
- Apply layering order commands to objects
- Group and ungroup objects
- Add new items, such as text, shapes, lines, and other pictures, to a *composite* (a group of objects placed together within a picture)

Using the Stack

The Stack is found along the right edge of the window (**Figure 6.2**). Whenever you add an item to the current project (such as a photo, shape, or text string), a thumbnail of the item appears at the top of the Stack. You can use the Stack to select an object to edit or move, delete objects, or change the layering order of objects.

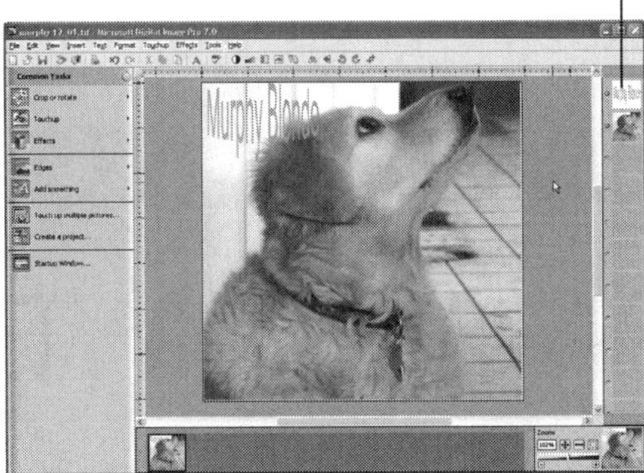

Figure 6.2 Every object in the current composite or project has its own thumbnail in the Stack.

To use the Stack:

- *Do any of the following:*
  - To select an object that you want to edit, click its thumbnail in the Stack. Selecting an object in the Stack simultaneously selects it in the workspace.
  - To change the layering order of items, select an item in the Stack and drag it up or down to a new position (indicated by the horizontal bar). When you release the mouse button, the layering change is executed.
  - To move an object one layer forward or backward, right-click the object in the Stack and then choose the appropriate command from the pop-up menu that appears (**Figure 6.3**).
  - To delete an object, select it (by clicking it in the Stack or the workspace). Then press Del, Delete, or Backspace; choose Edit > Delete; or right-click it in the Stack and choose Delete from the pop-up menu (see Figure 6.3).

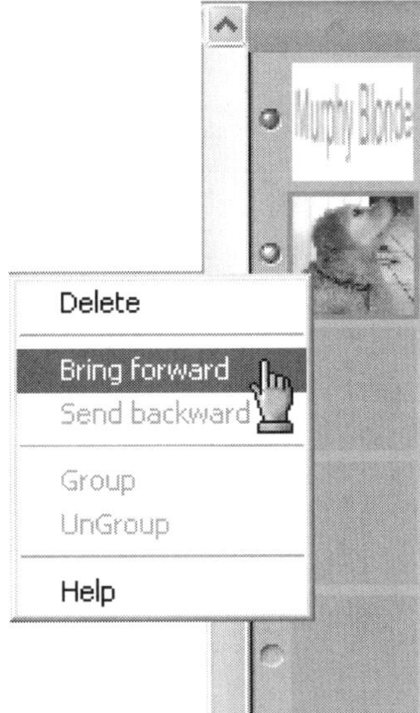

Figure 6.3 Change the layering order of an object by right-clicking it in the Stack and choosing a command from this pop-up menu.

✔ Tips

- You can directly select an object by clicking it in the workspace. However, you'll find that selecting it by using the Stack is often easier—especially when you're working with tiny objects or ones that are buried beneath several layers.
- When no object is selected, the radio buttons of all objects in the Stack are gray.

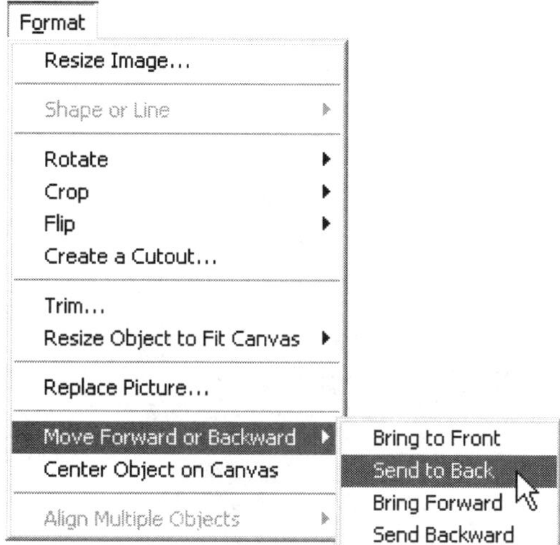

Figure 6.4 To change an object's layer, you can choose commands from the Format › Move Forward or Backward submenu.

Changing the Layering Order with Menus

Picture It! also provides menu commands that you can use to change the layering order of objects. Of course, whether you use these commands or manipulate the Stack directly is up to you. The result is the same.

To change the layering order using menus:

1. Select the object whose layering position you want to change. (Click the object in the workspace or in the Stack.)
2. Choose Format > Move Forward or Backward.
3. From the Move Forward or Backward submenu (**Figure 6.4**), do one of the following:
   - ▲ To move the selected object all the way to the front or back layer, choose Bring to Front or Send to Back, respectively.
   - ▲ To change the object's position by only a single layer, choose Bring Forward or Send Backward. (Repeat as necessary to move additional layers.)

✔ Tip

- While you *can* hide elements by placing them behind other layers, it's generally a better idea to delete them. Unused elements add unnecessarily to the file size and—if you intend to print the project with a PostScript printer—increase the printing time.

Grouping Objects

Working with multiple objects—each in its own layer—can sometimes be cumbersome. For example, suppose you want to apply a series of effects to all objects except your photo. It's much easier to accomplish this if you can treat the objects as a *group*, rather than as a set of unrelated items scattered over the workspace.

To group two or more objects:

1. Ctrl-click the items that you want to group (**Figure 6.5**).

   The Multiple Selection icon appears beneath the items.

2. To group the selected items, click the Multiple Selection icon or choose Edit > Group.

   The items will be surrounded by a single selection rectangle, and the icon will change (**Figure 6.6**).

✔ Tips

- Grouped items are represented in the Stack as a single, composite item on a single layer.
- To ungroup previously grouped items, select the group, and then click the Group icon or choose Edit > Ungroup. Note that some effects previously applied to the group may be removed by ungrouping the items.

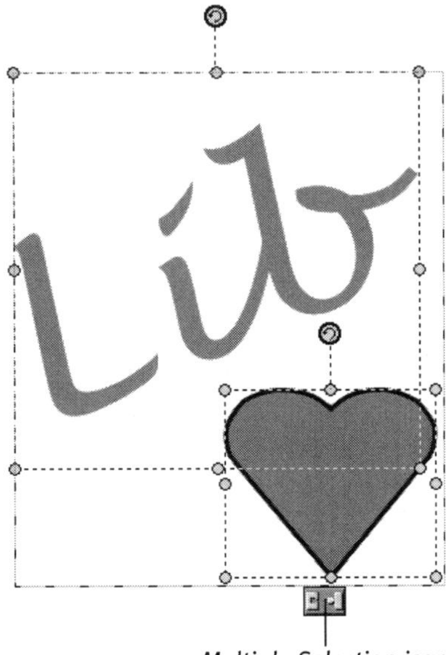

Figure 6.5 Select the items you want to group and click the Multiple Selection icon.

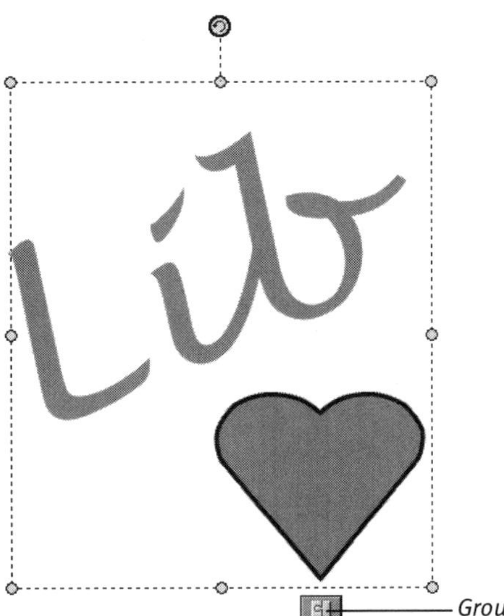

Figure 6.6 When grouped, the items can be selected as a unit. The icon changes to show that they're grouped.

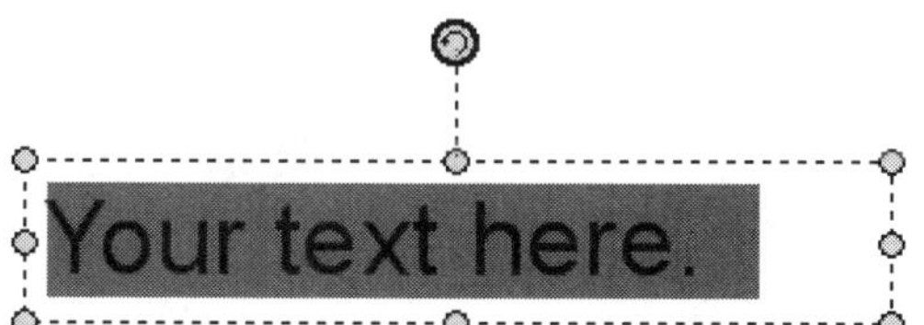

Figure 6.7 A sample text object appears in the workspace, ready for you to replace with your own text.

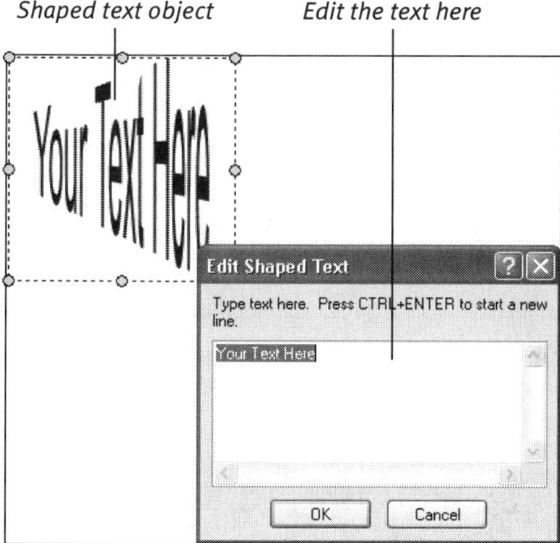

Figure 6.8 When placing shaped text, the sample and the Edit Shaped Text dialog box appear together.

Adding Objects

Much of the work you'll do with Picture It! will only involve a single object—generally, a photo that you're correcting, resizing, cropping, or saving in a new format. Occasionally, however, you may want to embellish a picture by adding text, shapes, lines, or other images to it.

Adding text

Picture It! allows you to add two types of text to your images: *normal text* and *shaped text* (text that's shaped by an invisible bounding box).

To add normal text to a picture:

1. *Do one of the following:*
   - ▲ Choose Text > Insert Text.
   - ▲ In the Common Tasks list, choose Add Something > Text.

   A text box containing some sample text appears in the workspace (**Figure 6.7**).
2. Edit the text, as desired.

To add shaped text to a picture:

1. *Do one of the following:*
   - ▲ Choose a shape from the Text > Insert Shaped Text submenu.
   - ▲ In the Common Tasks list, choose a shape from the Add Something > Shaped Text submenu.

   The Edit Shaped Text dialog box appears and a text box is added to the workspace (**Figure 6.8**).
2. Edit the text, as desired, and then click OK.

   The shaped text replaces the sample text in the workspace.

✔ Tip

- You can change the font, size, or color of all or selected text within any text object. For information on formatting text, see Chapter 7.

Adding lines

You can add straight or freehand lines to your pictures (as decorative elements or as callouts to important items, for example).

To insert and modify a straight line:

1. Choose Insert > Line, or choose Add something > Shape or lines > Line from the Common Tasks list.

   A straight line appears in the workspace (**Figure 6.9**).

2. To change the selected line's length or angle, click and drag one of its handles.

3. To change the line's thickness, choose Format > Shape or Line > Line Thickness. (You can also right-click the line and choose Change Shape or Line > Line Thickness.)

   In the Line Thickness dialog box (**Figure 6.10**), specify a new thickness (in points) by clicking an icon or by entering a number in the text box. Then click OK.

4. To change the line's color, choose Format > Shape or Line > Line Color. (You can also right-click the line and choose Change Shape or Line > Line Color from the pop-up color palette that appears.)

   In the Change Color dialog box (**Figure 6.11**) or palette, select a color or click More Colors to set a custom color. Then click OK.

✔ Tip

- You can also change a selected line's color or thickness by clicking the Line Color or Line Thickness toolbar icon, and then choosing an option from the drop-down palette or menu that appears, respectively.

Figure 6.9 An inserted line is initially always the same length, thickness, and color.

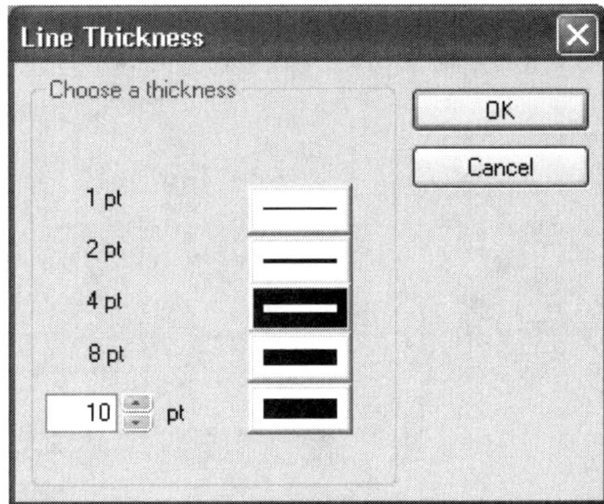

Figure 6.10 Line thickness is measured in points. (There are 72 points to an inch.)

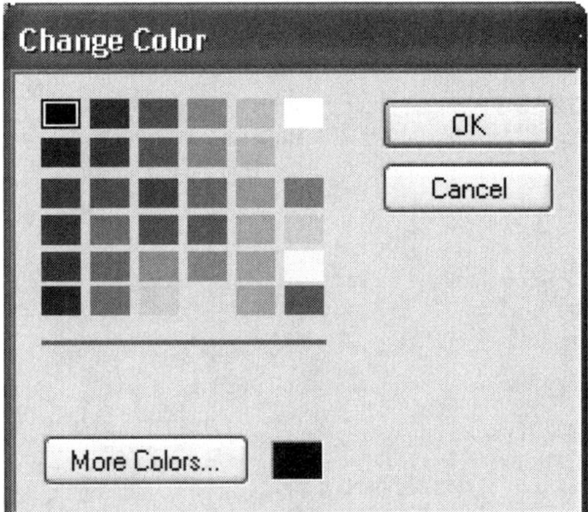

Figure 6.11 When you pick a new color, this dialog box or a palette appears. Click More Colors to select a color other than the ones displayed.

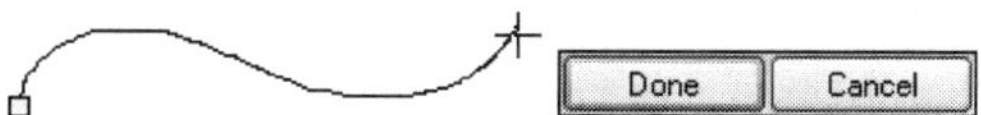

Figure 6.12 You can draw freehand lines in Picture It! After you click Done, you can change the line's attributes, such as its color and thickness.

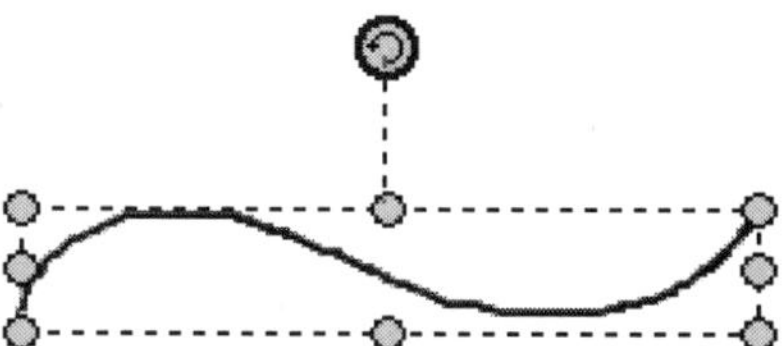

Figure 6.13 The line is selected, ready for any modifications you wish to make.

To draw a freehand line:

1. Choose Insert > Draw a Line, or choose Add something > Shape or lines > Draw a line from the Common Tasks list.
2. *Do one of the following:*
   - ▲ To draw a straight line, click once to set the starting point, and click a second time to set the end point.
   - ▲ To draw a curved line (**Figure 6.12**), click and drag.

   Repeat as necessary to draw additional line segments.
3. Click Done to complete the line.

   The new line is selected (**Figure 6.13**). To modify the line's attributes, refer to the instructions in the previous step list.

✔ Tip

- You change a line's properties *after* you insert or draw it. You must select the line—by clicking it in the workspace or the Stack—in order to change its properties.

Adding shapes

You can insert predrawn outlines of common shapes, as well as shape-related clip art from Picture It!'s collection.

To insert a shape:

- *Do one of the following:*
  - Choose an outline shape from the Insert > Shape submenu (**Figure 6.14**), or from the Add something > Shape or lines > Shapes submenu in the Common Tasks list.
  - Pick a clip art shape by choosing Insert > More Shapes, or choosing Add something > Shape or lines > More shapes from the Common Tasks list.

    Choose a Shapes category (geometric or other), select the desired shape (**Figure 6.15**), and click Open.

  The shape appears in the workspace.

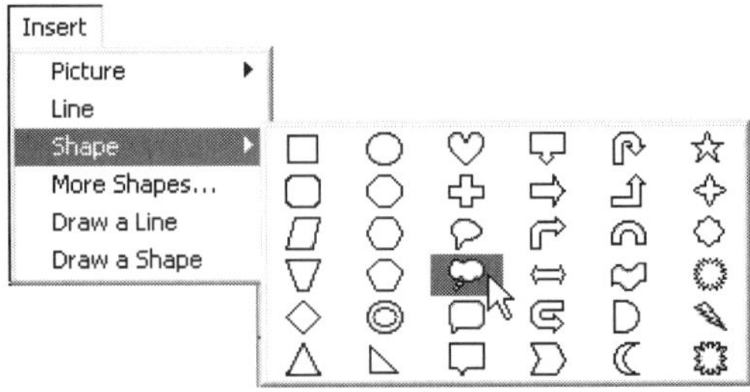

Figure 6.14 Choose a predefined outline shape from this submenu.

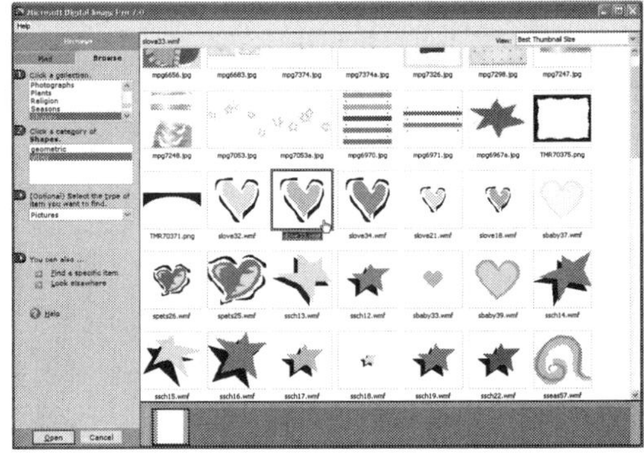

Figure 6.15 You can select a complex clip art shape from the Gallery images provided with Picture It!

✔ Tips

- To resize a shape, click and drag its handle. To add a fill color to an outline shape, click the Fill Color toolbar icon or choose Format > Shape or Line > Fill Color.
- To replace an outline shape with a different one, select the original shape in the workspace, click the Replace Shape toolbar icon, and choose another shape. (You can also choose a shape from the Format > Shape or Line > Replace Shape submenu.)
- You can also add *freehand* shapes of your own design. Choose Insert > Draw a Shape, or choose Add something > Shapes or lines > Draw a shape from the Common Tasks list. The procedure for drawing a shape is identical to that of drawing a freehand line (see the previous page), but the result is a closed object (**Figure 6.16**).

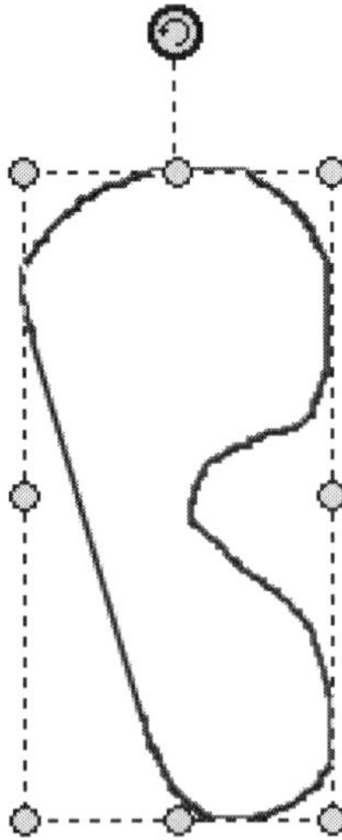

Figure 6.16 If you don't like the provided shapes, you can create your own.

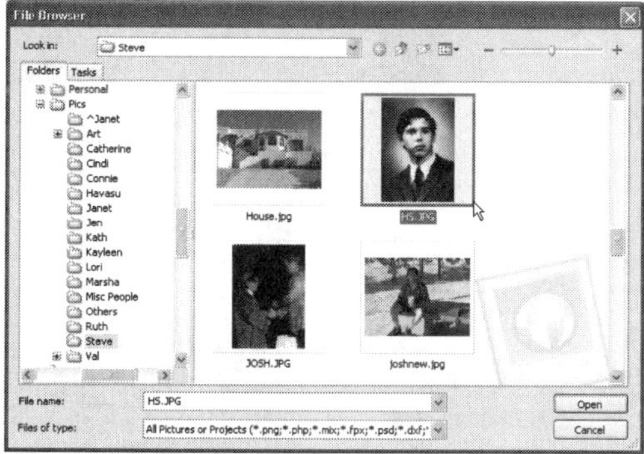

Figure 6.17 Use the File Browser to view and select images that are stored on disk.

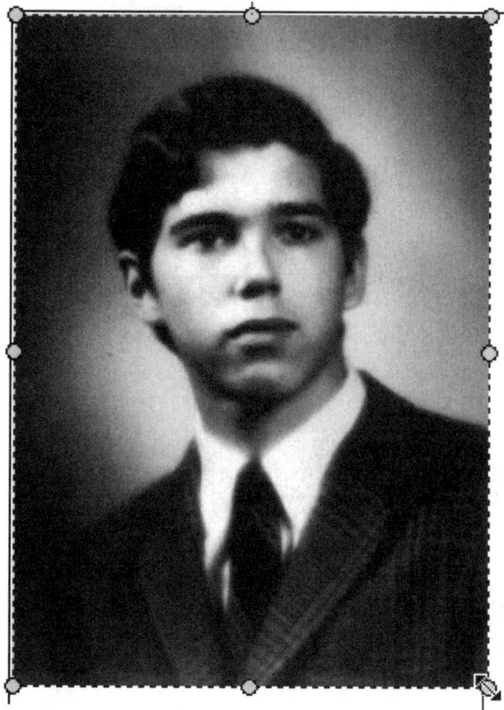

Figure 6.18 To resize an image proportionately, click a corner handle and drag.

Inserting other images

Although most of your pictures will probably contain only one main image, you can also insert additional images or clip art. For example, by adding a series of framed photos, you could create a miniature family album.

To insert a photo from your computer:

1. *Do one of the following:*
   - ▲ Open the picture with the File > Open command, adding it to the Tray. Click to select the original project in the Tray, and then drag the new image's thumbnail from the Tray into the workspace.
   - ▲ Choose Insert > Picture > From My Computer, or choose Add something > Picture from my computer from the Common Tasks list.

     The File Browser opens (**Figure 6.17**). Navigate to the desired drive and folder, select the image you want to add, and click the Open button.
2. Resize the image as necessary by clicking and dragging its handles (**Figure 6.18**.)

To insert another type of image:

- ◆ *Do one of the following:*
  - ▲ To insert an image from the Gallery, choose Insert > Picture > From Gallery, or choose Add something > Picture from Gallery from the Common Tasks list.
  - ▲ To scan an image into Picture It!, choose Insert > Picture > From Scanner, or choose Add something > Picture from scanner from the Common Tasks list.
  - ▲ To download an image from a digital camera or card reader, choose Insert > Picture > From Digital Camera, or choose Add something > Picture from digital camera from the Common Tasks list.

  For instructions on using a scanner, digital camera, card reader, or the Gallery to add images to Picture It!, refer to Chapter 2.

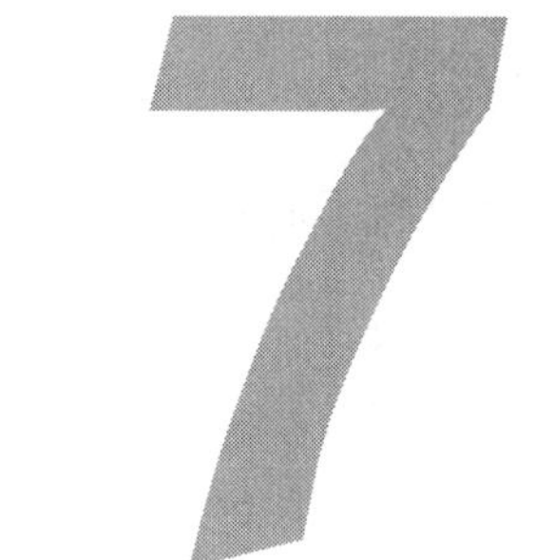

Working with Text

Shaped text

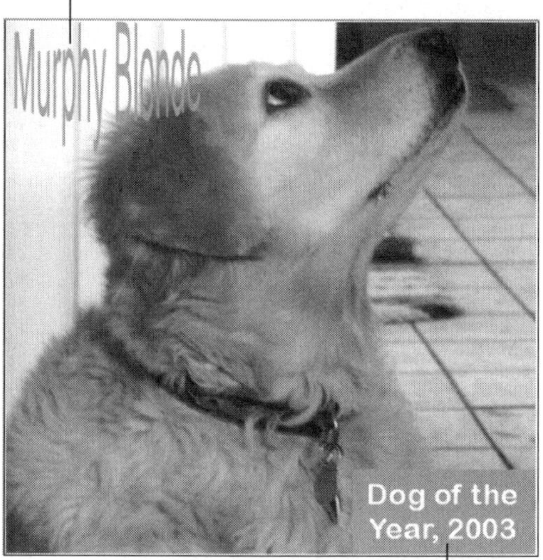

Normal text

Figure 7.1 Text can be normal or shaped, depending on the effect you want to achieve.

Occasionally, you may want to dress up your photos and projects by adding some text. Text is useful for creating posters, greeting cards, fliers, and business cards, as well as for labeling or titling photos.

As is the case with all objects in Picture It!, each text string that you add becomes a separate layer in the Stack. Text can be formatted on a character-by-character basis, word-by-word, or as an entire string. Picture It! also offers standard paragraph formatting options.

In this chapter, you'll learn to do the following:

- Add normal or shaped text to a project (**Figure 7.1**)
- Change the text position, size, color, and rotation angle, or wrap the text
- Modify character formatting, such as font, size, and color
- Set paragraph formatting properties
- Use the spelling checker to avoid embarrassing mistakes

Inserting Text

You can insert two types of text into a project: normal and shaped. *Normal text* corresponds to text that you might type as a title or figure callout. *Shaped text* is more artistic. It conforms to the shape of an invisible bounding box, such as a circle.

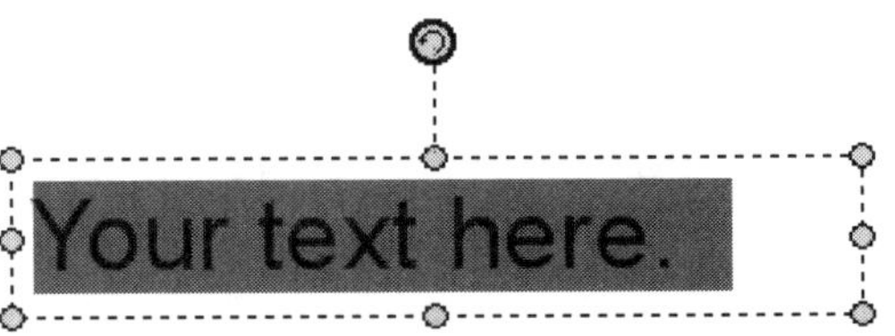

Figure 7.2 A sample text object appears in the workspace, ready for you to replace with your own text.

To insert normal text:

1. *Do one of the following:*
   - ▲ Choose Text > Insert Text.
   - ▲ From the Common Tasks list, choose Add something > Text.

   A text box containing some sample text appears in the workspace (**Figure 7.2**).
2. Edit the text, as desired.

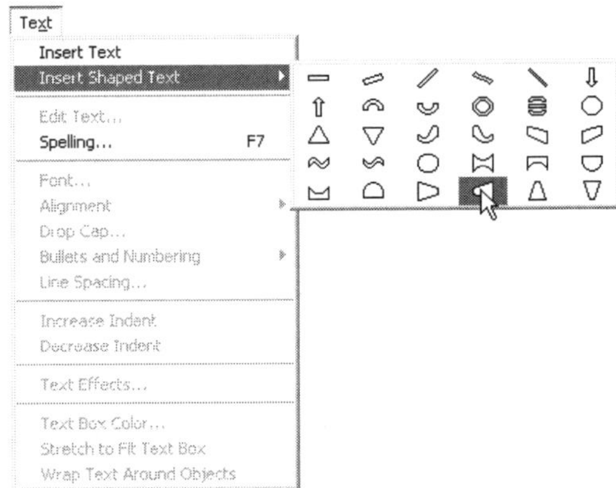

Figure 7.3 Choose a text shape from the submenu.

To insert shaped text:

1. *Do one of the following:*
   - ▲ Choose a shape from the Text > Insert Shaped Text submenu (**Figure 7.3**).
   - ▲ Choose a shape from the Add something > Shaped text submenu in the Common Tasks list.

   The Edit Shaped Text dialog box and a text box appear in the workspace (**Figure 7.4**).
2. Edit the text, and then click OK.

   The new text replaces the sample text in the workspace.

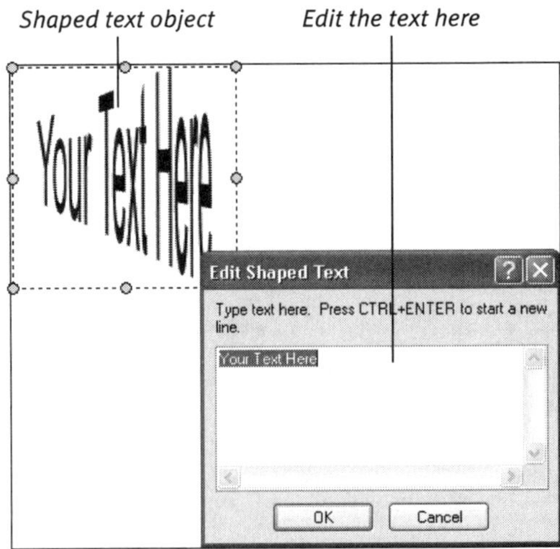

Figure 7.4 When placing shaped text, the sample and the Edit Shaped Text dialog box appear together.

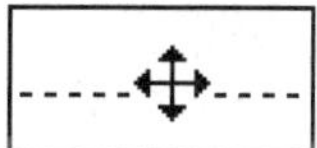

Figure 7.5 When this crosshair cursor appears, you can drag the text box to a new position.

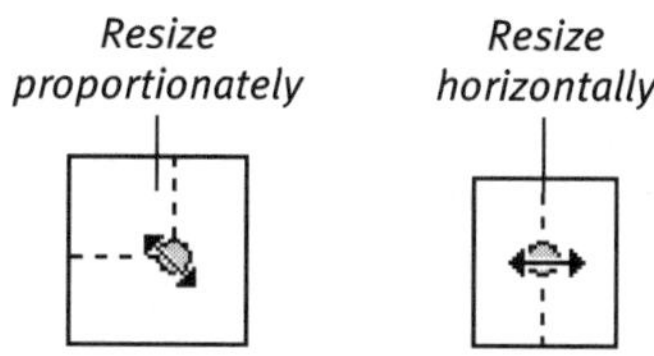

Figure 7.6 Click and drag a handle to resize the text box.

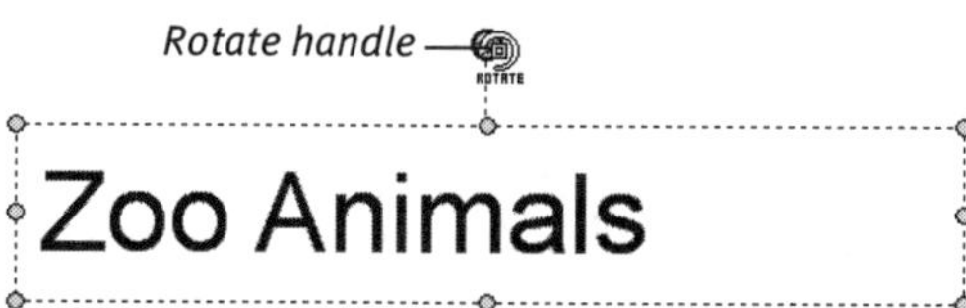

Figure 7.7 Click and drag the rotate handle at the top of the text box.

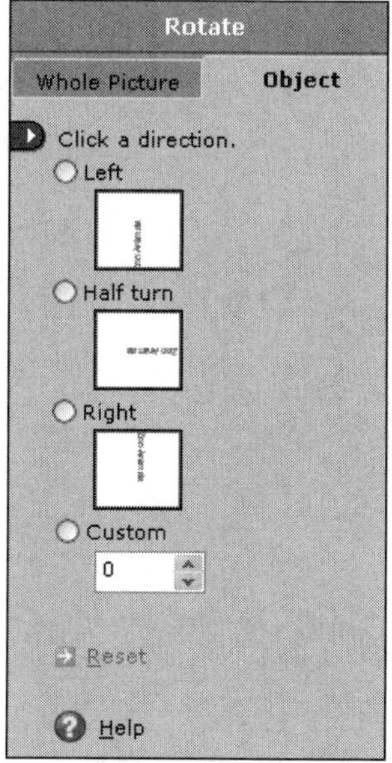

Figure 7.8 Use the Rotate pane to rotate to a specific angle or in 90-degree increments.

Modifying the Text Box

In addition to altering the text's formatting (as you can in a word processing program), you can modify the surrounding text box's properties: position, size/shape, rotation angle, color, and wrap.

To move a text box:

- Move the cursor over any edge of the text box. When it changes to a crosshair (**Figure 7.5**), you can click and drag the box.

To resize a text box:

- Move the cursor over any yellow handle. When it changes to a double-headed arrow (**Figure 7.6**), you can click and drag to resize the box.

  Drag a side or top handle to stretch or shrink the box; drag a corner handle to resize the box proportionately.

To rotate a text box:

- *Do one of the following:*
  - ▲ To manually rotate a selected text box to any desired angle, click the rotation handle at the top of the text box (**Figure 7.7**) and then drag.
  - ▲ To rotate a specific number of degrees, select the text box and choose Format > Rotate > Selected Object.

    In the Rotate pane (**Figure 7.8**), click the radio button that corresponds to the desired angle. To rotate to a different angle, click the Custom radio button and enter the angle (between 0 and 359) in the text box. (Note that this angle is relative to the text box's angle at the time the command is chosen, rather than being an absolute angle.)
  - ▲ To rotate a selected text box in 90-degree increments, click the Rotate Counterclockwise or Rotate Clockwise toolbar icon.

To set a text box's color:

1. Choose Text > Text Box Color.

   The Change Color dialog box appears (**Figure 7.9**).

2. *Do one of the following:*
   - ▲ Click a color icon and then click OK.
   - ▲ Click More Colors to pick a custom color.
   - ▲ Click No Fill to remove the color from the text box.

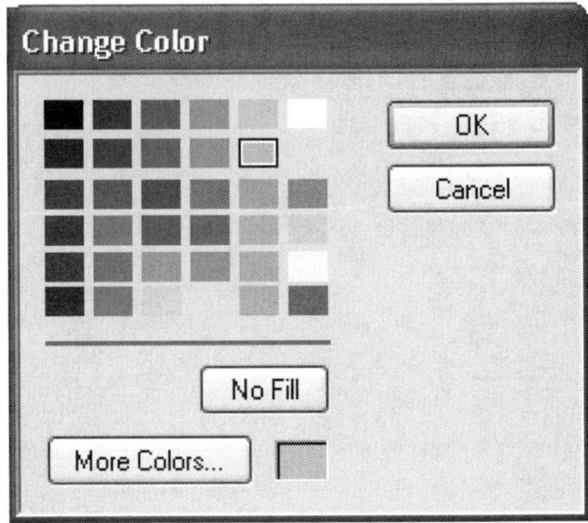

Figure 7.9 Select a background color for the text box.

To make text wrap around objects:

1. Select the text box.
2. Choose Text > Wrap Text Around Objects.

   The text now wraps around objects that would otherwise cover it (**Figure 7.10**).

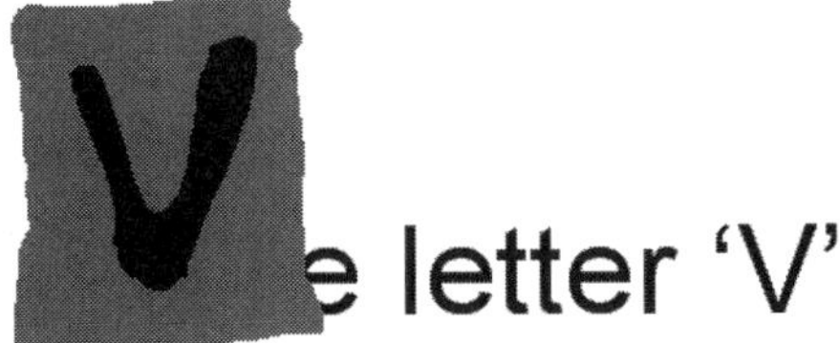

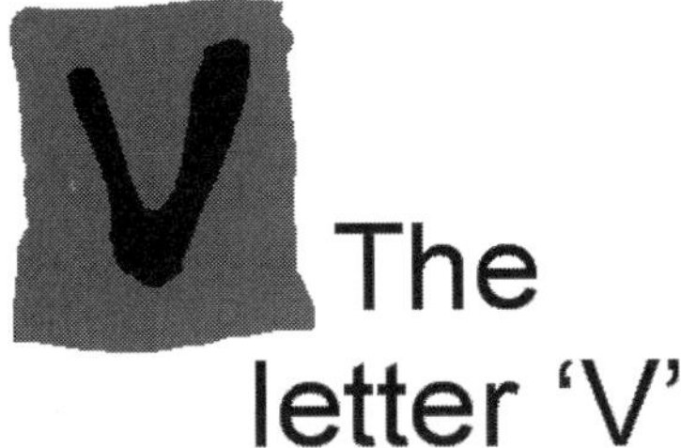

Figure 7.10 Without text wrap (top), text is obscured by objects placed over it. With wrap enabled (bottom), the text reforms around nearby objects.

✔ Tips

- ■ Text normally wraps to fit the size of the box in which it's contained. Resizing a text box only changes the size of the box, not the text within it. To change text size, use a formatting command (see the next section).

  The Text > Stretch to Fit Text Box command is the exception to this rule. When this command is enabled, resizing the box causes the text to shrink or expand to fit the box. Use this command when the size and shape of the box is more important than that of the text within it.

- ■ Both the Stretch to Fit Text Box and Wrap Text Around Objects commands work as toggles. When enabled, the command is preceded in the menu by a checkmark.

- ■ If you try to set the text box's color to the same color as the text within the box, a warning appears (**Figure 7.11**). If you don't choose different colors for the box and the text, the text will be unreadable.

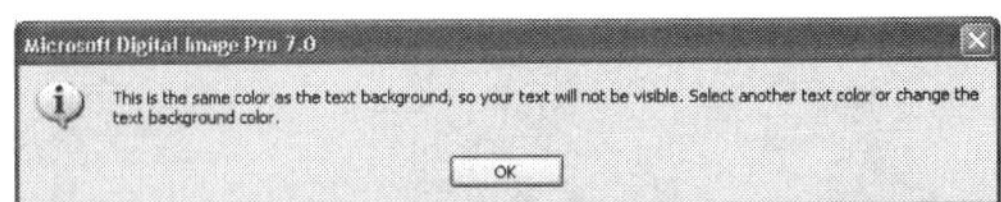

Figure 7.11 This warning appears if the text box and text are set to the same color.

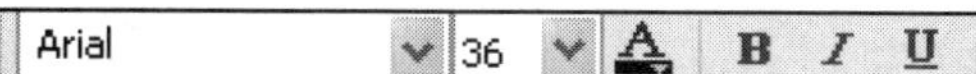

Figure 7.12 The toolbar contains many of the most common character formatting options.

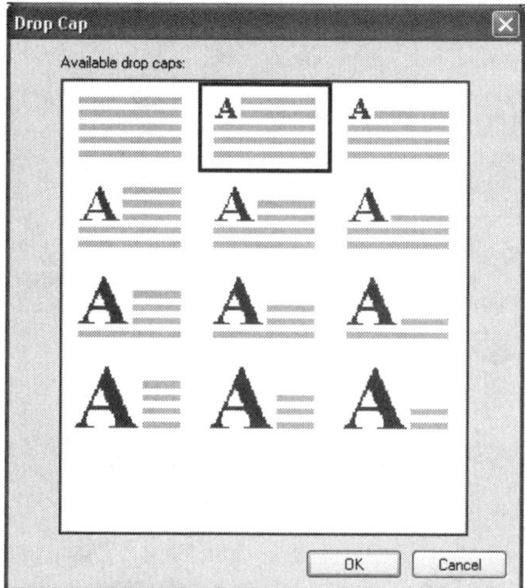

Figure 7.13 Select a drop cap size from this dialog box.

Font settings
Character spacing settings

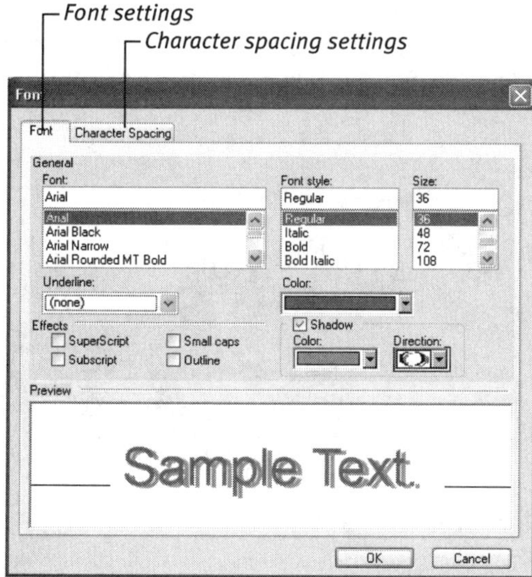

Figure 7.14 You can set advanced font formatting and character spacing options in the Font dialog box.

Character Formatting

Character formatting refers to any formatting that can be applied to selected text—from a single character to all the text in a text box. Just as you can do in a word processing document, you can apply character formatting to any text in your Picture It! projects.

To apply character formatting to text:

1. Select the text object (by clicking it or clicking its thumbnail in the Stack), and then select the specific text that you want to format.
2. *Do one of the following:*
   - ▲ To change the font, size, or color, choose options from the toolbar drop-down menus (**Figure 7.12**).
   - ▲ To apply boldface, italic, or underlining to the text, click the B, I, or U toolbar icon, respectively. To remove boldface, italic, or underlining, click the same toolbar icon again.
   - ▲ To begin the text with a drop cap, choose Text > Drop Cap. In the Drop Cap dialog box (**Figure 7.13**), choose a size for the drop cap and then click OK.
   - ▲ To make extensive character formatting changes, choose Text > Font. In the Font dialog box (**Figure 7.14**), make all necessary font and character spacing modifications, and then click OK.

✔ Tips

- To select all text in a text box, drag-select the text or simply click its icon in the Stack. To automatically select a single word, double-click anywhere within the word.
- Many character formatting options are *only* available in the Font dialog box.
- You can also use the following keyboard shortcuts: Ctrl B (Bold), Ctrl I (Italic), and Ctrl U (Underline).

Paragraph Formatting

Paragraph formatting refers to any text formatting that affects an entire paragraph. Picture It! paragraph formatting options include alignment, indents, bulleted and numbered points, line spacing, and text effects.

To apply paragraph formatting to text:

1. Select the text object (by clicking it or clicking its thumbnail in the Stack), and then select the paragraph(s) to be formatted.
2. *Do one of the following:*
   - ▲ To set the paragraph alignment, click the Alignment toolbar icon, choose an option from the Text > Alignment submenu, or use any of these keyboard shortcuts: Ctrl L (Left), Ctrl E (Center), Ctrl R (Right), or Ctrl J (Justify).
   - ▲ To change the paragraph indent, choose Text > Increase Indent or Text > Decrease Indent.
   - ▲ To create a bullet-point or numbered list, choose an option from the Text > Bullets and Numbering submenu (**Figure 7.15**) or from the Bullets and Numbers toolbar icon. To remove bullets or numbering from selected paragraphs, choose None.
   - ▲ To set line spacing for one or more paragraphs, choose Text > Line Spacing, choose a spacing from the Line Spacing dialog box (**Figure 7.16**), and click OK.
   - ▲ To create artistic text, choose Text > Text Effects. (Note that artistic fonts are applied to *all* text in the text box, not just to the selected paragraphs.) In the Text Effects pane, select a category and a specific effect. To change the color, click the Change color icon. Click Done to return to the workspace (**Figure 7.17**).

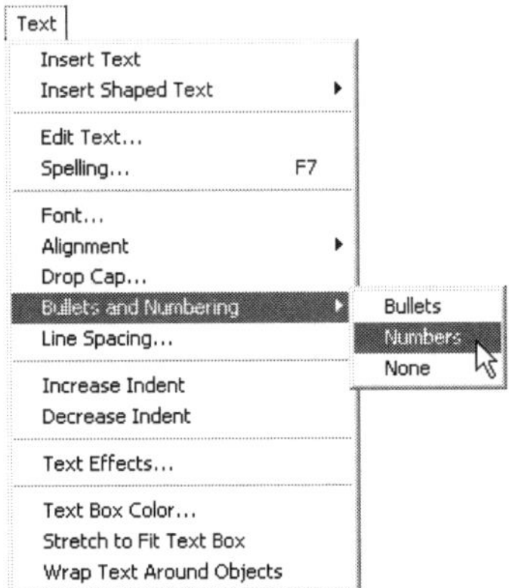

Figure 7.15 You can create bullet-point or numbered lists.

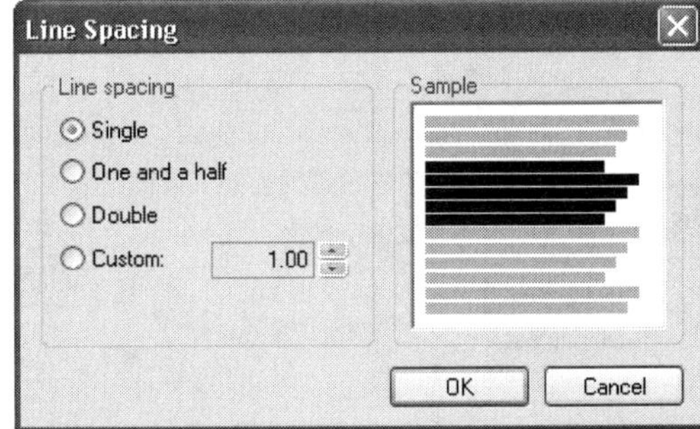

Figure 7.16 You can set a new line spacing for the selected paragraph(s) using this dialog box.

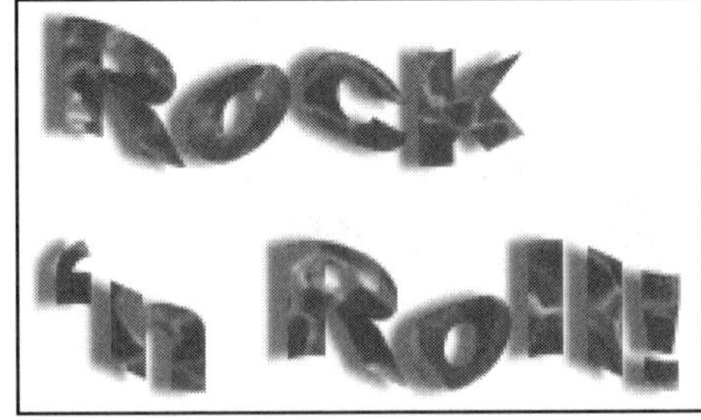

Figure 7.17 This is an example of an artistic text effect.

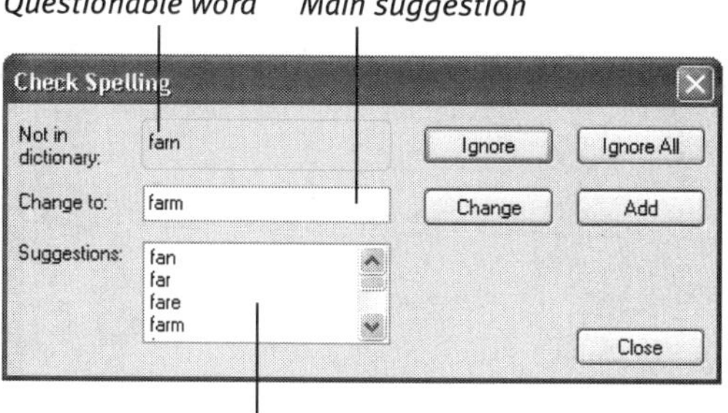

Figure 7.18 The Check Spelling dialog box.

Editing Text

In case it isn't obvious how you'd go about editing your text after composing it, here's what to do:

- To edit normal text, select the text box, position the insertion marker, and edit as you would in a word processor.
- To edit shaped text, select the text box, choose Text > Edit Text, edit the text in the Edit Shaped Text dialog box, and then click OK.

Writing the Text Elsewhere

If a project will contain a *lot* of text—as it might for a bullet-point list or a lengthy birthday poem, for example—you don't have to type it directly into Picture It! You can write in any word processing program, copy the text, and then paste it into your picture as a new text box. This copy-and-paste procedure retains the original fonts, styles, and colors. However, the original font size is ignored; all text is formatted as 36-point.

As a bonus, if you write in an advanced word processing application, such as Microsoft Word, you can take advantage of the program's grammar checker, thesaurus, and other writing tools.

Spell Checking

Using Picture It!'s spelling checker, you can check the spelling in all normal and shaped text boxes in a project. (There is no selective spell checking; it's an all-or-nothing procedure.) When you initiate a spell check, Picture It! automatically moves from one text box to the next until all text has been examined.

To perform a spell check:

1. Choose Text > Spelling, press F7, or click the Spelling toolbar icon.

   The Check Spelling dialog box appears (**Figure 7.18**), and the first questionable word—if there is one—is displayed.

2. *Do one of the following:*
   - To accept the change suggested in the Change to box, click Change or press Enter.
   - To use a word from the Suggestions list, highlight the word and then click Change or press Enter.
   - To accept the questionable word as is for the current instance only, click Ignore.
   - To accept the questionable word for this and any additional instances in the current document, click Ignore All.
   - To accept the questionable word as is and add it to the dictionary (so it will be accepted in future spell checks), click Add.

   The next questionable word appears, if there is one. The spell check continues until no additional questionable words are found. (You can end the spell check at any time by clicking Close.)

✔ Tip

- Rather than accept one of the suggested words, you can manually edit the word in the Change to box and then click Change to accept the edited word.

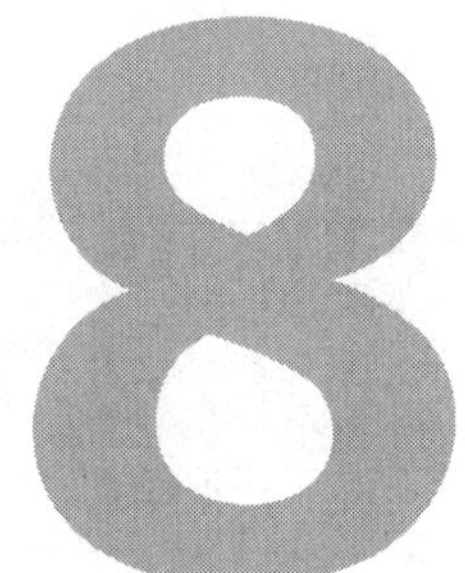

FILTERS AND EFFECTS

Effects
- Antique
- Black and White
- Negative
- Diffuse Glow...
- Distort...
- Filters ▸
- Plug-in Filters...
- Colorize Brush...
- Distortion Brush...
- Paint Brush ▸
- Fill with Texture or Color...
- Transparent Fade ▸
- Shadow...
- Skew Object...
- Emphasize...
- Edges ▸

Figure 8.1 The Effects menu.

If you'd like to change your projects and photos into other-worldly images or works of art, Picture It! provides effects and filters that you can apply to images, objects, or an entire project.

The effect and filter commands can be found in the Effects menu (**Figure 8.1**). Unfortunately, the difference between filters and effects isn't obvious. The Effects menu looks more like a hodgepodge than a logical grouping based on functional similarities between commands.

In trying to make sense of how the Effects commands go together, I've decided to impart my own organization on them. In this chapter, I'll discuss all effects and filters that can be applied to an entire image or object. Others, such as those for selective editing and painting, can be found in Chapter 5. For examples of special effects, see the color section of this book

In this chapter, you'll learn how to accomplish the following tasks:

- Applying filters and effects to an image
- Using Adobe Photoshop filters to alter images (Digital Image Pro only)

Note that the available effects and filters depend on which variation of Picture It! you own. As you'd expect, Digital Image Pro provides the most filters and effects, while Picture It! Express has none.

Applying Effects

The three effects at the top of the Effects menu (Antique, Black and White, and Negative) can each be applied by simply selecting the command. What could be simpler?

Other effects (Diffuse Glow, Distort, Transparent Fade, and Skew Object) require you to set options as they are applied to a selected image or object.

To apply the antique, black and white, or negative effect:

1. Select an image or object.
2. *Do one of the following:*
   - ▲ From the Effects menu, choose Antique, Black and White, or Negative.
   - ▲ From the Common Tasks list, click Effects and then choose Antique, Black and white, or Negative.

   The chosen effect is applied to the image or object (**Figure 8.2**).

✔ Tips

- The antique and black-and-white effects are options in some digital cameras. That is, you may be able to create these effects as you shoot.
- The antique effect is also known as a *duotone*.

To apply the diffuse glow effect:

1. To apply the effect to particular objects, select one or more images or objects.

   Even if you want to apply diffuse glow to an entire project consisting of multiple images or objects, you must first select at least one image or object.
2. Choose Effects > Diffuse Glow.

   The Diffuse Glow pane appears, open to the Object(s) tab (**Figure 8.3**). The default settings are applied to the selected object.

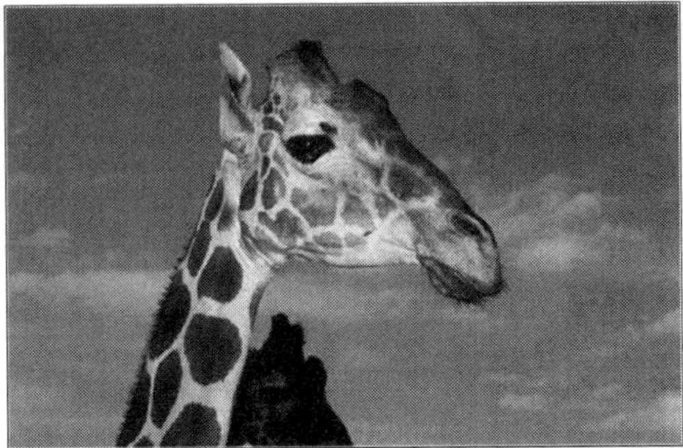

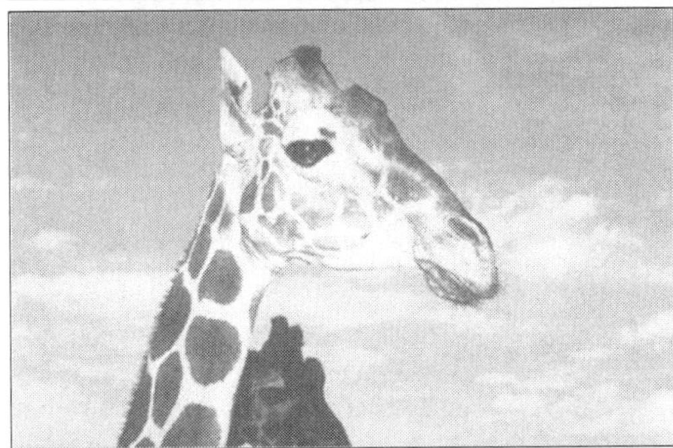

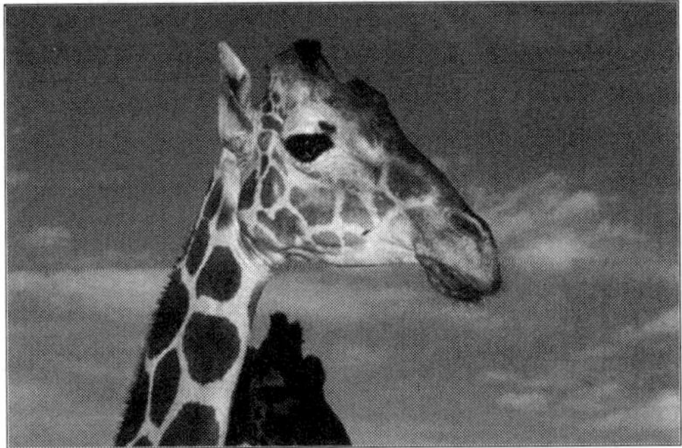

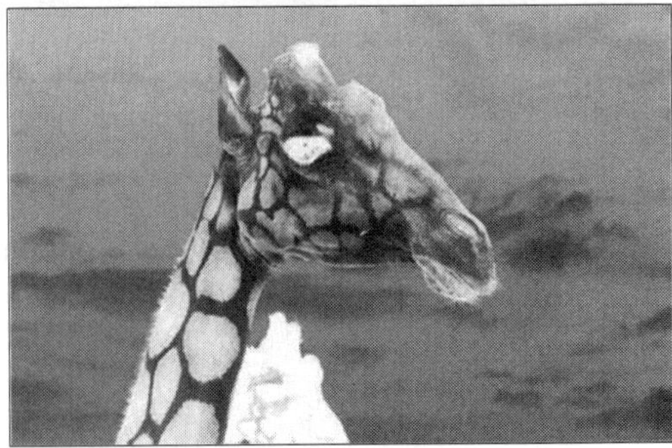

Figure 8.2 From the top: the original image, antique, black and white, and negative.

Sliders

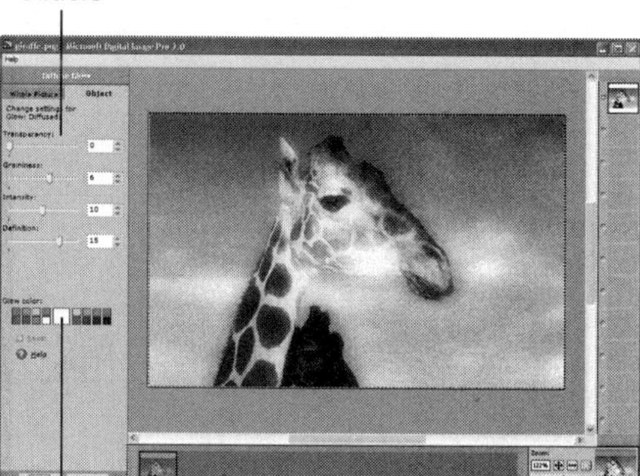

Glow color palette

Figure 8.3 To set diffuse glow for a selected object, drag the sliders and/or select a glow color.

Distort options

Click to view all options

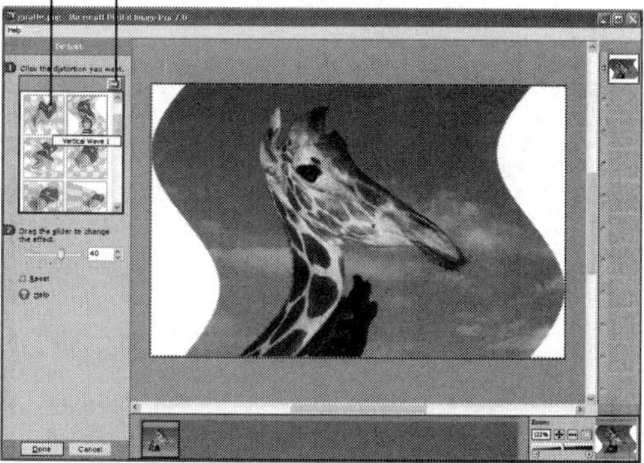

Figure 8.4 Select a distort option from the scrolling list.

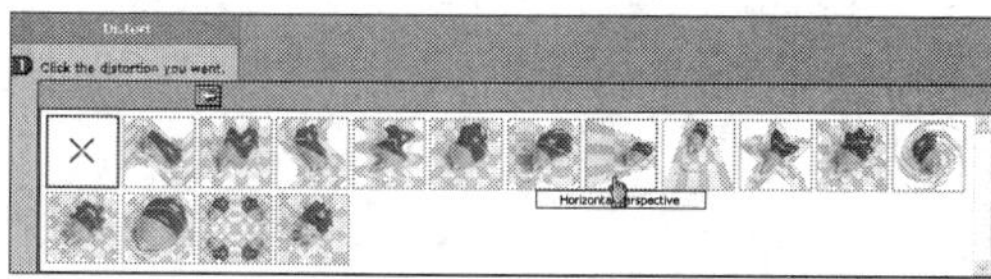

Figure 8.5 It can be easier to select an option if you can see them all.

3. *Do one of the following:*
   - ▲ When applying diffuse glow to only a selected object or image, you can alter the settings by moving the sliders and selecting a new glow color.
   - ▲ To apply the default settings to the entire project, click the Whole Picture tab.
4. Click Done to return to the workspace.

✔ Tips

- To apply the same diffuse glow to several objects or images, Ctrl-click each item, group them (see Chapter 6), and then apply diffuse glow. Note that ungrouping them later will remove the effect. Be sure that you're done editing the items before grouping and applying the effect.
- It's often difficult to tell exactly what the effect looks like—especially with a small image. Zoom in before finalizing the settings.

To apply the distort effect:

1. Unless the project contains only one image or object, you must first select the item(s) to which you want to apply the effect.

   To select multiple objects, Ctrl-click them.
2. Choose Effects > Distort, or choose Effects > Distort from the Common Tasks list.

   The Distort pane appears (**Figure 8.4**).
3. Select a distortion effect from the scrolling list or click the arrow button to view all possible effects (**Figure 8.5**).
4. *Optional:* Drag the slider to change the intensity of the selected effect.
5. Click the Done button to accept the effect and return to the workspace.

To apply a transparent fade:

1. Unless the project contains only one image or object, you must first select the item(s) to which you want to apply the effect.

   To select multiple objects, Ctrl-click them.

2. *Do one of the following:*
   - ▲ Choose Effects > Transparent Fade > Even. In the Transparent Fade - Even pane, drag the slider to set the amount of transparency (**Figure 8.6**).
   - ▲ Choose Effects > Transparent Fade > Gradual. In the Transparent Fade - Gradual pane, select a gradient to use for the transparency effect (**Figure 8.7**). To reverse the gradient, click Flip the direction of the gradient.

3. Click the Done button to accept the effect and return to the workspace.

✔ Tip

- To learn how to fade only a portion of an image or object using the Transparency Brush, see Chapter 5.

To skew an image or object:

1. Unless the project contains only one image or object, you must first select the item to which you want to apply the effect.

   Skew can only be applied to a single item at a time.

2. Choose Effects > Skew Object.

3. Drag a handle to achieve the desired skew (**Figure 8.8**).

4. Click the Done button to accept the effect and return to the workspace.

✔ Tip

- Skewing often requires experimentation to obtain the desired effect. If you want to start over, click the Reset icon.

Set the transparency percentage

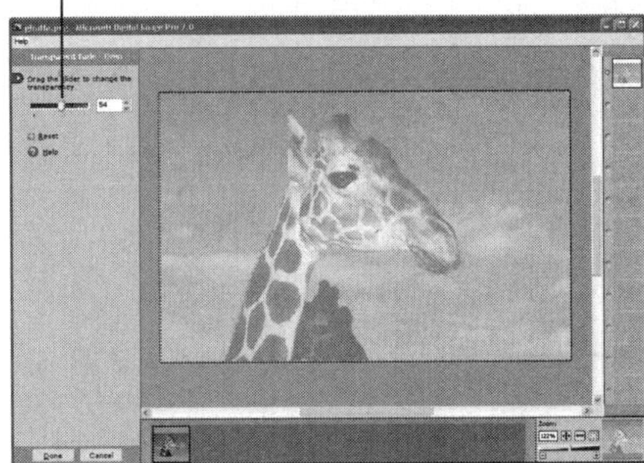

Figure 8.6 Apply an even transparent fade when you want to fade an image uniformly.

Select a transparency gradient

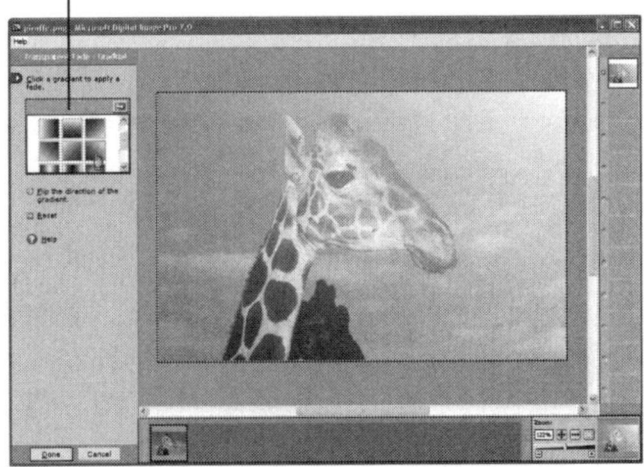

Figure 8.7 In a gradual transparent fade, an applied gradient determines the areas that will be faded.

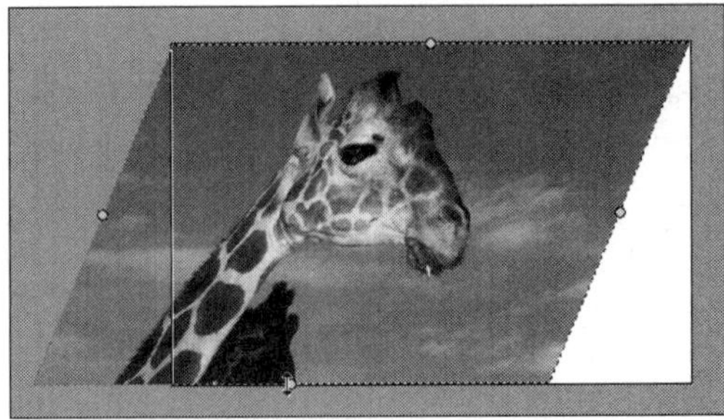

Figure 8.8 To skew a selected image or object, drag a handle until you achieve the desired effect.

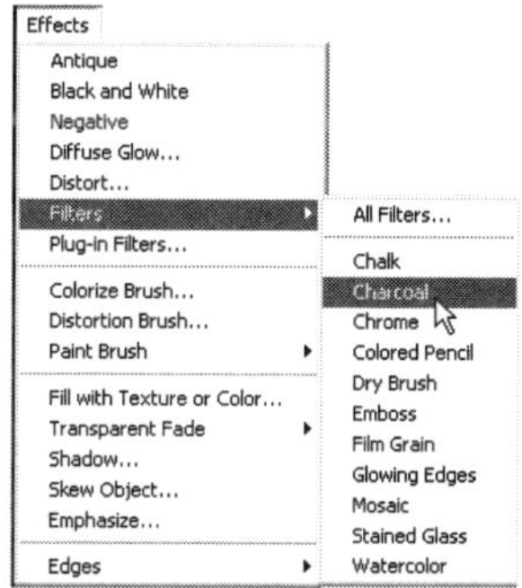

Figure 8.9 Common filters can be chosen from this submenu.

Click to view all filters

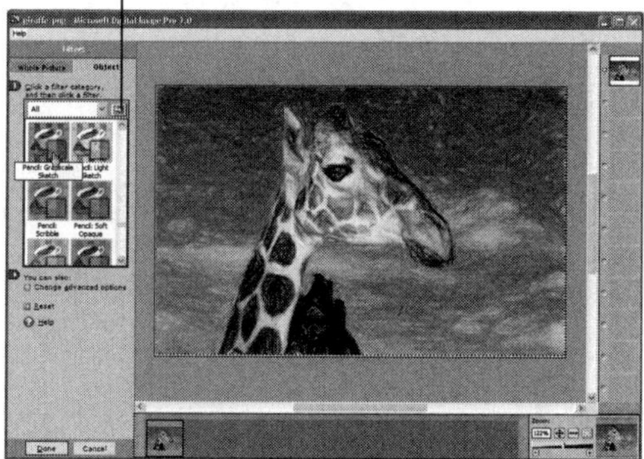

Figure 8.10 You can select other filters from this pane.

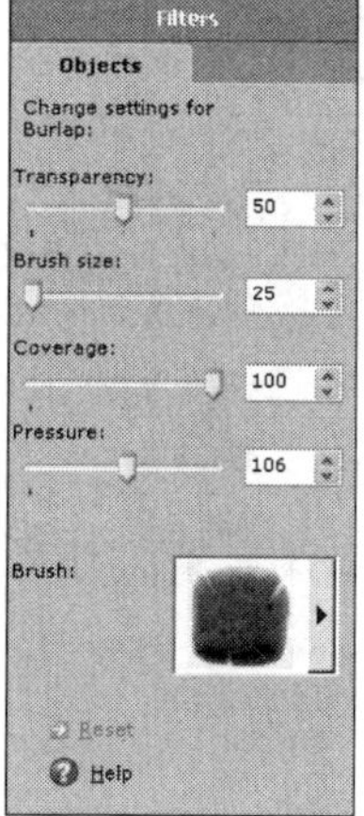

Figure 8.11 You can tweak the filter's settings, if the default ones aren't appropriate.

Applying Filters

With the aid of filters, you can transform photos or objects into artwork. You might want to change a scenic view into a watercolor or an Impressionist painting, for instance. Doing so can be as simple as clicking an icon. In fact, to apply any of the most common filters, you can choose one from the Effects > Filters submenu (**Figure 8.9**). See the color section of this book for examples.

If you use Digital Image Pro, you can supplement the Picture It! filters with Photoshop-compatible filters that you've purchased or downloaded.

To apply a built-in filter:

1. Unless the project contains only one image or object, you must first select the item(s) to which you want to apply the filter.

   To select multiple objects, Ctrl-click them.

2. Choose Effects > Filters > All Filters, or choose Effects > Filters from the Common Tasks list.

   The Filters pane appears (**Figure 8.10**), open to the Object(s) tab.

3. *Optional:* Click the Whole Picture tab if the project contains multiple items and you want to apply the filter as though all items were on the same layer, rather than applying the filter separately to each selected item.

4. Select a filter from the scrolling list or click the arrow button to easily view and select from all possible filters.

5. *Optional:* To more precisely control the filter, click Change advanced options.

   A new pane appears with sliders that are specific to the selected filter (**Figure 8.11**). Set options and click Done.

6. Click the Done button to return to the workspace.

To apply a Photoshop filter:

1. Unless the project contains only one image or object, you must first select the item to which you want to apply the filter.
2. Choose Effects > Plug-in Filters.

   The Plug-in Filters pane appears (**Figure 8.12**).
3. Select a plug-in filter from the list of installed plug-ins and then click Launch plug-in filter.

   A dialog box for the filter appears (**Figure 8.13**).
4. Set options for the plug-in and click OK.

   The filter is applied to the selected image or object.
5. Click the Done button to return to the workspace (**Figure 8.14**).

✔ Tips

- You can change the location(s) on disk in which Picture It! looks for plug-ins. For instructions, see *Setting the Plug-Ins Folder* in Chapter 14.
- While Picture It! is designed to use Photoshop-compatible plug-ins, it cannot use the Adobe plug-ins that are built into Photoshop or Photoshop Elements.
- Free, shareware, and demo versions of compatible plug-ins are readily available on the Web. Use your favorite search engine (such as *www.google.com*) to search for "Photoshop plug-ins."

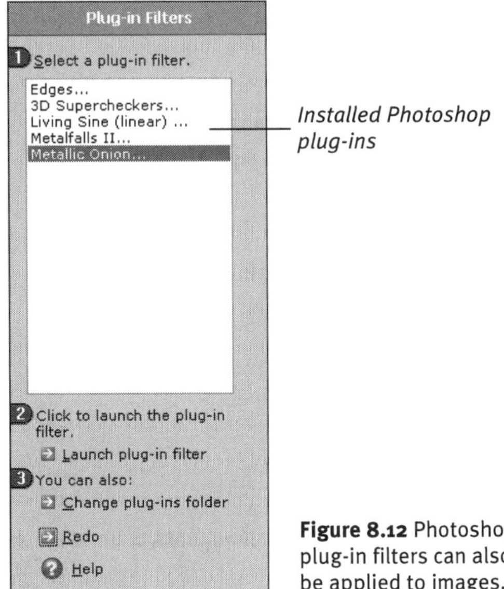

Figure 8.12 Photoshop plug-in filters can also be applied to images.

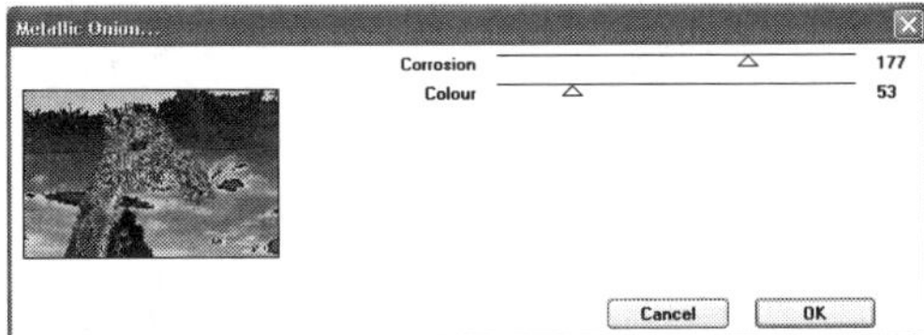

Figure 8.13 The plug-in displays a dialog box with filter options.

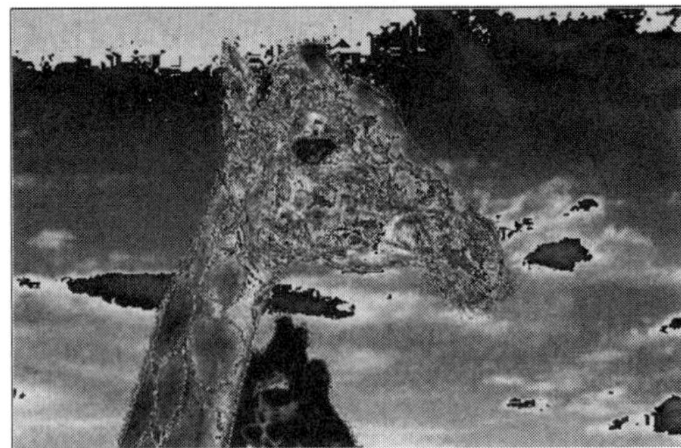

Figure 8.14 This is our giraffe as modified by the Metallic Onion plug-in *(http://photoshop.msk.ru)*.

Editing with the Mini Lab

It's not unusual to want to correct a bunch of pictures at the same time. You may have downloaded images from the Web, received a batch of family photos from a relative, or taken a series of pictures with your digital camera, for example. While you can certainly edit photos one by one, you may find it a bit faster to use the Mini Lab. The purpose of the Mini Lab is *batch editing* (making the same type of correction to a set of images)—either all at once or one-by-one, depending on the type of correction selected.

You can perform the following kinds of image corrections in the Mini Lab:

- Levels auto fix
- Rotate clockwise or counterclockwise
- Crop
- Set brightness and contrast
- Fix red eye
- Adjust tint

Note: The Mini Lab is not available to Picture It! Express users. However, all of the Mini Lab features *are* available as normal editing options (to be used on a picture-by-picture basis).

Mini Lab Essentials

Many of the Mini Lab procedures (as well as the options available to you) are identical, regardless of the type of edit or correction you're making. Rather than repeat them in each of this chapter's step lists, I'll explain them here.

To use the Mini Lab:

1. Open the images that you want to edit. (Alternately, you can open the pictures *after* you've opened the Mini Lab.)
2. *Do one of the following:*
   - ▲ Choose Touchup > Multi-photo Edit in Mini Lab.
   - ▲ In the Common Tasks list, click Touch up multiple pictures.
   - ▲ In the Startup Window, click Edit Multiple Pictures.

   The Mini Lab pane appears (**Figure 9.1**). All pictures in the Tray are shown as thumbnails (**Figure 9.2**). If you need to open additional pictures, click Open more files.
3. Before performing an edit procedure, you must select the picture(s) to which the edit will be applied.

   Click Select all pictures in the Mini Lab pane or Ctrl-click specific pictures. (You can deselect a previously selected image by Ctrl-clicking it again.)
4. Click an editing option in the Mini Lab pane.

   Some procedures (such as Levels auto fix) are simultaneously applied to all open pictures. Edits that must be applied individually are performed on one picture at a time. (Picture It! steps you through the selected images.)

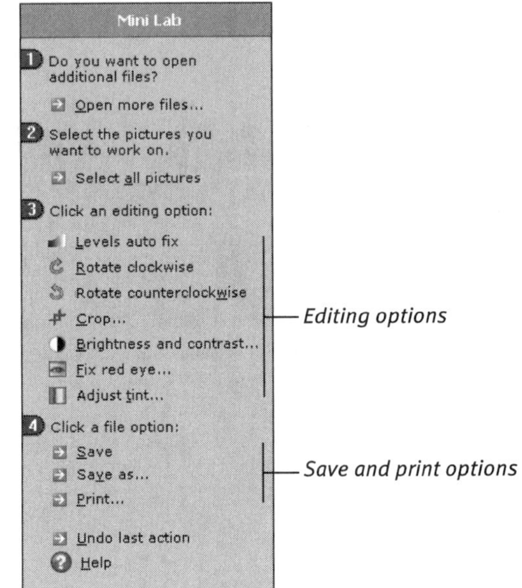

Figure 9.1 Batch edits are performed with the aid of the Mini Lab pane.

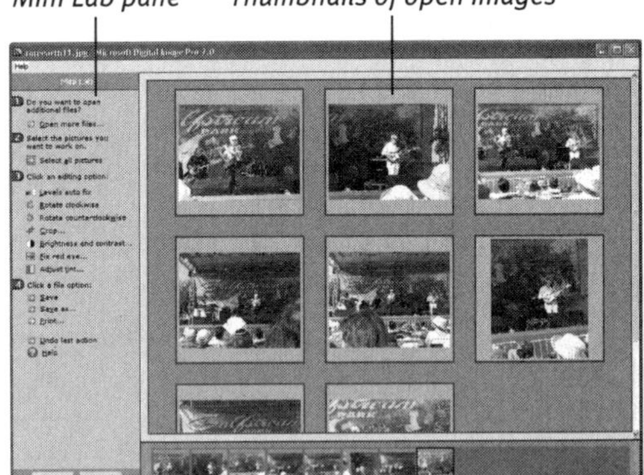

Figure 9.2 Edits are done only on the selected images.

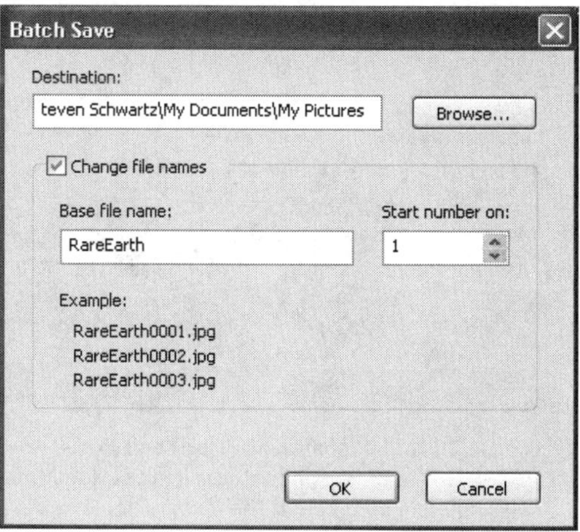

Figure 9.3 When saving the edited images, you can specify a new location on disk and/or rename the images with a constant series name.

5. *Optional:* When you're through editing, you can select thumbnails and then perform any of the following options:
   - Click Save to resave edited images using their original file names and disk locations. (No dialog box appears.) This has the effect of replacing (overwriting) the original files with the new versions.
   - Click Save As to resave images using new file names and/or locations, rather than overwriting the original files.

     In the Batch Save dialog box (**Figure 9.3**), select a destination disk and folder by clicking the Browse button. To optionally rename the files as a numbered sequence, enter the base file name in the text box, set a starting number for the sequence, and then click OK.
   - Click Print to print the selected images. (For details about printing and print options, see Chapter 11.)
6. To close the Mini Lab pane, click Done.

✔ Tips

- If you don't like the results of a given batch procedure, you can reverse it by clicking Undo last action.
- Unless you issue the Save or Save As command in Step 5, edited images are not saved to disk; that is, their files are unchanged. However, when you close the altered images or quit from Picture It!, you will be given an opportunity to save the changes.
- Picture It! also has batch file commands. If you open the File Browser (by choosing File > Open) and click the Tasks tab, you can perform a batch copy, move, rename, or duplication. For details, see Chapter 3.

Performing Mini Lab Procedures

Some Mini Lab procedures are instantly performed on all selected images when you click a command. For others, a new Mini Lab pane appears, and the procedure is repeated for every selected image.

To perform a single-step procedure:

1. With the Mini Lab pane displayed and the necessary images open in the Tray, select the thumbnails of the picture(s) to which the procedure will be applied.
2. Click one of the following in the Mini Lab pane:
   - ▲ Levels auto fix
   - ▲ Rotate clockwise
   - ▲ Rotate counterclockwise

   The command is simultaneously carried out for all selected images. The thumbnails change to reflect the edit(s).

To perform an image-by-image procedure:

1. Select the thumbnails of the picture(s) to which the procedure will be applied.
2. Click one of the following in the Mini Lab pane:
   - ▲ Crop
   - ▲ Brightness and contrast
   - ▲ Fix red eye
   - ▲ Adjust tint

   The first selected image is displayed and the Mini Lab pane changes to enable you to perform the procedure (**Figure 9.4**).
3. Perform the procedure as you would if you were editing without using the Mini Lab (by clicking icons, dragging sliders, and so on).
4. If there are more images to be edited, click Next. Otherwise, click Done after editing the final image.

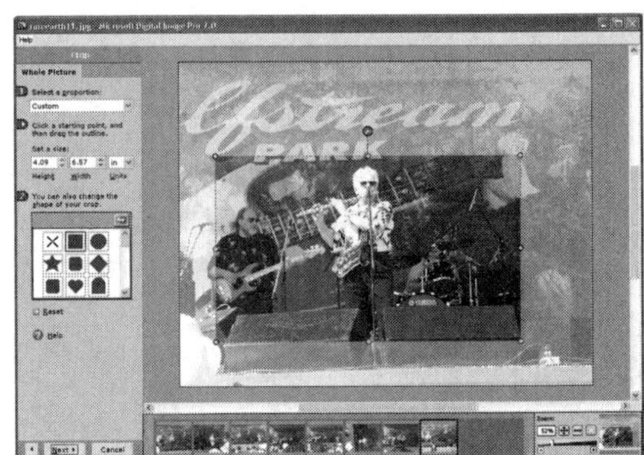

Figure 9.4 For batch commands that can't be performed simultaneously on multiple images, the Mini Lab pane steps you through the images one by one.

10

Adding Edge Effects

To add an artistic or finishing touch to a photo or collage, you can surround images with borders, edges, mats, or frames. While they're no substitute for *real* mats and frames, they can give a similar feel to pictures that you want to share on the Internet or mail to relatives, for example.

In this chapter, you'll learn to do the following:

- Create simple or decorative borders for pictures and objects
- Apply any of Picture It!'s impressive edge effects, including highlight, designer, soft, art stroke, photo stroke, and stamped edges
- Add a textured mat around a photo
- Choose a thematic frame or create one from any of Picture It!'s textures

Adding a Border

You can add a rectangular border around an object or the entire canvas. A border can be as simple as a colored outline, decorative (such as a scalloped pattern), or whimsical (such as push pins or clocks).

When applied to the canvas or a picture that fills the canvas, the border will be within the canvas edges. When applied to a smaller object placed on the canvas, the border appears outside of the object.

To add a border around an object:

1. Select the object or picture to which you want to add a border.
2. Choose Effects > Edges > Borders.
   The Borders dialog box appears (**Figure 10.1**).
3. Choose a border category from the Select a category drop-down menu.
4. Select a specific border. (As you click different borders, an image of the border appears in the Preview box.)
5. Set a size (in points) in the Border size box.
6. *Optional:* To see what the border will look like around the selected object or picture, click the Preview button. (If necessary, you can move the Borders dialog box out of the way by dragging its title bar.)
7. Repeat Steps 3–6 until you're satisfied with your choices, and then click OK (**Figure 10.2**). Click Cancel if you decide not to add the border.

✔ Tips

- A new border applied to an object replaces any previously applied border.
- If no image fills the canvas, Picture It! automatically applies the border to the entire canvas—even if a different object is currently selected.

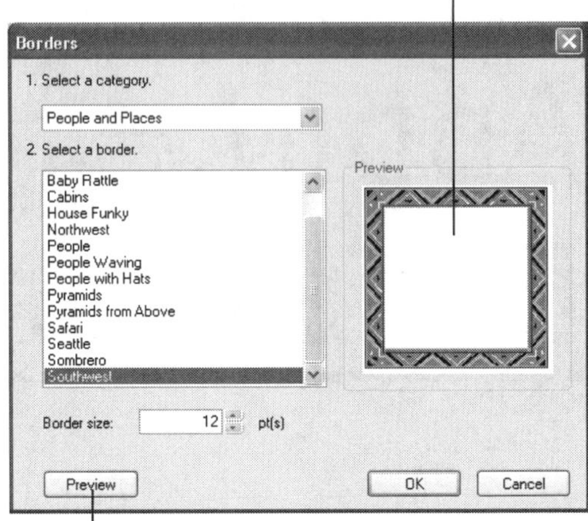

Figure 10.1 Select a border category and style. A sample of the selected style appears in the Preview box.

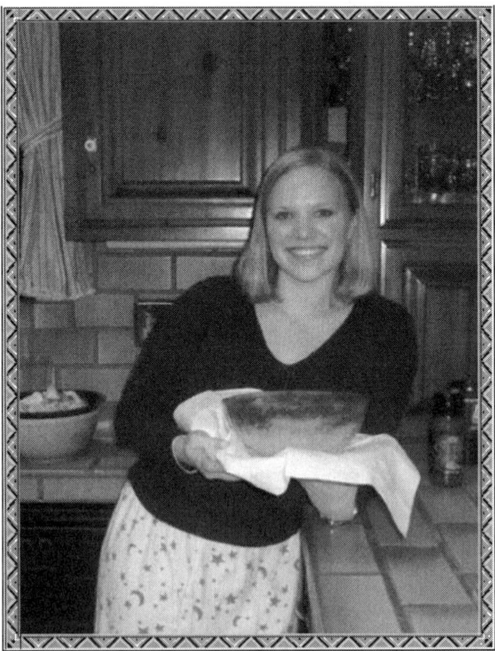

Figure 10.2 A carefully chosen border can make an image stand out.

Remove a highlighted edge

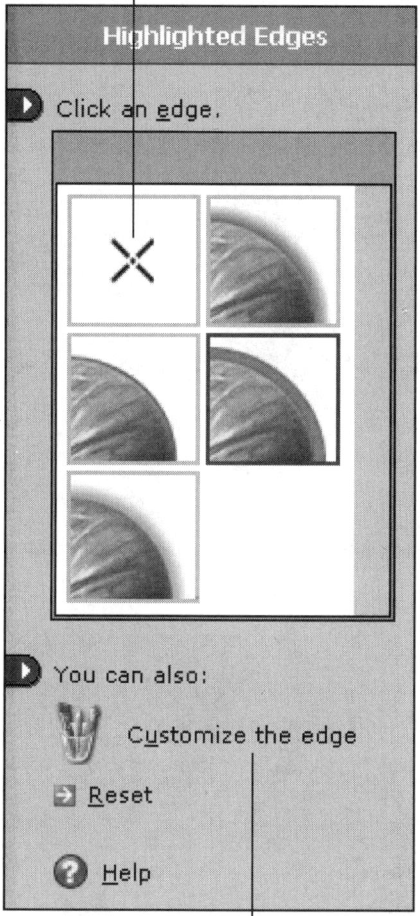

Highlighted Edges

Click an edge.

You can also:

Customize the edge

Reset

Help

Set options

Figure 10.3 Select a highlighted edge style. If you like, you can change the default color, shape, and width of the applied edge.

Adding an Edge Effect

You can also add an edge to a selected object. Edges differ from borders in two important ways. First, edges are created by overlaying the existing edges of the selected object. Borders are decorative designs that are added *around* an object. Second, if you apply additional edges, they are cumulative; they do not replace the previous edge as borders do.

Some of the edge effects described here are not available in all versions of Picture It! 7.0.

Highlighted edges

Apply *highlighted edges* to create a neon-style, colored border around an object or picture.

To add a highlighted edge:

1. Select the object or picture to which you want to apply the effect. (If the workspace contains only one object, it isn't necessary to preselect it.)
2. Choose Effects > Edges > Highlighted Edges, or choose Edges > Highlighted edges from the Common Tasks list.

   The Highlighted Edges pane appears (**Figure 10.3**).
3. Click to select one of the highlight styles. (To remove a previously applied highlight, click the No Edge style—the X.)

   As you click different highlight styles, they are applied to the selected picture or object.
4. *Do one of the following:*
   - ▲ If you're satisfied with the effect, click Done.
   - ▲ If you'd like to change the highlight's color, shape, or width, click Customize the edge and continue with Step 5.

continues on next page

5. In the new pane (**Figure 10.4**), you can modify the edge by doing any of the following:
   - ▲ Click to select a new color. To pick a color other than the ones displayed, click More color choices.
   - ▲ Choose a new edge shape by clicking the pop-out menu.
   - ▲ Change the edge width by choosing a percentage (1–100%) from the slider.
6. When you're satisfied with the changes, click Done.

   You return to the original pane. Click Done to close the pane.
7. If the selected object filled the entire canvas (as a normally opened photo would), a warning appears to inform you that the newly edged object has areas that are outside of the canvas.

   Click OK and then resize the object so it fits on the canvas.

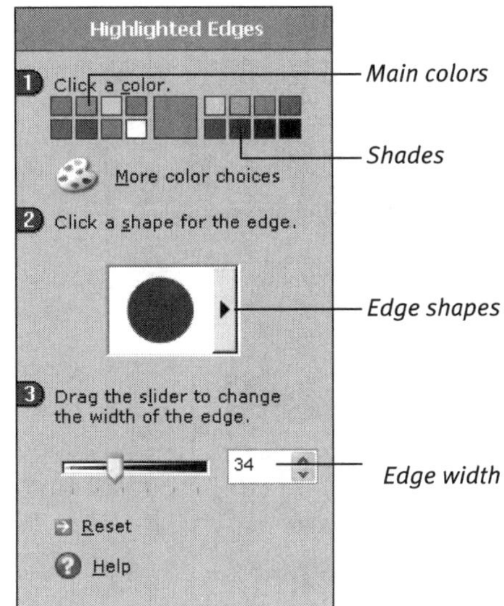

Figure 10.4 Specify the color, shape, and width of the edge.

✔ Tip

- ■ When changing the edge color, start by clicking a basic color on the left side of the pane. Additional shades of the clicked color appear on the right side of the pane.

Designer edges

Think of *designer edges* as decorative cutouts that overlay an image, obscuring all parts of the image that aren't beneath the cutouts.

To add a designer edge:

1. Select the picture to which you want to apply the effect. (If the workspace contains only one picture, it isn't necessary to preselect it.)
2. Choose Effects > Edges > Designer Edges, or choose Edges > Designer edges from the Common Tasks list.

   The Designer Edges pane appears.
3. Select an edge category (**Figure 10.5**).

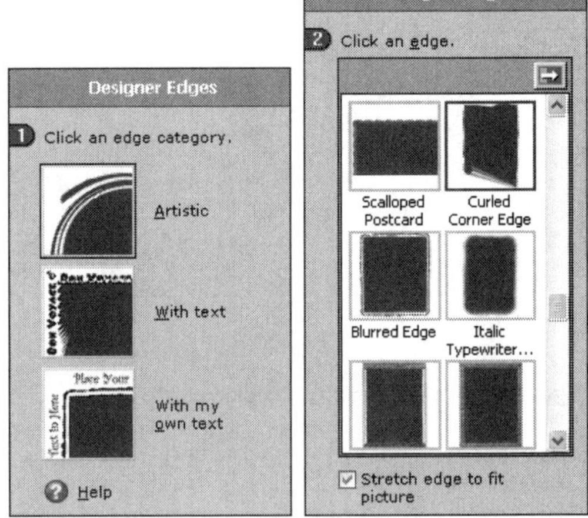

Figure 10.5 After you select a category (left), a choice list appears (right).

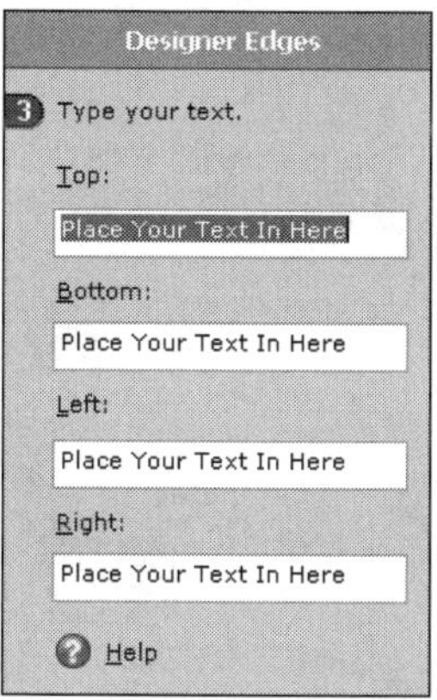

Figure 10.6 Enter text strings for the edges.

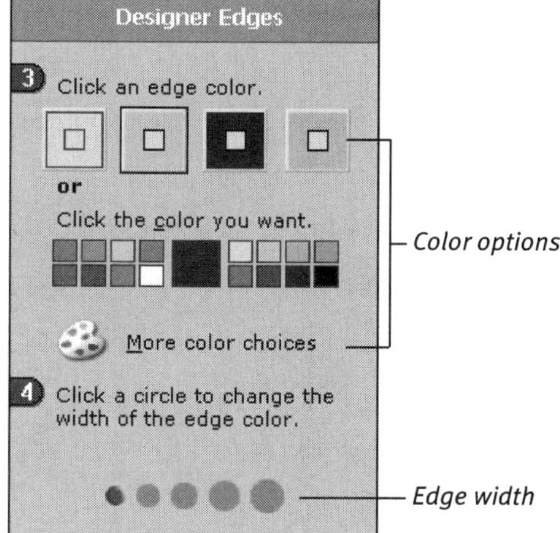

Figure 10.7 You can also select an edge color and a width.

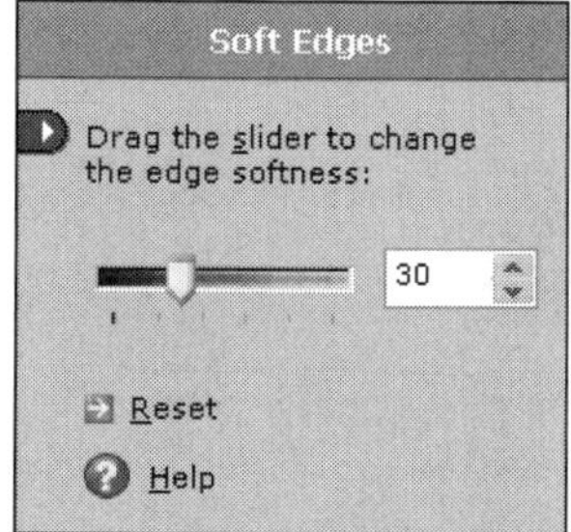

Figure 10.8 Set the amount of the edge/image to be softened.

4. The pane changes to show a list of edge designs (see Figure 10.5). Click an edge design.

   The design is applied to the selected picture.
5. *Optional:* To show more of the underlying picture, click the Stretch edge to fit picture check box.
6. Click the Next button.
7. If you chose With my own text as the category in Step 3, enter your text for the four sides (**Figure 10.6**) and then click Next.

   To eliminate the text on a given edge, leave the text box blank.
8. *Optional:* Select a new edge color and/or width (**Figure 10.7**). Then click the Next button.
9. You can move, resize, and/or rotate the underlying image so the desired area is beneath the designer edge.
10. Click the Done button.

Soft edges

You can use *soft edges* to give a dreamlike quality to portraits and nature scenes. When applied to an image, it's as though you're viewing the edges through a milky gauze.

To add soft edges:

1. Select the picture to which you want to apply the effect. (If the workspace contains only one picture, it isn't necessary to preselect it.)
2. Choose Effects > Edges > Soft Edges, or choose Edges > Soft edges from the Common Tasks list.

   The Soft Edges pane appears (**Figure 10.8**).
3. Drag the slider to the right to increase the effect or to the left to decrease it.
4. When you're satisfied with the effect, click the Done button.

Art stroke edges

Art stroke edges simulate paint brush strokes. You can set the stroke style, width, color, and transparency.

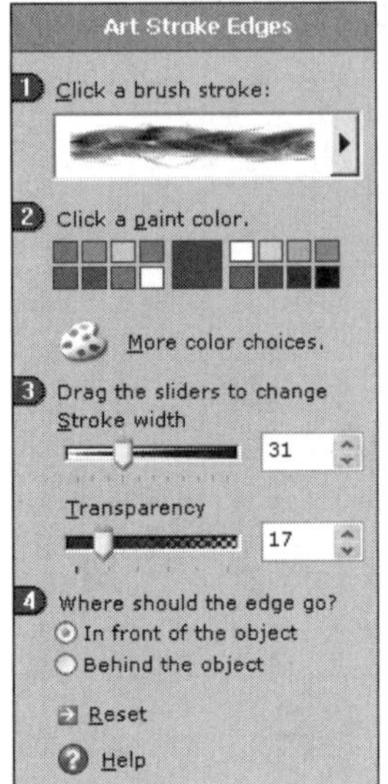

Figure 10.9 All settings for a paint brush stroke edge are selected in this pane.

To add art stroke edges:

1. Select the picture to which you want to apply the effect. (If the workspace has only one picture, it isn't necessary to preselect it.)
2. Choose Effects > Edges > Art Stroke Edges.
   The Art Stroke Edges pane appears (**Figure 10.9**).
3. Select a brush stroke style from the pop-out list.
4. Set the stroke width and transparency by dragging the sliders.
5. Specify whether the stroke will be applied in front of or behind the selected object by clicking the appropriate radio button.
6. Click the Done button.
7. If the selected object filled the entire canvas (as a normally opened photo would), a warning appears.
   Click OK to close the dialog box. Resize the highlighted object so it fits on the canvas.

Photo stroke edges

Photo strokes are created by stretching real objects (such as a rope, pipe, or ribbon) around a photo or object.

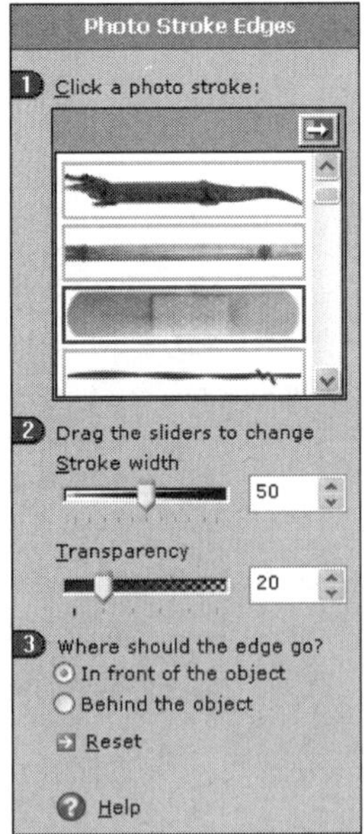

Figure 10.10 A photo stroke is created from a single real photo or image.

To add photo stroke edges:

1. Select the picture to which you want to apply the effect. (If the workspace has only one picture, it isn't necessary to preselect it.)
2. Choose Effects > Edges > Photo Stroke Edges.
   The Photo Stroke Edges pane appears (**Figure 10.10**).
3. Select a photo stroke style from the drop-down list.

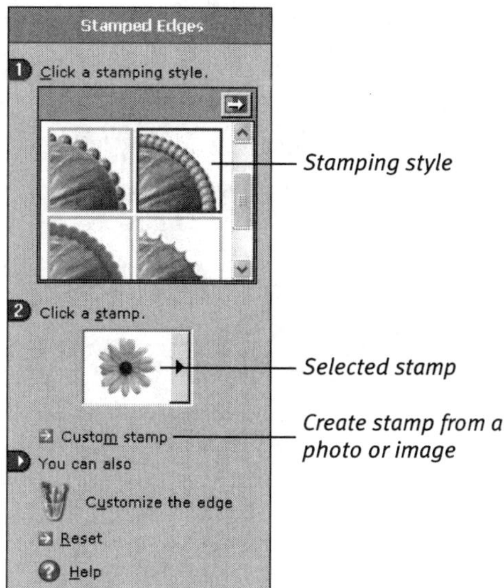

Figure 10.11 Select a stamping style and the particular stamp you want to use.

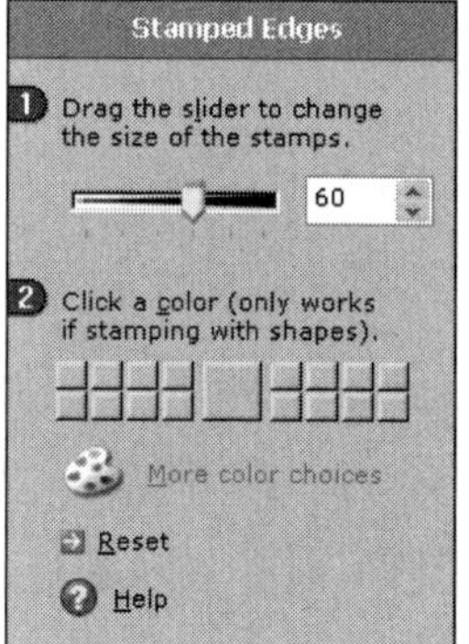

Figure 10.12 You can alter the stamp's size or color.

4. Set the stroke width and transparency by dragging the sliders.
5. Specify whether the stroke will be applied in front of or behind the selected object by clicking the appropriate radio button.
6. Click the Done button.
7. If the selected object filled the entire canvas (as a normally opened photo would), a warning appears.

   Click OK to close the dialog box. Resize the highlighted object so it fits on the canvas.

Stamped edges

Stamped edges are a repeating pattern around a photo or object, formed from a single design, image, or cutout object.

To add stamped edges:

1. Select the picture to which you want to apply the effect. (If the workspace contains only one picture, it isn't necessary to preselect it.)
2. Choose Effects > Edges > Stamped Edges.

   The Stamped Edges pane appears (**Figure 10.11**).
3. Select a stamping style and then select the stamp that you want to use.

   The stamp appears around the object.
4. *Optional:* To change the size or color of the stamp, click Customize the edge. In the new pane that appears (**Figure 10.12**), drag the slider to set a different stamp size and click to choose a new color. Click Done.
5. Click Done.

✔ Tips

- You can create a stamp from clip art, a photo, or any other image. Click Custom stamp (see Figure 10.11).
- Color can only be changed for some stamps.

Adding a Mat

Framed photos and artwork are often matted. A *mat* is made of textured mat board and is used to surround the image within a frame. In Picture It!, you can simulate a mat by surrounding your photo with a texture chosen from the Gallery.

To add a mat:

1. Choose Effects > Edges > Frames and Mats, or choose Edges > Frames and mats from the Common Tasks list.

   The Pick a Design window appears.

2. Select Build Your Own theme and then click the Photo simple mat thumbnail.

   The Simple Mat pane appears.

3. *Do one of the following:*
   - ▲ If the picture is the one that's already open in the workspace, click Next.
   - ▲ If the picture you want to use is in the Tray, double-click it.
   - ▲ If the picture is on disk, is in your connected digital camera, or you want to scan one, click the appropriate icon.

   The Browse window appears, open to the Textures category (**Figure 10.13**).

4. Click the texture that you want to use as the mat. (If you prefer, you can select a texture or other image that's stored on disk by clicking Look elsewhere.)

   The Simple Mat pane appears.

5. Select a mat size by clicking a radio button (**Figure 10.14**).

   The mat texture appears around the image in the chosen size.

6. Click the Next button.

7. *Optional:* To reshape the visible part of the picture, choose a shape from the list (**Figure 10.15**). Click the Next button.

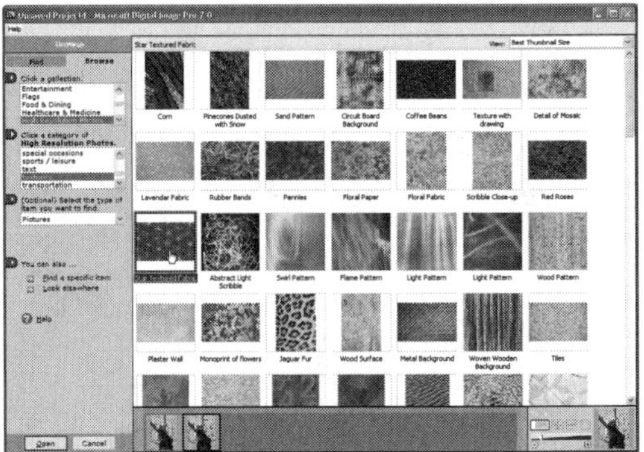

Figure 10.13 Choose one of these textures for your mat or use own of your own images.

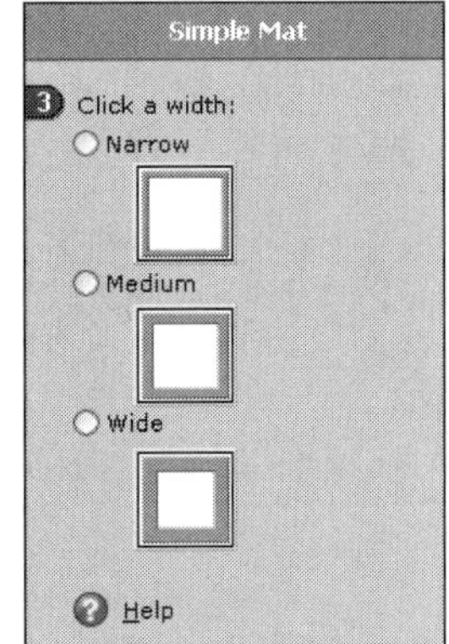

Figure 10.14 Choose one of these three mat sizes.

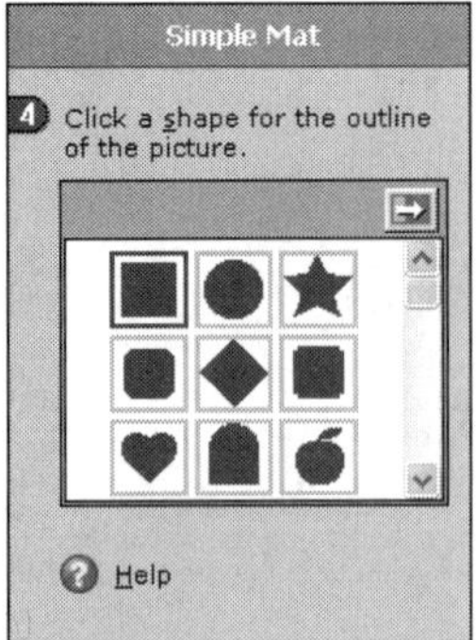

Figure 10.15 You can reshape the photo.

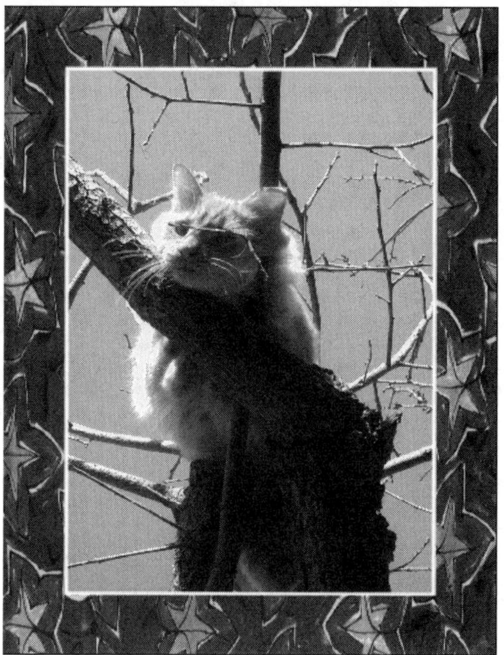

Figure 10.16 An example of a matted photo.

8. To change the mat color, click a color icon or click Choose your own color.

   If you don't like the effect and want to return to the original color, click Reset.

9. Click the Next button.

10. As needed, move or resize the picture. Click Done to complete the process (**Figure 10.16**).

Adding a Frame

Like Picture It!'s mats, a frame mimics a real picture frame. An added frame automatically surrounds all images and objects in the picture—including any borders, edges, or mats. You can pick a frame from Picture It!'s selection or create a custom one from the same textures that are used to make mats.

To add a normal frame:

1. Choose Effects > Edges > Frames and Mats, or choose Edges > Frames and mats from the Common Tasks list.

   The Pick a Design window appears.

2. Select a theme from the scrolling list and then click the thumbnail of the frame style that you want to use (**Figure 10.17**).

   The frame appears in the workspace.

3. *Do one of the following:*
   - ▲ If the picture you want to use is in the Tray, drag it into the frame.
   - ▲ If the picture is on disk, is in your connected digital camera, or you want to scan one, click the appropriate icon.

4. Click the Next button.

5. If necessary, move or resize the image that you placed in the frame.

   If you wish, you can also flip the image vertically or horizontally by clicking the appropriate icon.

6. Click Done (**Figure 10.18**).

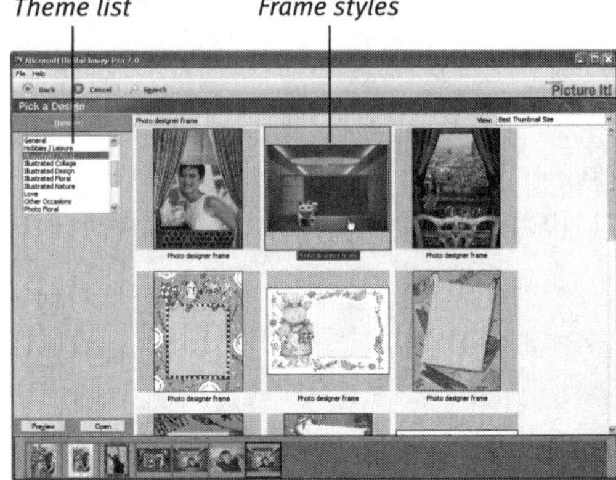

Figure 10.17 After selecting a theme, click the frame that you'd like to use.

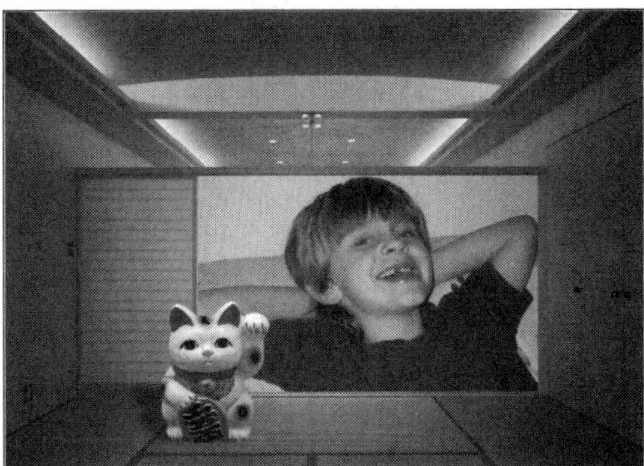

Figure 10.18 An example of a framed photo.

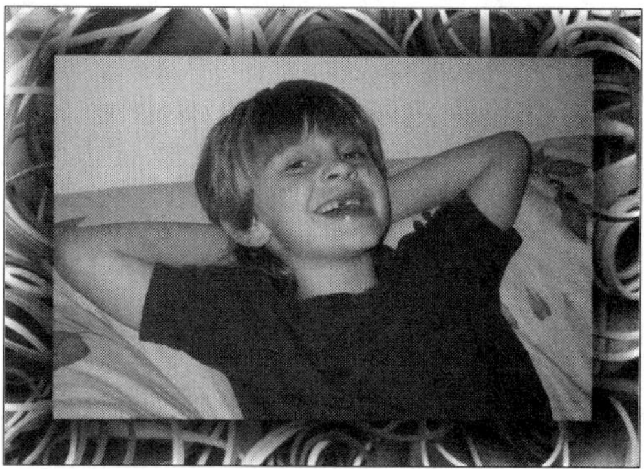

Figure 10.19 This rubber band texture makes a visually interesting frame.

To add a texture frame:

1. Choose Effects > Edges > Frames and Mats, or choose Edges > Frames and mats from the Common Tasks list.

   The Pick a Design window appears.

2. Select Build Your Own theme and then click the Photo simple frame thumbnail.

   The Simple Frame pane appears.

3. *Do one of the following:*

   ▲ If the picture is the one that's already open in the workspace, click Next.

   ▲ If the picture you want to use is in the Tray, double-click it.

   ▲ If the picture is on disk, is in your connected digital camera, or you want to scan one, click the appropriate icon.

   The Browse window appears, open to the Textures category (see Figure 10.13).

4. Click the texture that you want to use as the frame. (If you prefer, you can select a texture or other image that's stored on disk by clicking Look elsewhere.)

   The Simple Frame pane appears.

5. Select a frame size by clicking a radio button (see Figure 10.14).

   The frame—in the chosen size—appears around the image.

6. Click the Next button.

7. To change the frame color, click a color icon or click Choose your own color.

   If you don't like the effect and want to return to the original color, click Reset.

8. Click the Next button.

9. As needed, move or resize the picture. Click Done to complete the process (**Figure 10.19**).

11

PRINTING

Printing is the culminating event of many Picture It! projects. Given the cost of printing high-resolution pictures with an inkjet, you probably won't print *all* the digital photos you take, but you're sure to want to print the best ones. And many Picture It! projects (such as greeting cards, business cards, and labels) are pointless unless printed.

In this chapter, you'll learn to do the following:

- Create standard image printouts
- Generate multi-photo prints and labels using special papers
- Print *index sheets* (thumbnail images from a particular folder)
- Create two-sided printouts for projects such as half-fold greeting cards
- Order professional photographic prints of your favorite images

Basic Printing

If you're like the majority of Picture It! users, most of your print jobs are pretty basic. That is, you want to print a photograph or scan on standard printer or photo paper, for example. All such print jobs are set up and executed in the Print pane. More advanced procedures, such as two-sided printing, are discussed later in this chapter.

When setting options in the Print pane, the onscreen image is a preview of the parts of the project that will be printed, the image size, and how everything will fit on the page. As you change print options, they're reflected on the canvas.

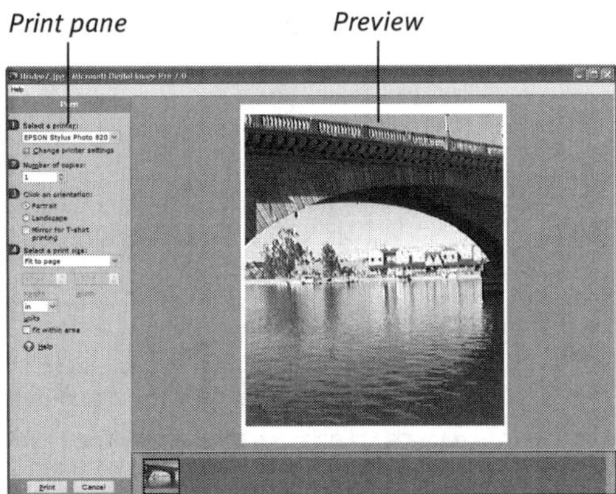

Figure 11.1 Unlike in most Windows programs, all printing options are selected in a Print pane, rather than in Print and Print/Page Setup dialog boxes.

To print an image on standard paper:

1. *Do one of the following:*
   - ▲ Choose File > Print or press Ctrl P.
   - ▲ Click the Print toolbar icon.
   - ▲ Choose File > Print Special > Standard Paper.

   The Print pane appears (**Figure 11.1**).
2. Select an installed printer to use.
3. *Optional:* To review or change print options for the selected printer, click Change printer settings.

   The Properties dialog for the printer appears (**Figure 11.2**). The options presented depend on your printer and its installed software. Set options and click OK.
4. Specify the number of copies to print.
5. Select a print orientation: Portrait (normal) or Landscape (sideways).
6. *Optional:* To reverse the printout (when printing a T-shirt transfer, for example), click the Mirror for T-shirt printing check box.

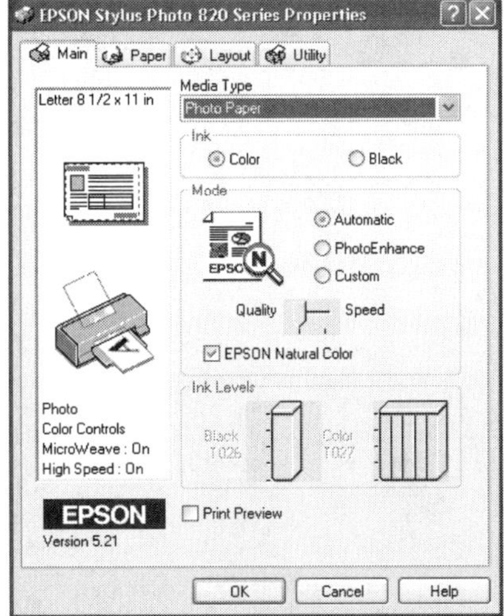

Figure 11.2 Use your printer's Properties dialog box to set printer-specific options.

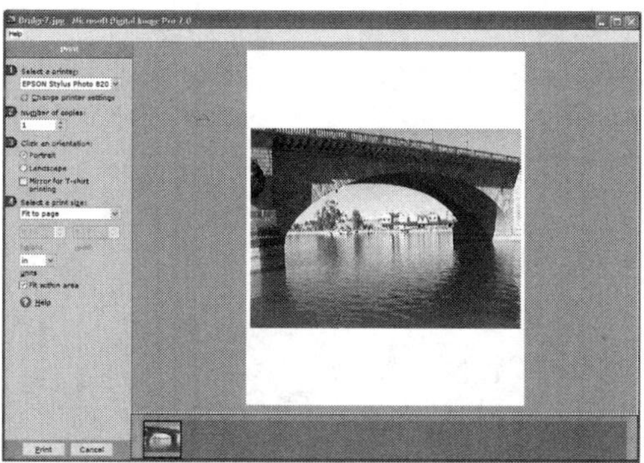

Figure 11.3 With Fit within area checked, the image is fully displayed, but may be reduced in size to fit the page.

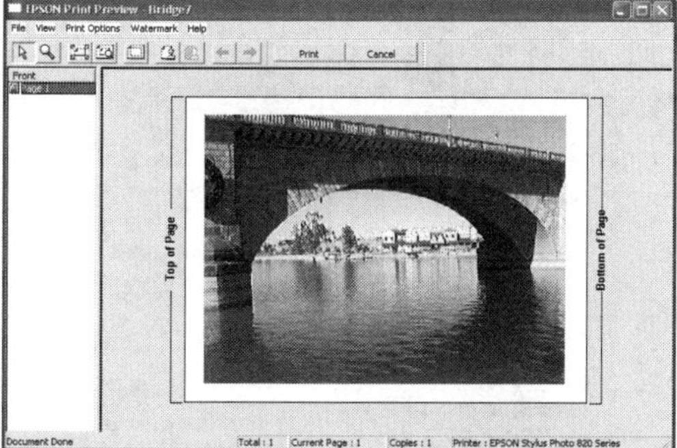

Figure 11.4 Epson printers may be able to generate a print preview in response to a Print command. The preview can show additional settings chosen in the Properties dialog box, such as this sepia tone print.

7. Select a print size from the drop-down list.

   In addition to the specific sizes and formats listed, you can choose the following:

   ▲ *Exact Size.* Print the image using its actual dimensions.

   ▲ *Fit to Page.* Proportionately expand or reduce the image so it comes as close as possible to filling the page.

   ▲ *Custom.* Specify a custom size for the image by entering the desired height and width in any of three measurement units: inches, centimeters, or millimeters.

8. *Optional:* Depending on your size choice in Step 7, the image may be cropped on some edges in order to fit the paper. To avoid this automatic cropping, click the Fit within area check box (**Figure 11.3**).

9. Click the Print button.

✔ Tips

- Items that are in the workspace but not on the canvas won't be printed. Any part that's off the canvas will be clipped at the canvas edge.
- Be sure to examine your printer's options before printing (Step 3). In other programs, this is the equivalent of issuing the File > Print Setup/Page Setup command. It is here that you can specify the size and quality of paper to be used, whether to print in color or black-and-white, and set special printer options (such as color correction). Owners of Epson printers, for example, can request a print preview from this dialog box (**Figure 11.4**).

Printing Multiple Photos

Using the Print Special > Multi-photo Sheet command, you can print a single photo several times on the same page or several different photos on a page...just like the photo sheets you order each year from your kid's school!

To generate a multi-photo printout:

1. Open all of the projects that you intend to print on the same page.

   All photos must be in the Tray before you issue the Print Special command.
2. Choose File > Print Special > Multi-photo Sheet.

   The Print Multiple pane appears.
3. Select an installed printer to use.
4. *Optional:* To view or change print options for the printer, click Change printer settings.

   Be sure that the proper options are specified for this printout, such as paper quality, color settings, and so on.
5. Click Next to continue.
6. In the next pane (**Figure 11.5**), select a paper category from the scrolling list, select a paper type thumbnail in the main window, and click a radio button to indicate whether your image(s) should be printed in portrait or in landscape mode.
7. *Optional:* To fine-tune the printout, click View advanced options. Doing so enables you to set *bleed* (eliminating white space around each image) and *fine-tuning* (adjusting for slight print alignment problems).
8. Click Next to continue.
9. In the next pane (**Figure 11.6**), click a radio button to indicate whether you want to print One project or Several projects. Click Next to continue.

   A new pane appears with shaded areas in which to place the projects (**Figure 11.7**).

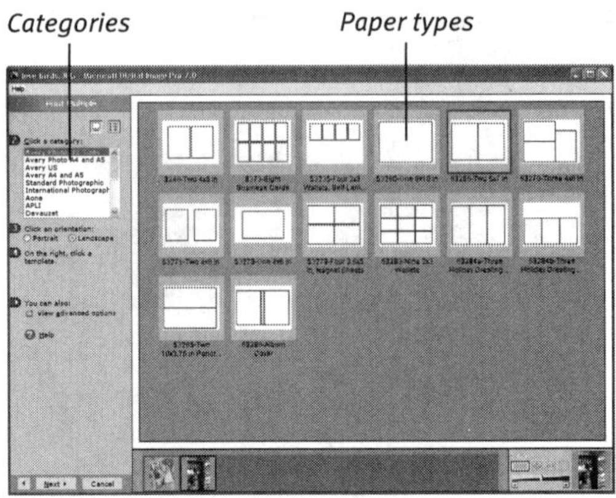

Figure 11.5 Select a paper category, select the paper stock that you'll use, and specify the orientation.

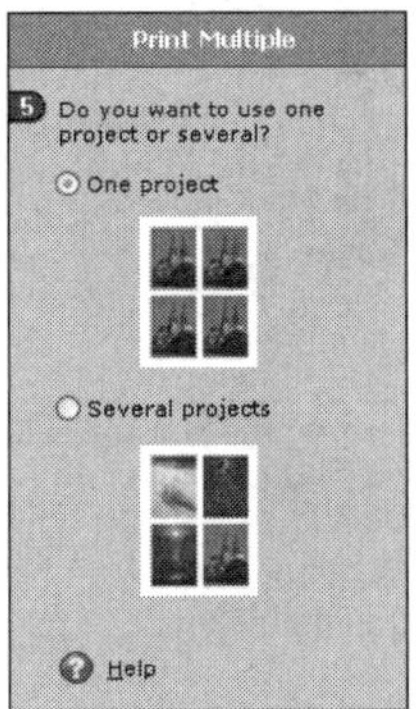

Figure 11.6 Indicate whether you want multiple prints of one project or whether several projects will be printed.

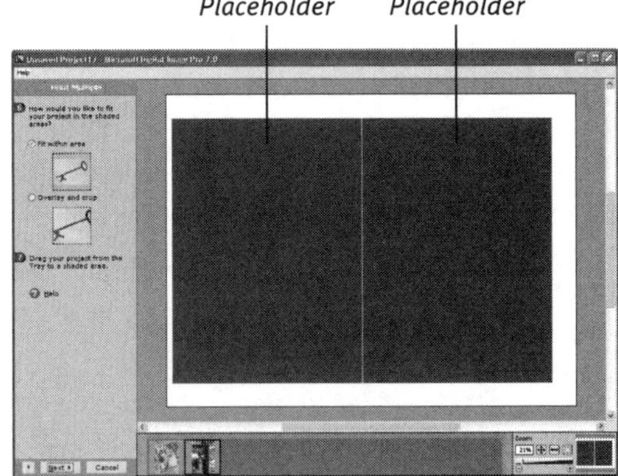

Figure 11.7 Select a placement method, and then drag images into the placeholders.

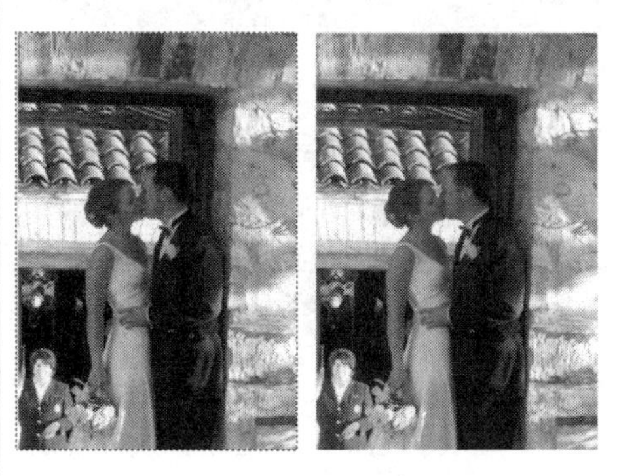

Figure 11.8 When printing one image several times, you only need to drag it into one placeholder.

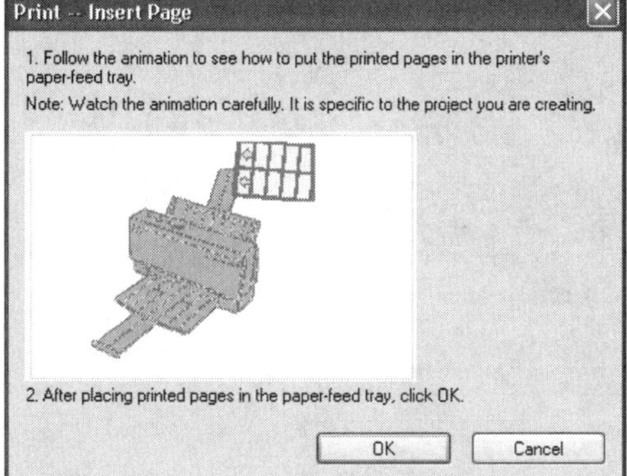

Figure 11.9 This animation shows the proper way to insert the selected paper stock into your printer.

Labels and Special Papers

Don't use File > Print to print labels or print on special paper, such as paper for business cards, greeting cards, or 4" x 6" photos.

To print on label stock or a special paper, follow the steps for creating a multi-photo printout, but choose File > Print Special > Labels or Special Paper (rather than Multi-photo Sheet).

10. Click a radio button to indicate how you wish to place the projects. All projects will be placed using this setting.
    - ▲ *Fit within area.* Select this option to enlarge or shrink each project as needed to fit within the blue areas.
    - ▲ *Overlay and crop.* If this option is selected and a placed project doesn't fit within the blue area, the project will be left at its original size, but any portions outside the blue area will be eliminated.
11. Drag a project from the Tray into a blue area.

    If you chose *One project* in Step 9, Picture It! will automatically copy the project to all blue areas (**Figure 11.8**). If you chose *Several projects* in Step 9, drag each additional project into a blue area.

    After placing the projects, if you don't like the effect of the choice made in Step 10, click the other radio button and drag the project(s) in again.
12. Click Next to continue.
13. In the new pane, specify the number of copies to print and then click Print.

    The Print -- Insert Page dialog box appears (**Figure 11.9**).
14. Insert the paper into the printer in the manner shown in the animation, and then click OK.

✔ Tip

- As you probably noticed in Step 6, you can't mix and match project orientations. When creating multi-photo printouts, be sure that all projects are designed to print in portrait mode or in landscape mode.

Printing an Index Sheet

Once you have more than a handful of images stored on disk, Picture It! provides a way for you to document and find them again. You can print a *photo index* (similar to a photographic contact sheet) for selected images in any folder.

To create and print an index sheet:

1. *Optional:* An index sheet can be created from all images in the Tray or selected ones that are on disk. To create an index from the Tray, open the desired images and close the ones that you don't want to include.

   Regardless of whether the images are in the Tray or on disk, however, you must have at least one open image in order to issue the Index Sheet command.
2. Choose File > Print Special > Index Sheet.

   The Print Index Sheet pane appears.
3. *Do one of the following:*
   - ▲ Click In the Tray to create the index from all currently open images.
   - ▲ Click On my computer to select the images from a location on disk. The File Browser appears (**Figure 11.10**). Navigate to the folder in which the images are stored, select them by Ctrl-clicking or pressing Ctrl A (Select All), and then click the Open button.

   A new pane appears (**Figure 11.11**).
4. Click a radio button to indicate whether file names will appear under the images, and select an installed printer from the drop-down list.
5. *Optional:* To review or change print options for the selected printer, click Change printer settings.
6. Click the Next button to continue.

   A new pane appears (**Figure 11.12**).

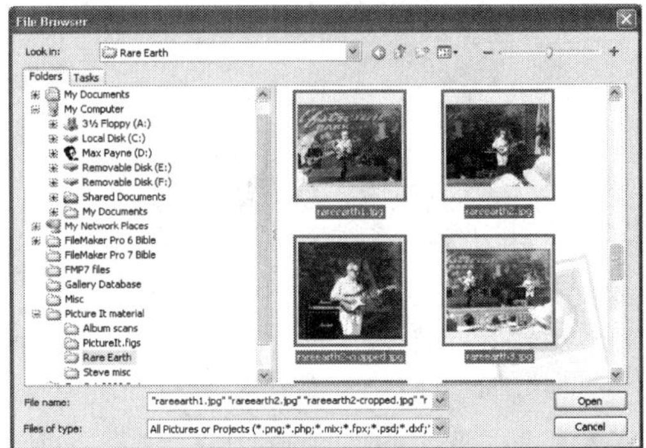

Figure 11.10 Open the folder that contains the images, select those that you want to include, and click Open.

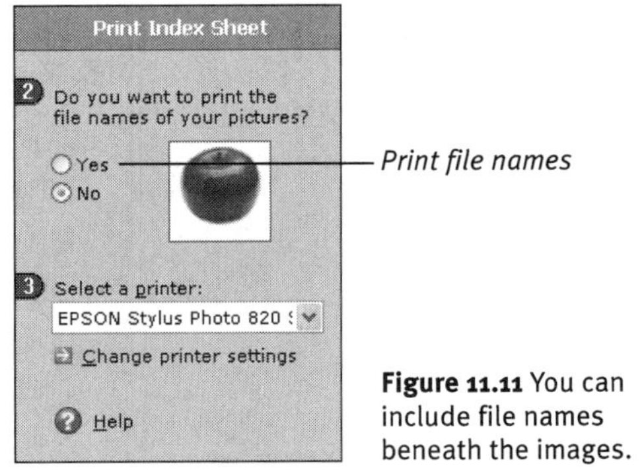

Figure 11.11 You can include file names beneath the images.

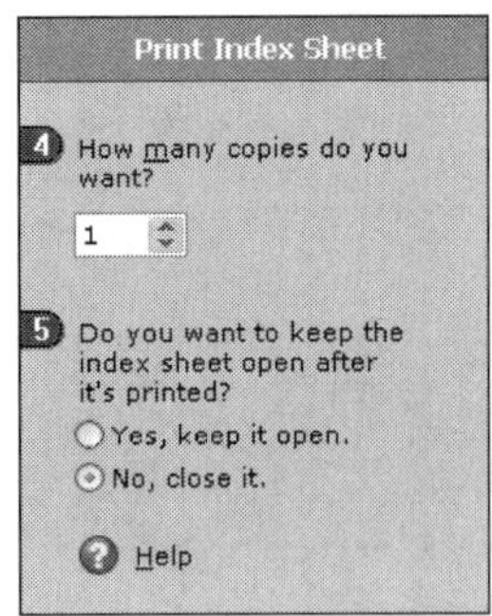

Figure 11.12 Specify the number of copies and whether the index sheet should be placed in the Tray following printing.

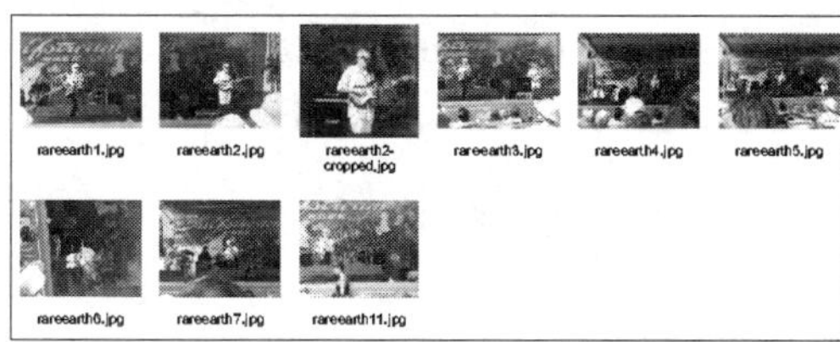

Figure 11.13 Here's an example of a small index for a photo shoot.

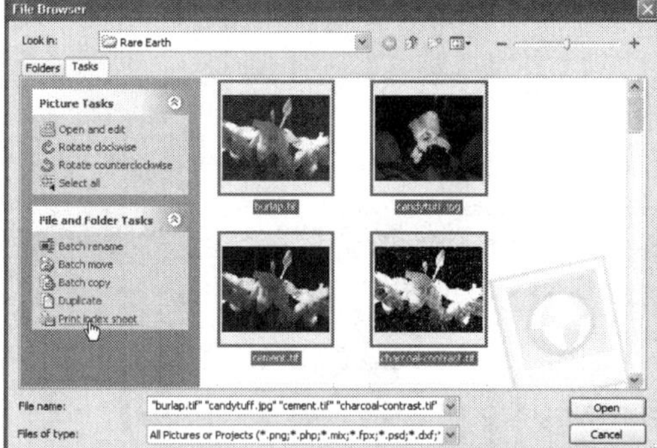

Figure 11.14 You can also generate an index by selecting images in the File Browser and clicking Print index sheet.

7. Specify the number of copies to print and whether you want the resulting index sheet to remain open after it is printed.
8. Click the Print button.

   The photo index is printed (**Figure 11.13**). If you've selected more images than can fit on a single page, additional pages will be generated and printed as necessary.

✔ Tips

- If you keep the index sheet open after printing, you can save it as a new file.
- When using the Select All command (Ctrl A) to select all images in a folder, Picture It! automatically ignores subfolders, as well as any files that are of an incorrect type (such as word processing or ZIP files).
- You can also print an index sheet from within the File Browser (**Figure 11.14**). Choose File > Open, navigate to the correct folder, click the Tasks tab, select the files, and click Print index sheet in the File and Folder Tasks area of the dialog box.
- One of the problems with photo indexes is that there isn't an option to label the page. It would be more useful if you knew what folder the images were from, for example.

  There are two ways to add a label to the printout. First, you can choose to leave the index sheet in the Tray after it's printed and then edit it by adding a text label. Second, if your printer software has a print preview option, select it, and cancel the printing when the preview appears. Add the text label, and then print the index sheet as you would any other project.

Two-sided Printing

While most printers are incapable of automatically printing on both sides of a page, you *can* flip the paper over when it's necessary. The first time you try to print a two-sided project (such as a half-fold card), Picture It! presents a series of dialog boxes that determine how your printer handles a two-sided print job.

To prepare for two-sided printing:

1. Open a project that requires printing on both sides of the paper.
2. Choose File > Print, press Ctrl P, click the Print toolbar icon, or choose File > Print Special > Standard Paper.

   A dialog box appears, notifying you of the printer test.
3. Turn your printer on, and click OK to begin the test.
4. In the new dialog box that appears (**Figure 11.15**), click the picture that most resembles your printer and then click Continue.
5. In response to the next dialog box (**Figure 11.16**), insert a sheet of letter-sized printer paper and then click OK.

   The first test page prints.
6. Remove the test page and reinsert it into the printer with the arrow side up and pointing toward the printer. Then click OK.

   Another test is printed on the page.
7. When the printing finishes, click OK.
8. Hold the test page with the arrow pointing up and then click the radio button of the animation that matches the test page (**Figure 11.17**). If you don't see a matching animation or aren't sure, click the top radio button to perform the test again.
9. The test concludes (**Figure 11.18**). Click OK to print the current document, or click Cancel if you don't want to print at this time.

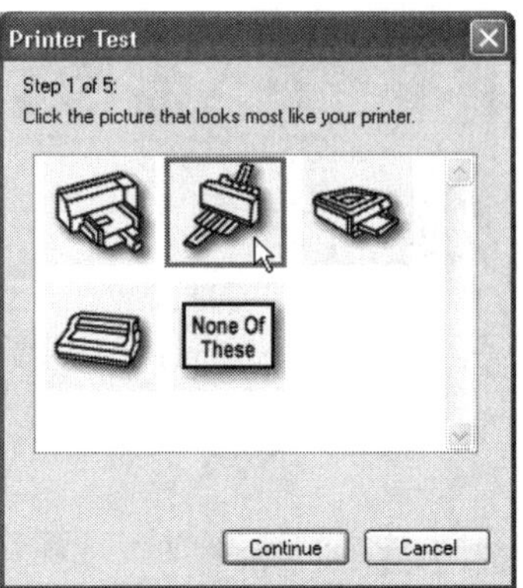

Figure 11.15 Select your printer type from this dialog box.

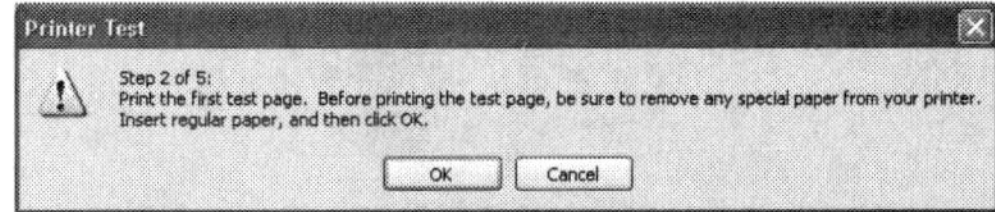

Figure 11.16 Insert paper and click OK to print the initial test page.

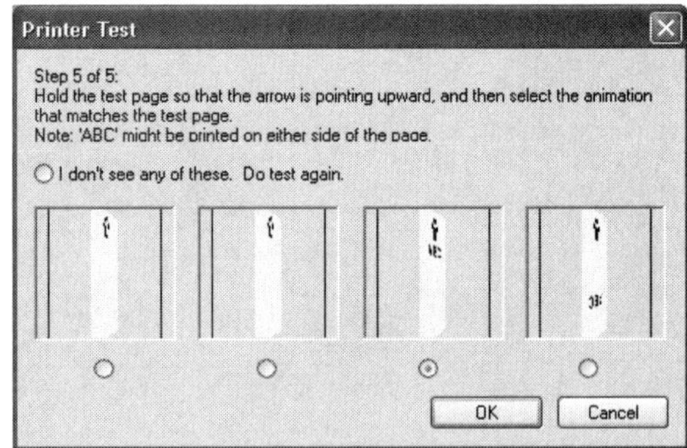

Figure 11.17 Compare the test page to the animations in this dialog box.

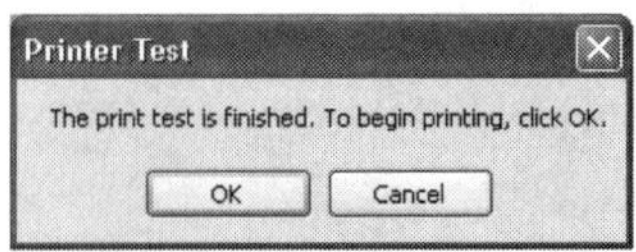

Figure 11.18 Click OK to print the project, or click Cancel to quit without printing.

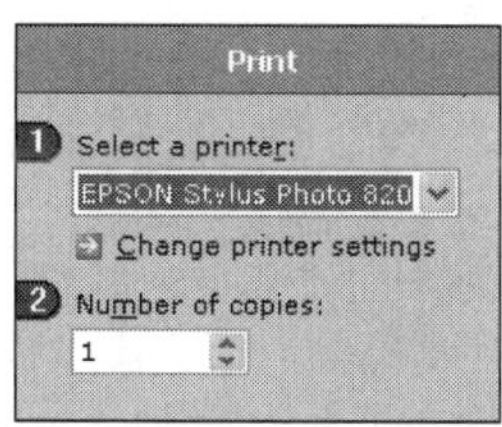

Figure 11.19 Select your printer and specify the number of copies.

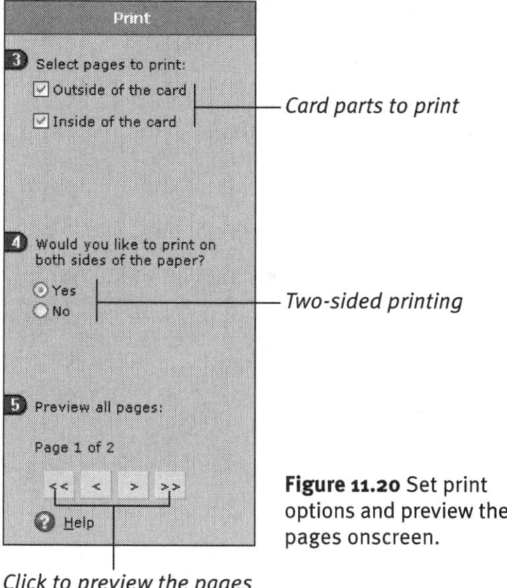

Figure 11.20 Set print options and preview the pages onscreen.

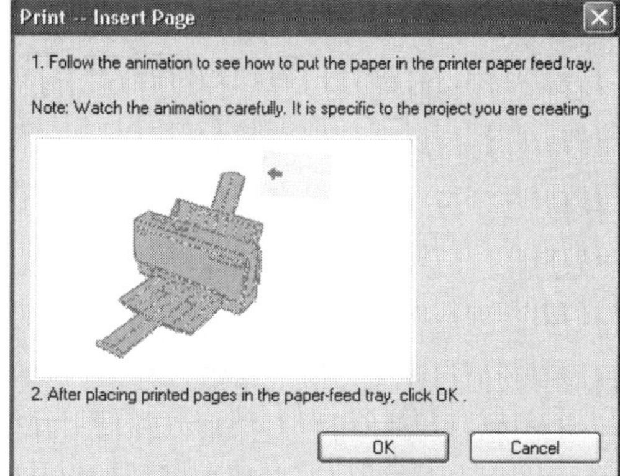

Figure 11.21 Insert the paper as directed and then click OK.

To print a two-sided document:

1. Open a project that requires printing on both sides of the paper.
2. Choose File > Print, press Ctrl P, click the Print toolbar icon, or choose File > Print Special > Standard Paper.

   The Print pane appears (**Figure 11.19**).
3. Select an installed printer to use.
4. *Optional:* To review or change print options for the selected printer, click Change printer settings.
5. Specify the number of copies to print and click Next.
6. In the new pane (**Figure 11.20**), ensure that both check boxes are checked and that the Yes radio button is selected (indicating that this is a two-sided print job). You can preview the pages by clicking the arrow buttons in the Preview all pages section.
7. Click the Print button.

   A dialog box appears, indicating that the front page is being printed.
8. When the front(s) are done printing, click OK.

   The Print -- Insert Page dialog box appears (**Figure 11.21**).
9. Insert the printed page(s) into the printer in the manner shown in the animation, and then click OK.

   The second side of each page is printed.

Ordering Prints Online

Are you dissatisfied with the quality and longevity of the photo prints you're getting from your inkjet or other type of printer? You can order professional prints of your favorite Picture It! images on photographic paper.

To order prints online:

1. In Picture It!, open the images that you want to have professionally printed.

   The images must all be in the Tray.

2. Choose File > Print Professionally Online > Prints and Enlargements.

   The Prints and Enlargements pane appears (**Figure 11.22**).

3. Click a radio button to indicate whether you want to order prints of The current picture or All open pictures in the Tray.

4. If you're printing only one picture, but it isn't the current one, click the correct picture's thumbnail in the Tray.

   If printing multiple pictures, but you still need to add or remove some from the Tray, click Add or remove pictures.

5. When the proper image is displayed or all images in the Tray are correct, click Next.

   Using your active Internet connection, you are taken to the MSN Photos Web site (**Figure 11.23**).

6. Review the prices and click Order Prints.

   If you aren't currently signed in to your .NET Passport or Hotmail account, you will be asked to do so now.

7. Follow the onscreen instructions to place your order.

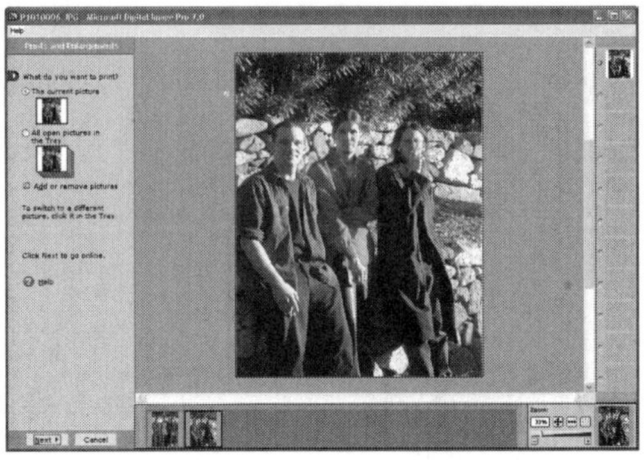

Figure 11.22 You can order prints of just the current image or all images in the Tray.

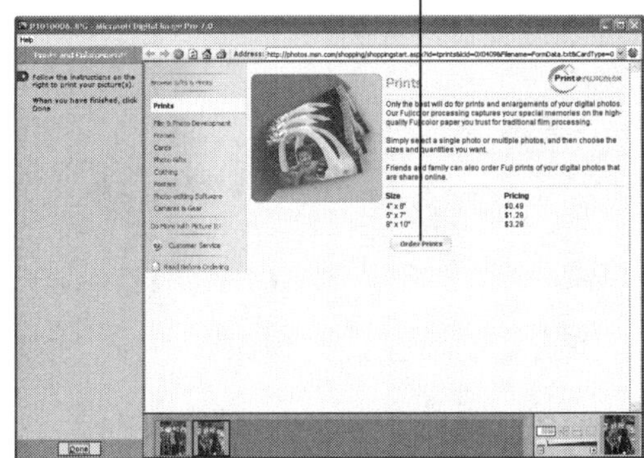

Figure 11.23 The MSN Photos Web site lists photo prices and provides complete instructions for placing your order.

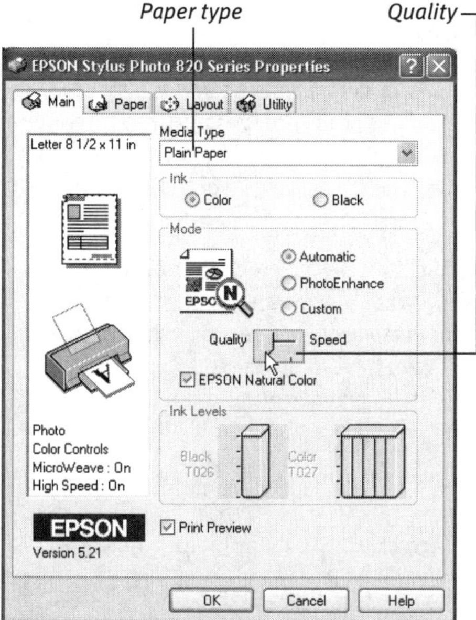

Figure 11.24 In your printer's Properties dialog box, you can often set print quality and select a paper stock.

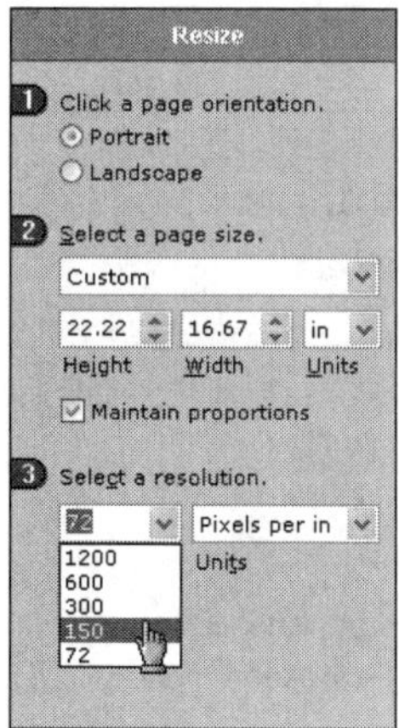

Figure 11.25 Selecting a new resolution automatically adjusts image size.

Planning Before Printing

The size and resolution of your photo determine how large of a print you can make while achieving close to photo quality. Many digital cameras create huge photos but at a very low (72 dpi) resolution. There are several things you can do to assure the highest image quality possible in your prints:

- Set your printer for the desired quality. (Click the Change printer settings icon in the Print pane.) Chances are excellent that the Properties dialog box for your printer (**Figure 11.24**) will have options for setting the print quality.

  The same dialog box may also let you specify the type of paper being used. Select the proper paper type to enable the printer to adjust its print options to match.

  You may also choose different color settings to ensure a better match with the image's colors onscreen or for the particular type of image, such as a photo. Refer to your printer manual or Help for details.

- Use a paper that is rated for printing at your chosen resolution or higher, such as 1200 dpi. A high-resolution printout on inexpensive copier paper will often cause the ink to soak through the paper, resulting in a blurry mess.

- Reduce the size of the image. Doing so has the effect of *magically* increasing the resolution. While a poster-sized photo printed at 72 dpi will look mediocre, it may be perfectly acceptable—or even gorgeous—printed as an 8" x 10" image or smaller.

  For those versions of Picture It! that offer this feature, choose Format > Resize Image. In the Resize pane (**Figure 11.25**), select a higher resolution. Picture It! will automatically reduce the image's size to match the new resolution.

Inkjet Printing Tips

If you're printing in Picture It!, chances are excellent that you're using an inkjet printer. With almost any current inkjet, you can print on photo paper, generating paper images that rival the ones from photo processing places. To help you obtain superior printouts and handle some of the typical problems that can arise, this section provides a series of—what I hope you will find to be—useful inkjet tips.

Learn about indicator lights. Common problems are often signalled by a printer indicator light. On an Epson printer, for example, a flashing light may indicate that an ink cartridge is *almost* empty, while a solid light shows that it *is* empty. (Any empty cartridge stops the printer from printing. If the color cartridge is dry, for instance, you won't even be allowed to print in black-and-white until the color cartridge is replaced.) Review the printer manual for the meanings of all indicators.

Run cleaning cycles. When you start seeing *banding* (blank strips) in your printouts, it's probably time to run a cleaning cycle. (Banding is a sign of clogged printheads.) What you may not know is that it can take multiple cycles to unclog them—as many as six for some printers.

The bad thing about cleaning cycles is that they use ink—significant amounts of ink. Running multiple cleaning cycles can seriously reduce the number of printed pages you'll get from the cartridges. If your printheads need frequent cleaning, just consider it part of the cost of inkjet ownership.

Buy cheap replacement cartridges. When you saw the price of that new inkjet, you probably thought you were getting a bargain. But after running through the initial cartridges and pricing replacements, the truth became apparent. For between $50 and $60, a standard set of cartridges can print about half a ream of paper (250 pages). Some bargain, huh?

You can ease the pain by buying compatible cartridges, rather than ones made by the printer manufacturer. For example, I recently bought a pack of 12 cartridges (8 black and 4 color) for $36. That comes to $3 apiece! To compare sources of compatible cartridges, visit *http://dealink.com.*

Use the right paper. When using an inkjet printer to print photos, scanned images, or other artwork, normal printer or copier paper is barely sufficient for low-resolution printouts. Because images of this type tend to have large areas of color, low-quality paper can get saturated. To print at higher resolutions (such as 1200 dpi), be sure that your paper is rated for that resolution or higher.

Similarly, most inkjet paper is designed to be printed only on one side. If you can't tell which side is the correct one from examining the paper (and, frankly, I usually can't), you may find the answer printed on the outside of the paper ream.

Use archival inks and papers. Although your printed photos may look like normal photos, they won't last as long. Unless you intend to reprint them every few months or years, you may want to find out if archival inks and paper are available for your printer.

Creating Photo Projects

12

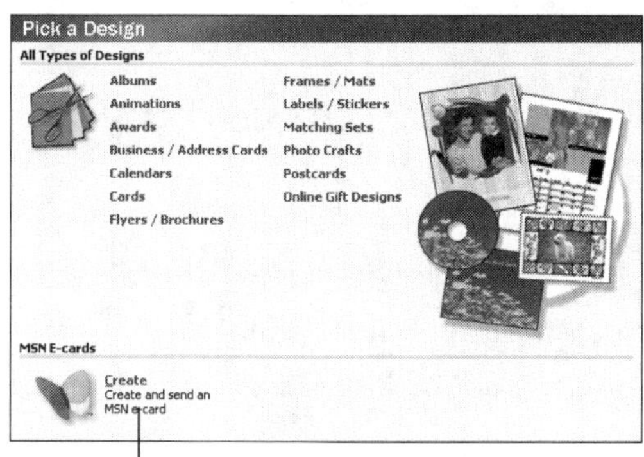

Create an electronic greeting card

Figure 12.1 Choose the project you want to create from the list on the Pick a Design screen.

Online Projects

In addition to those projects that you can create and print on your own printer, you can also design projects to be professionally printed (for a fee) by MSN Photos. You can order prints of your favorite digital photos, as well as mouse pads, coasters, T-shirts, caps, and the like—all of which will sport an image that you've created and edited in Picture It!

To design a project for professional printing, choose Online Gift Designs on the Pick a Design screen or just open your image and choose an option from the File > Print Professionally Online submenu.

Other than Express, all versions of Picture It! can help turn your photos into useful, eye-catching projects. As shown in **Figure 12.1**, you can use Picture It! to create photo albums and collages, award certificates, business cards, calendars, greeting cards, stickers, labels, fliers, and more.

Rather than illustrating every possible project and variation, this chapter highlights a handful of the more interesting ones. As you'll learn by checking out these projects, the process of creating a project is basically the same—regardless of the type of project.

To create a photo project:

1. Choose File > Create a Project, or choose Create a project from the Common Tasks list.
2. Select a project type (see Figure 12.1).
3. Pick a theme, and then select a template.
4. Replace the picture placeholders with your own photos. If necessary, move and resize the photos to fit the placeholders.
5. Edit and reformat the text placeholders to suit the project.

✔ Tip

- Certain projects, such as business cards, work better if you use the original images or clip art, rather than substituting your own photos.

Creating a Magazine Cover

How about putting yourself, spouse, child, or pet on their own magazine cover? Printed on high-quality photo paper, it makes a great gift.

To create a magazine cover:

1. Choose File > Create a Project, or choose Create a project from the Common Tasks list.

   The Pick a Design screen appears (see Figure 12.1).

2. Click the Photo Crafts category. On the next screen, click the Magazine Covers subcategory.

   A list of magazine thumbnails appears (**Figure 12.2**).

3. To select a cover, *do one of the following:*
   - ▲ Click a cover to open it.
   - ▲ Select a cover and click Open.
   - ▲ Select a cover and click Preview. In the Preview Design window (**Figure 12.3**), flip through the covers by clicking the Previous Design and Next Design buttons. When you find the one you want to use, click Open This Design.

4. To insert a picture, *do one of the following:*
   - ▲ If the picture that you want to insert is in the Tray, drag it into the dotted picture placeholder on the cover.
   - ▲ If the picture isn't in the Tray, click the appropriate text icon to load the picture from disk, camera, or scanner.

   Some covers have multiple picture placeholders. Repeat this step until all of the placeholders contain the desired images. Click the Next button.

5. Move, resize, or flip the placed pictures, if necessary. Then click the Done button.

6. To complete the cover, edit the text placeholders, as needed (**Figure 12.4**). You can also change the font, font size, or color.

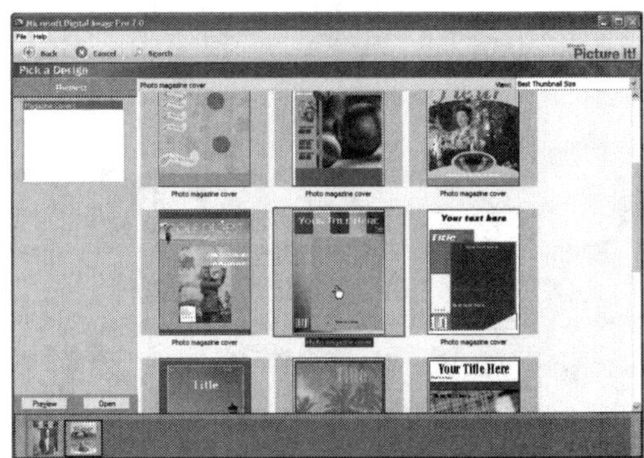

Figure 12.2 Select a cover from this scrolling list.

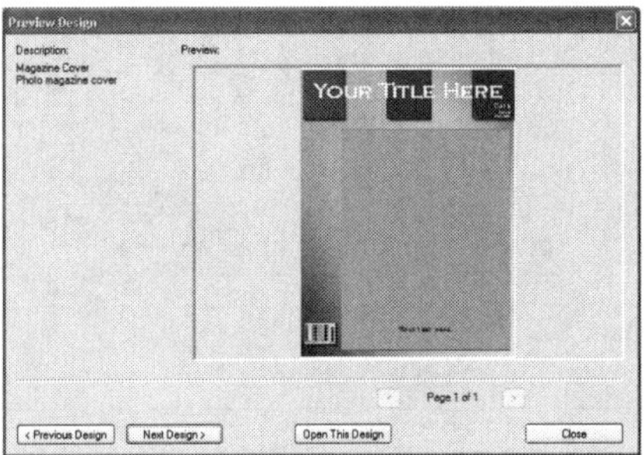

Figure 12.3 You can preview cover images in this window.

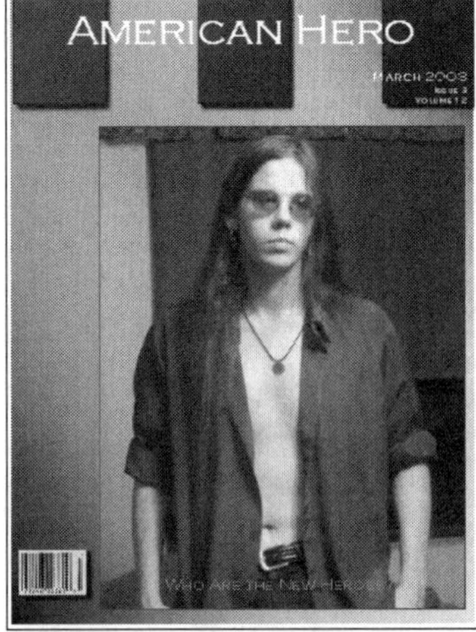

Figure 12.4 This is an example of a finished cover.

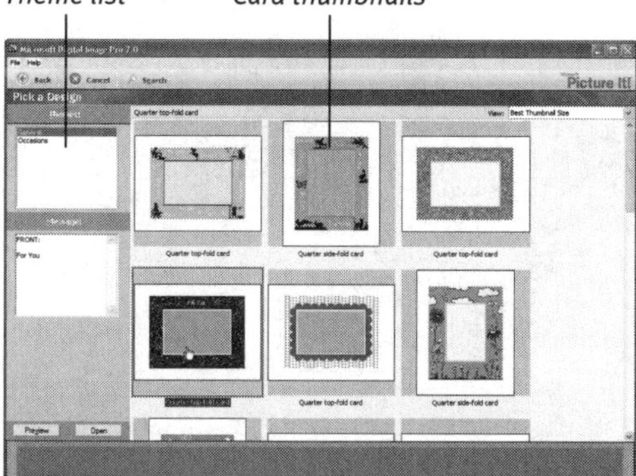

Figure 12.5 Pick a card thumbnail. Be sure to select one with a placeholder that matches your photo's orientation.

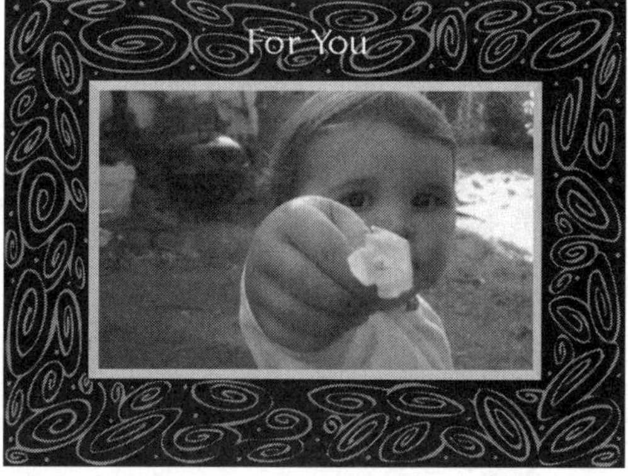

Figure 12.6 What grandparent could resist this card?

✔ Tips

- To view the different parts of the card (front, inside spread, and back), click the icons beneath the Common Tasks list.
- The first time you print something complex in Picture It! (like a two-sided card), you'll be walked through a one-time printer test. See Chapter 11 for details.

Creating a Greeting Card

If you're looking for a cheap source of greeting cards, check out the Cards project category. For most, no customizing is required—just pick a card design and print it. On the other hand, if you're more interested in showing off *your* originality rather than Picture It!'s, here's how to create a custom greeting card that features your personalized text and images.

To create a custom greeting card:

1. Choose File > Create a Project, or choose Create a project from the Common Tasks list.

   The Pick a Design screen appears (see Figure 12.1).
2. Click the Cards category. On the next screen, click the Photo Cards subcategory.

   The Themes screen appears (**Figure 12.5**).
3. Select a theme from the list box.
4. To select a card style, *do one of the following:*
   - ▲ Click a card to open it.
   - ▲ Select a card and click Open.
   - ▲ Select a card and click Preview. In the Preview Design window (see Figure 12.3), flip through the card styles by clicking the Previous Design and Next Design buttons. When you find the one you want to use, click Open This Design.
5. To insert a picture, *do one of the following:*
   - ▲ If the picture that you want to insert is in the Tray, drag it into the dotted picture placeholder.
   - ▲ If the picture isn't in the Tray, click the appropriate text icon to load the picture from disk, camera, or scanner.
6. Move, resize, or flip the placed pictures, if necessary. Then click the Done button (**Figure 12.6**).
7. *Optional:* Edit the text, font, font size, and font color, if desired.

Creating a Calendar

In my opinion, the personalized calendars are among Picture It!'s best projects. By using a favorite snapshot as the background and then printing the calendar on photo paper, you can quickly make an inexpensive gift for friends and relatives that will be viewed and enjoyed for an entire year.

To create a one-year calendar:

1. Choose File > Create a Project, or choose Create a project from the Common Tasks list.

   The Pick a Design screen appears (see Figure 12.1).

2. Click the Calendars category. On the next screen, click the Year subcategory.

   The Themes screen appears.

3. Select a theme from the list box.

4. Click a calendar thumbnail, or select a calendar and click Open (**Figure 12.7**).

5. In the Calendar Project pane (**Figure 12.8**), choose a year for the calendar and choose the day of the week that will be displayed at the beginning of each calendar line.

6. Click the Next button to continue.

7. To replace the default picture, *do one of the following:*

   - If the picture that you want to insert is in the Tray, drag it into the dotted picture placeholder.
   - If the picture isn't in the Tray, click the appropriate text icon to load the picture from disk, camera, or scanner.
   - To use the picture placeholder rather than one of your own photos, do nothing.

8. Click the Next button to continue.

9. Move, resize, or flip the placed picture, if necessary. Then click the Done button (**Figure 12.9**).

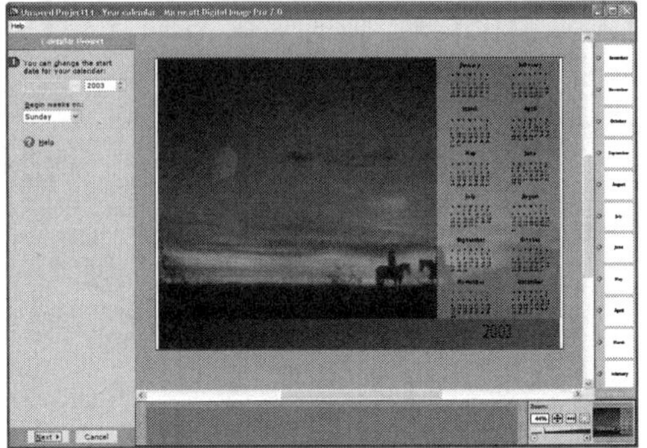

Figure 12.7 The selected calendar template opens, ready for you to customize.

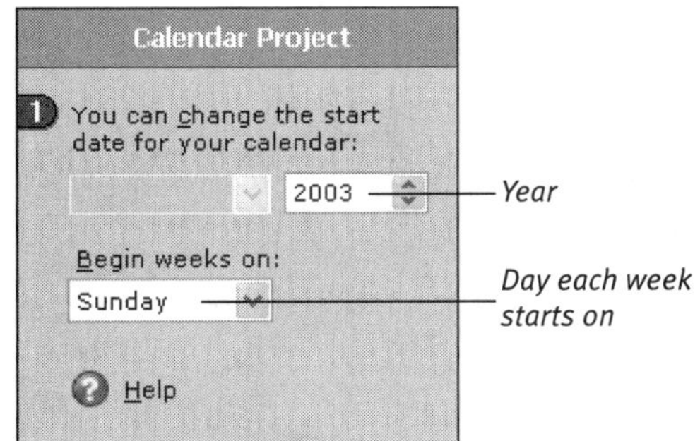

Figure 12.8 Set options for your calendar in this pane.

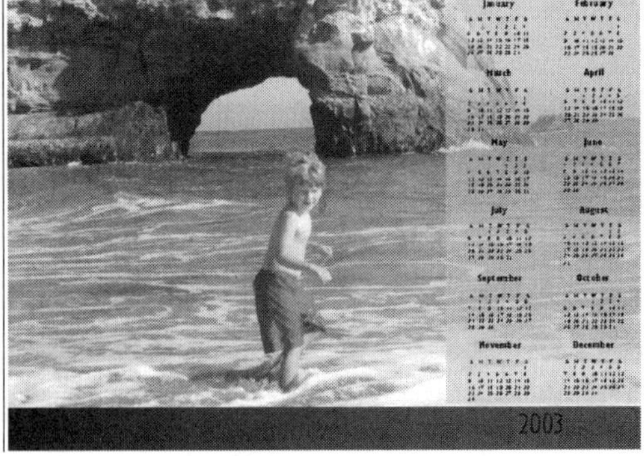

Figure 12.9 Depending on the photo you want to use, be sure to choose a layout that will show the photo to good advantage.

Picture placeholders

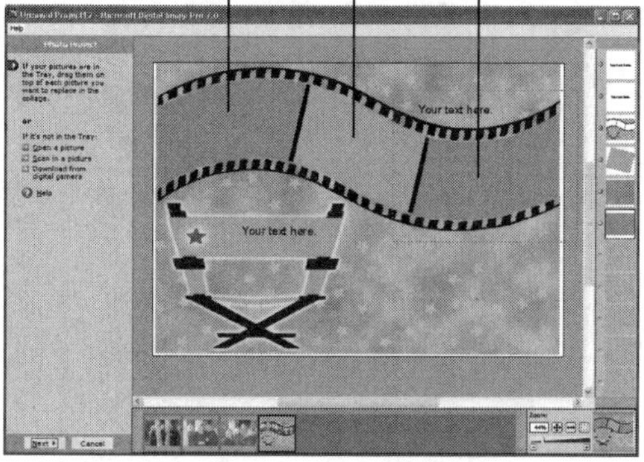

Figure 12.10 This collage template has placeholders for three photos.

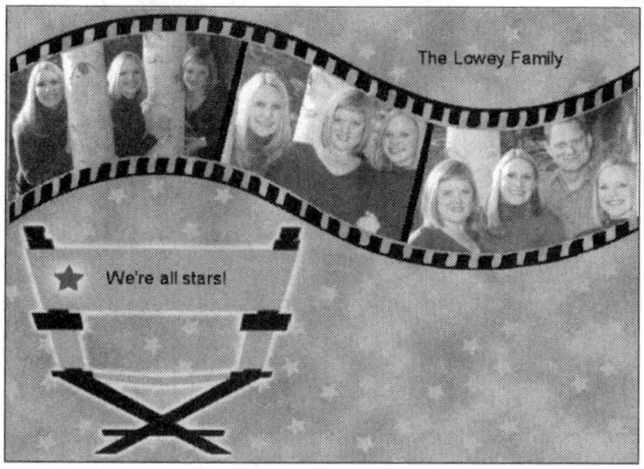

Figure 12.11 Here's the finished collage. Note that the text strings were moved to slightly different positions.

Creating a Photo Collage

You can make a collage from treasured family photos or shots of college friends, for example.

To create a photo collage:

1. Choose File > Create a Project, or choose Create a project from the Common Tasks list.

   The Pick a Design screen appears (see Figure 12.1).

2. Click the Albums category. On the next screen, click the Collages subcategory.

   The Themes screen appears.

3. Select a theme from the list box.

4. To select a collage layout, *do one of the following:*
   - ▲ Click a layout to open it (**Figure 12.10**).
   - ▲ Select a layout and click Open.
   - ▲ Select a layout and click Preview. In the Preview Design window (see Figure 12.3), flip through the layouts by clicking the Previous Design and Next Design buttons. When you find the one you want to use, click Open This Design.

5. To insert a picture, *do one of the following:*
   - ▲ If the picture that you want to insert is in the Tray, drag it into the dotted picture placeholder.
   - ▲ If the picture isn't in the Tray, click the appropriate text icon to load the picture from disk, camera, or scanner. Drag it into the dotted placeholder.

   Repeat this step as many times as necessary to fill all of the picture placeholders. Then click the Next button.

6. Move, resize, or flip the placed pictures, if necessary. Then click the Done button.

7. Edit the text, font, font size, or font color. You can also move the text to more aesthetically pleasing positions (**Figure 12.11**).

Creating a Web Slide Show

If you've done any Web surfing, you've seen—and probably been annoyed by—animated pictures on Web pages. They're often used in advertisements, for example. Many of these are *animated GIFs*, a variation of the GIF image format that combines multiple pictures that play in sequence when viewed in a browser.

Digital Image Pro can create two such types of images: *Web animations* (uses a special effect such as a gradual fade when displaying a single image) and *flipbooks* (generates an animated sequence from multiple images). Since most of us aren't animators, nor do we have images that are suitable to create an animation, I'll show you how to use the Flipbook feature to create a slide show from your favorite photos.

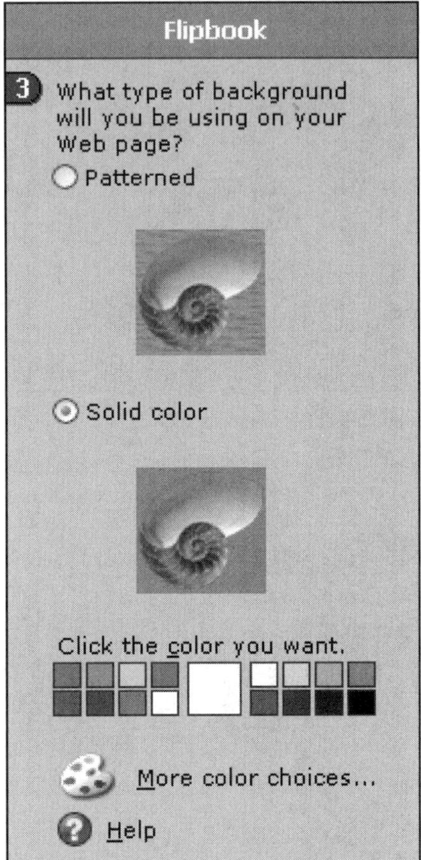

Figure 12.12 If some images are smaller than others, the selected background color will be used to fill in any blank areas around the smaller images.

To create a Web slide show:

1. In Digital Image Pro, open the image files that you want to use in your slide show.

   The animation will be created from all images in the Tray. Close any that won't be used in the animation.

2. Choose Tools > Flipbook.

   The Flipbook pane appears.

3. If you want to include additional pictures that aren't in the Tray, click the appropriate text icon to load the picture from disk, camera, or scanner.

4. The animation is created from the pictures based on their order in the Tray. If necessary, change the order by dragging thumbnails to the left or right. Click Next to continue.

5. Click a radio button to indicate the type of Web page background that the animation will be placed on (**Figure 12.12**). Click Next.

   If you click the Solid color radio button, select a color icon, too. If the correct color isn't shown, click More color choices.

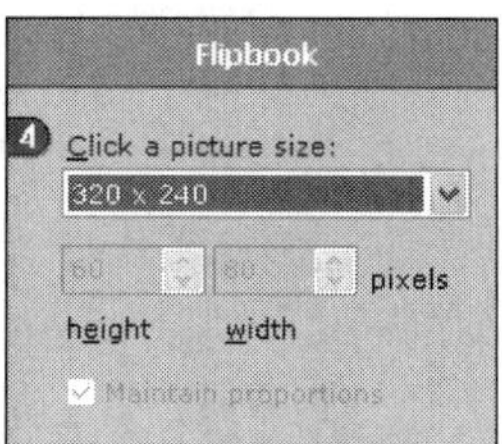

Figure 12.13 Set the size of the images in the finished flipbook.

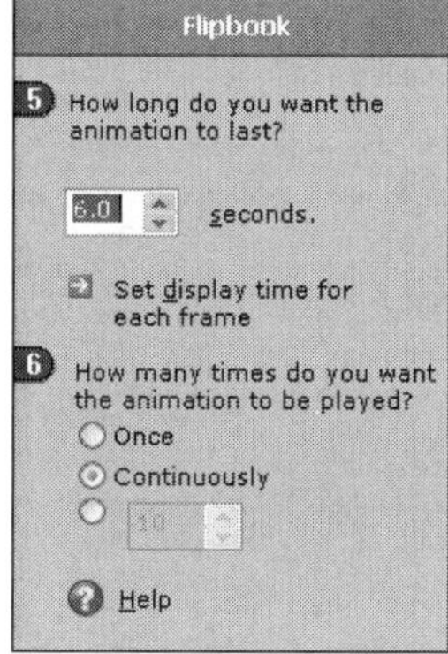

Figure 12.14 Set the total time for the animation and the number of times it will play.

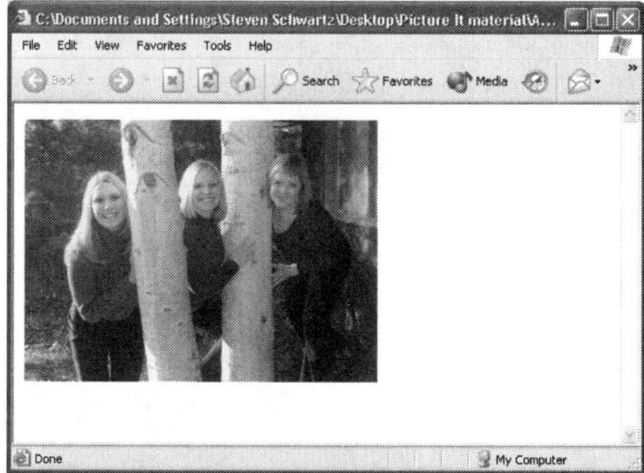

Figure 12.15 When viewed in a browser, the flipbook animated GIF plays automatically.

6. Choose a size (in pixels) for the images in the flipbook (**Figure 12.13**). Click Next.
7. On the next screen (**Figure 12.14**), specify the total time that the finished flipbook will take to display all the images, as well as whether it will play once, continuously, or a specific number of times.

   By default, each image is displayed for the same length of time: one second. To set the display time for each image individually, click Set display time for each frame. Double-click each image in the Tray to set its play time.
8. Click the Next button.

   The flipbook is generated and plays for you.
9. To save the flipbook, click Save it. Then click Done.

✔ Tips

- To view the finished flipbook, open it in any Web browser, such as Internet Explorer (**Figure 12.15**), or in Windows Picture and Fax Viewer (a part of Windows XP). As soon as the flipbook loads, it plays using the settings you specified.
- You can email a flipbook to friends and relatives. Just be sure to tell them to open it in a Web browser or in Windows Picture and Fax Viewer. Otherwise, all they'll see is the first image, rather than the slide show.
- Since flipbooks are designed for Web viewing, you can also include them in personal or business Web pages. You could make a small flipbook of your bestselling products, for instance.
- Image size and number affect the flipbook's resulting size. Before posting or emailing a flipbook, check its file size by right-clicking its file icon and choosing Properties. If necessary, you can reduce the file size by using fewer images or choosing a smaller display size.

Designing CD/DVD Labels

After making a backup copy of a CD/DVD or having painstakingly transferred the contents of a favorite LP or cassette onto a CD, do you find yourself reaching for a marker to scribble out a label? With a box of blank CD labels, a label that you've designed and printed in Picture It!, and a label applicator such as the CD Stomper *(www.cdstomper.com)*, you can handle the labeling job with aplomb.

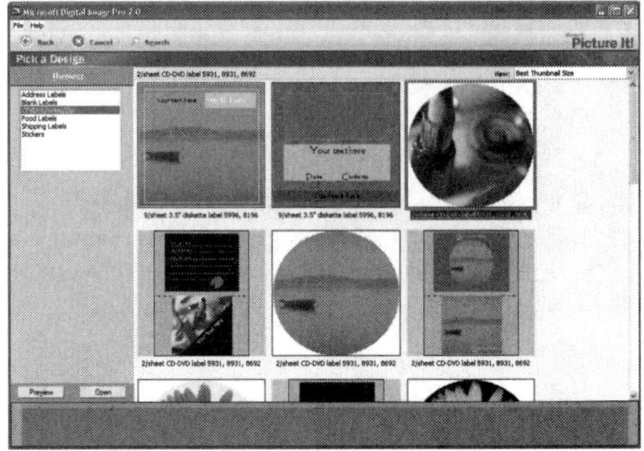

Figure 12.16 Select a CD/DVD template that matches your label stock.

To design a CD or DVD label:

1. Choose File > Create a Project, or choose Create a project from the Common Tasks list.

   The Pick a Design screen appears (see Figure 12.1).

2. Click the Labels/Stickers category.

   The Themes screen appears.

3. Select the CD/Disk/Video/Zip theme (**Figure 12.16**).

4. To select a CD/DVD label template, *do one of the following:*

   - Click a label.
   - Select a label and click Open.
   - Select a label and click Preview. In the Preview Design window (see Figure 12.3), flip through the label styles by clicking the Previous Design and Next Design buttons. When you find the one you want to use, click Open This Design.

   Be sure to choose a template that matches your label stock. Supported label part numbers are listed below each template.

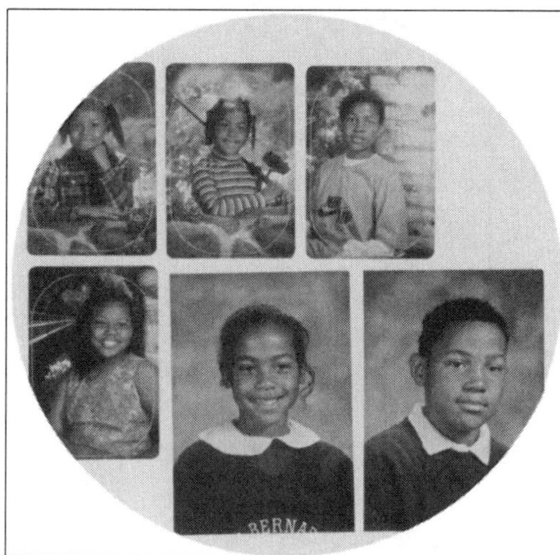

Figure 12.17 You could use a photo collage of your kids to serve as a CD label for some of their favorite songs.

Select a label manufacturer *Select the label type*

Figure 12.18 You can also use the Create a Label Sheet command to generate labels.

5. To replace the default picture, do one of the following:
   - ▲ If the picture that you want to insert is in the Tray, drag it into the dotted picture placeholder.
   - ▲ If the picture isn't in the Tray, click the appropriate text icon to load the picture from disk, camera, or scanner.
   - ▲ To use the picture placeholder rather than one of your own photos, do nothing.
6. Move, resize, or flip the placed picture, if necessary. Then click the Done button.
7. *Optional:* Add a normal or shaped text box so you can include the album, CD, or DVD's title on the label (**Figure 12.17**).

✔ Tips

- If you intend to replace the template picture with one of your own, it really doesn't matter which template you choose—as long as you pick one that matches your label stock.
- If you want to make a really impressive label, consider scanning the album, CD, or DVD cover and using it for the label image.
- Another easy way to create labels with Picture It! is to choose File > Create a Label Sheet. A series of panes step you through the process for your particular label stock (**Figure 12.18**).
- The Create a Label Sheet command is especially useful if you aren't using Avery labels. This wizard supports labels made by more than a dozen other manufacturers.
- When you're ready to print the CD/DVD label, choose File > Print Special > Labels or Special Paper. For instructions, see Chapter 11.

13 Sharing Via the Internet

Since so many people now have Internet access, one of the easiest ways to share photos with relatives, friends, classmates, and colleagues is to use the Internet. You're probably familiar with using your email program to send photos and other images as file attachments. And if you have a personal or business Web page, you may also know how to post images to a Web site where everyone can view them. However, as a Picture It! user, you can also accomplish these tasks without having to leave Picture It! to launch other programs.

In this chapter, you'll learn how to use Picture It! to accomplish the following tasks:

- Send photos as email attachments
- Alter images so they're ready for posting and viewing on the Web
- Preview photos in your Web browser
- Create a Web page from any project
- Post pages to a Web site
- Use the MSN Photos site to share photos

Emailing Photos

You can send the current photo or project to anyone who has an email account. In addition to sending images as unmodified *attachments* (files that are attached to an email message), you can send them as *executable* attachments that—when opened—automatically launch the person's Web browser to display the image.

To email an image as an attachment:

1. The image to be sent must be the active one. If it isn't currently displayed in the workspace, click its icon in the Tray.
2. Choose File > Send As > Picture Attachment.

   The Send or Save for E-mail pane opens (**Figure 13.1**).
3. Picture It! will resize the image prior to sending it. Choose a final image size from the drop-down menu.

   For any chosen image size, the pane shows the resulting file size and transmission time.
4. Click the Next button to continue.
5. *Do one of the following:*
   - To immediately attach the image to a new email message, click Put the project in an e-mail message.

     A new message opens in your default email program with the file attached (**Figure 13.2**). Address the message, edit the Subject and body text as desired, and then send it.
   - To store the resized image as a new file that you can later attach manually to an email message (from within your email program), click Save the Project to e-mail later.

     The Save As dialog box opens. If you wish, you can edit the file name and/or location in which it will be saved. Then click the Save button.

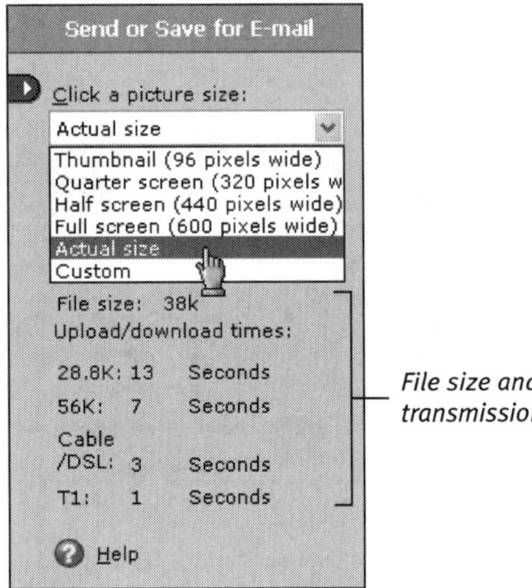

Figure 13.1 Resize the image by choosing a new size from this list.

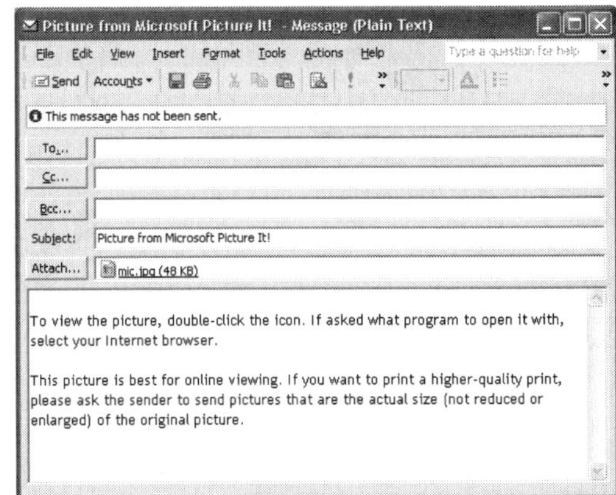

Figure 13.2 Picture It! offers image emailing for the terminally lazy. If you don't feel like writing a personal note, the image is accompanied by a "canned" one.

✔ Tip

- Pay attention to the file size information shown onscreen in Step 3 (see Figure 13.1). If an image is very large (over 2 MB, for instance), many mail servers will refuse to send or deliver it. If one of your picture files is refused for this reason, try sending a smaller version of the same image.

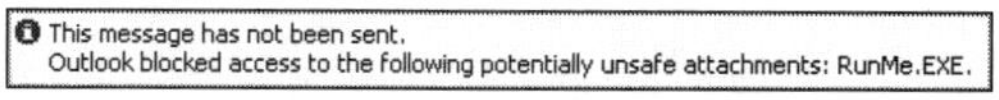

This message has not been sent.
Outlook blocked access to the following potentially unsafe attachments: RunMe.EXE.

Figure 13.3 Microsoft Outlook automatically prevents you from emailing .exe file attachments. This warning text appears at the top of such a message.

To email an image as an executable program:

1. The image to be sent must be the active one. If it isn't currently displayed in the workspace, click its icon in the Tray.
2. Choose File > Send As > EXE Attachment.

   An executable version of the image named RunMe.exe is created and attached to a new message in your default email program.
3. Address the message, edit the Subject and body text as desired, and then send it.

✔ Tips

- If you don't see an appropriate image size in the drop-down menu, choose Custom and specify the image width (in pixels).
- To set your default email program, choose File > Send As > Options. If your program isn't listed, choose As an attachment in an e-mail message. For additional information, see Chapter 14.

Executable Email Attachments

In general, it's a terrible idea to send an image as an executable attachment. Common viruses are frequently delivered as executable programs, so smart users who receive .exe files normally just delete them.

If you decide to use the option anyway, you should note that many email programs (Microsoft Outlook, for example) prevent you from sending executable files (**Figure 13.3**). Some programs, as well as some Internet service providers, also prevent the *delivery* of such files. Even if the attachment is successfully delivered, users of any computing platform other than Windows will be unable to run or open it.

Finally, do you really want to encourage your computer novice friends to blithely open .exe files? My advice is to pretend that the Send As EXE Attachment command doesn't exist. Don't use it.

Sharing Images on the Web

Another way to share photos over the Internet is to publish them on a Web site. Although the most common way of accomplishing this is to post them to your own personal or business Web site, Picture It! provides a host of Web publishing options—and several of them don't require you to have a site of your own.

The following Web-related options are available in Picture It! 7:

- Saving images as Web-ready pictures
- Previewing images in a Web browser
- Creating a Web page from any image or project
- Posting images to a Web site
- Using the MSN Photos Web site to share photos with anyone who has a browser

These options are all available in two program submenus: File > Save Special (**Figure 13.4**) and File > Save to the Web (**Figure 13.5**).

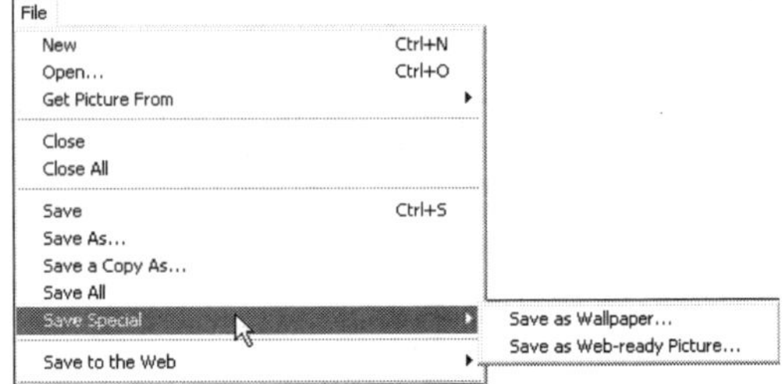

Figure 13.4 Using the Save Special submenu, you can save the current image so it's ready for display on the Web.

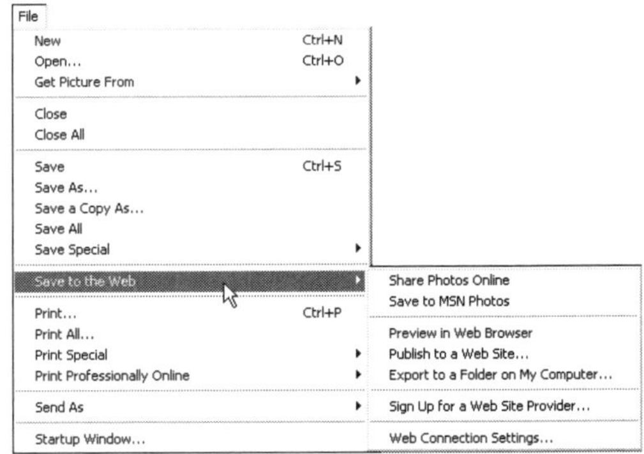

Figure 13.5 The other Web-related commands can be found in the Save to the Web submenu.

Saving images as Web-ready

Using the Save as Web-ready Picture command, you can save any image so that it's appropriate for viewing in a Web browser. The procedure is very similar to the one used when preparing images for email.

To save an image for the Web:

1. Open the image and make it the active one by clicking its thumbnail in the Tray.
2. Choose Save Special > Save as Web-ready Picture.

   The Save for the Web pane opens (**Figure 13.6**).
3. Choose an image size from the drop-down menu.

   For any chosen image size, the pane shows the resulting file size and transmission times.

Select an image size

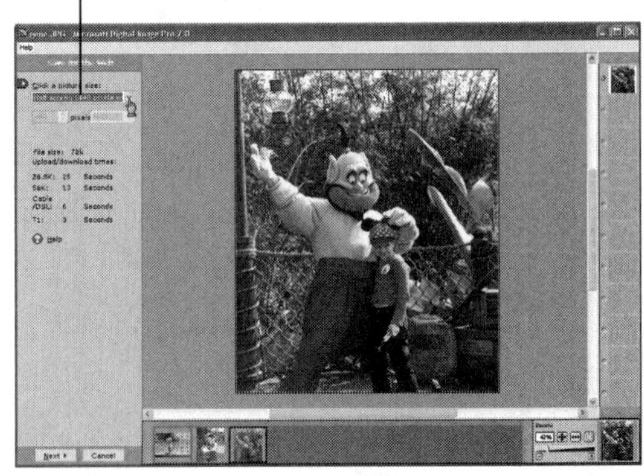

Figure 13.6 Choose a final image size from the Save for the Web pane.

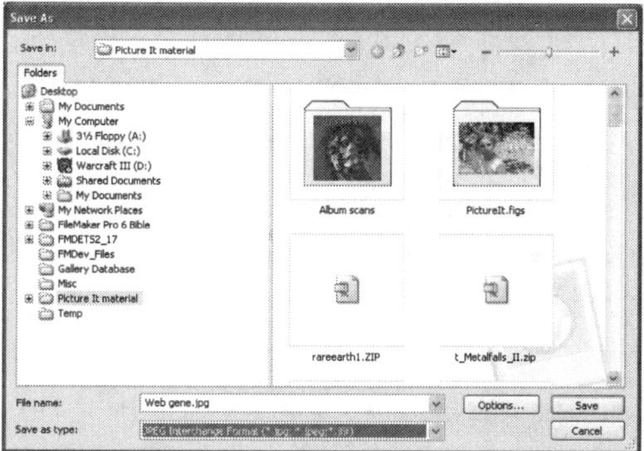

Figure 13.7 Specify a file name and location for the resulting image.

4. Click the Next button to continue.

   The Save As dialog box appears (**Figure 13.7**). The proposed name is the original file name with the word *Web* preceding it, such as Web calendar.jpg. The file type is JPEG, regardless of the file's original type.

5. *Optional:* To change the amount of compression, click the Options button.

6. *Optional:* If desired, you can edit the file name and choose a new location for the file.

7. Click the Save button.

   The new file is saved, and the original file remains open in Picture It!

✔ Tips

- You may want to open the new Web file so you can compare it with the original. Doing so will enable you to verify its clarity and colors.

- Any image—regardless of its original file type—can be readied for the Web with this command. Note, however, that images with layers will be "flattened," since JPEG files cannot contain layers.

Saving an image as a Web page

Two related commands enable you to save the current image as a separate Web page, ready for posting to a Web site.

To save an image as a Web page:

1. Open the image and make it the active one by clicking its thumbnail in the Tray.
2. Choose Save to the Web > Export to a Folder on My Computer.
   The Publish to a Folder dialog box appears (**Figure 13.8**).
3. In the top text box, type or select a name for the resulting Web page. The file extension should be .htm.
4. Specify a folder in which to save the Web page and the converted image by typing its path or by clicking the Browse button (to use the Select Folder dialog box).
   In order to work, the resulting HTML file and graphic must be stored in the same folder. If an appropriate folder doesn't exist, you can create a new one by clicking the New Folder button in the Select Folder dialog box (**Figure 13.9**).
5. Click the OK button.
   If the selected folder already contains files, a warning dialog appears. Click Yes to use the folder, or click No to select another one. The HTML and JPEG files are created and stored in the selected folder.
6. Click OK to dismiss the final dialog box.

✔ Tips

- To view the new Web page in your default browser (**Figure 13.10**), click or double-click the new HTML file icon.
- To view the image without creating permanent HTML and JPEG files, choose Save to the Web > Preview in Web Browser.

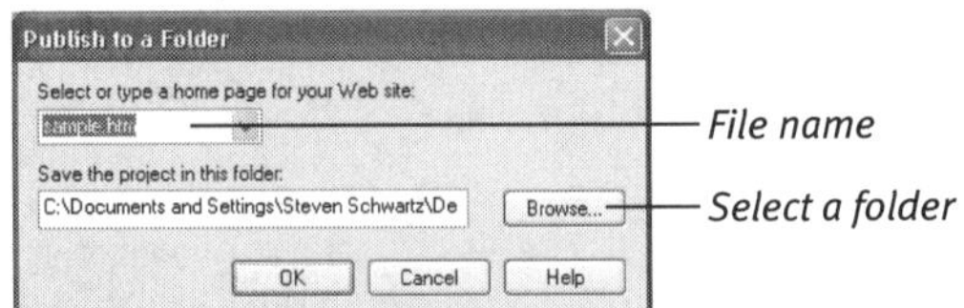

Figure 13.8 Specify a file name and location for the new Web page.

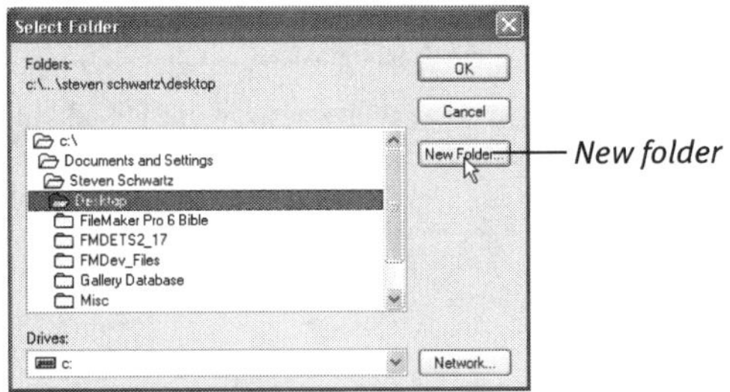

Figure 13.9 You can select an existing folder or create a new one.

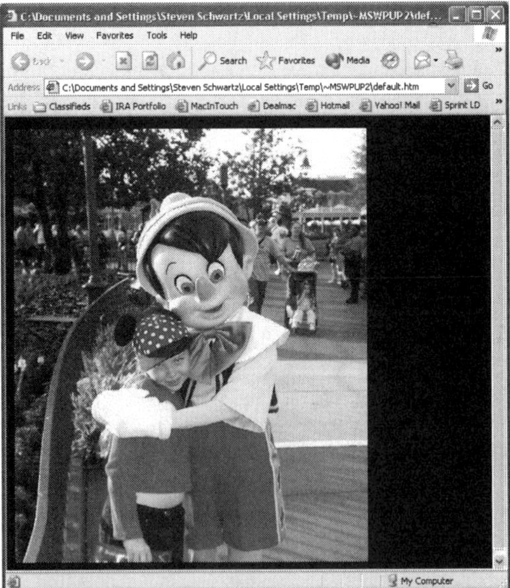

Figure 13.10 The Web page displays the image on a black background. You can use an HTML editor to change the background, if you like.

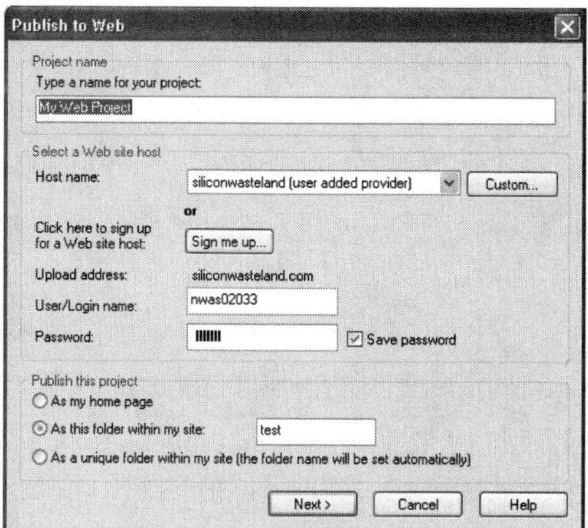

Figure 13.11 Specify the host name, your login name and password for the hosting service, and the folder to which the page will be uploaded.

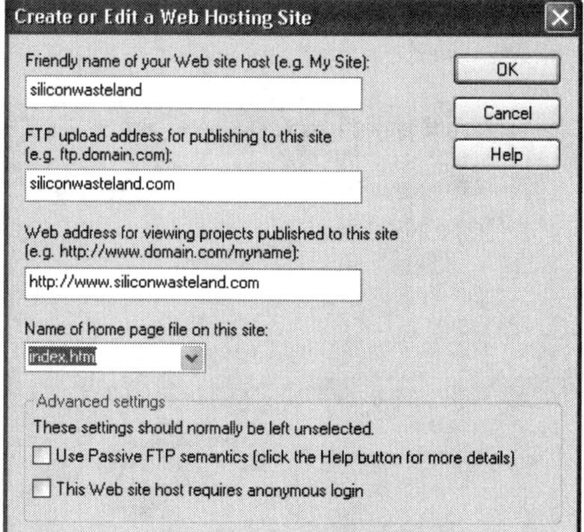

Figure 13.12 If your hosting site isn't listed, you can enter its information as a new custom site.

Publishing an image as a Web page

In addition to changing a picture into a Web (HTML) page, Picture It! can also publish the page on your personal or business Web site. As long as you have the information needed to upload pages to your Web site and recognize Picture It!'s limitations, you may find this capability useful.

To publish an image as a Web page:

1. Open the image and make it the active one by clicking its thumbnail in the Tray.
2. Choose Save to the Web > Publish to a Web Site.

   The Publish to Web dialog box appears (**Figure 13.11**).
3. *Optional:* Enter a name for this project.
4. *Do one of the following:*
   - ▲ Open the Host name drop-down list and select your Web site host.
   - ▲ If your site host isn't listed, click the Custom button. In the Custom Web Host dialog box, click New. In the Create or Edit a Web Hosting Site dialog box (**Figure 13.12**), enter the information provided by your site host, click OK, and then click Close.
5. Enter your user name and password. (Click the Save password check box to have Picture It! remember your password for use in later sessions.)
6. In the Publish this project section, select one of the following options:
   - ▲ *As my home page.* Use this page as your new home page.
   - ▲ *As this folder within my site.* Save the page and image to this existing folder.
   - ▲ *As a unique folder within my site.* Save the page to a new folder named using today's date, such as 03142003.

continues on next page

7. Click the Next button.

   The Web page is uploaded to your site (**Figure 13.13**).

8. *Optional:* Click any of the check boxes, if you wish.

9. Click the Close button.

✔ Tips

- In Step 4, as long as the Web page is named index.html, index.htm, default.html, or default.htm, you only need to specify its directory in your browser's address box, such as *www.siliconwasteland.com/test/*. The page's name isn't required.

- Where your new page can be found on your Web site depends on the option you selected in Step 6.
  - ▲ If you set it as your home page, all you need to do is type your site address, such as *www.mysite.com.*
  - ▲ If you set it to an existing folder (test, for example), type the address of the folder, such as *www.mysite.com/test/.*
  - ▲ If you set it to a unique folder (which will be named as today's date), type the site address followed by the date, such as *www.mysite.com/03142003/.*

  These instructions assume that you named the Web page as index.html, index.htm, default.html, or default.htm in Step 4. If you used a different name, append the page name to the ones listed here.

- Step 8 will only result in the correct link being displayed, emailed, or copied if you uploaded the image as your new home page. Otherwise, you will have to edit the link as indicated in the previous tip.

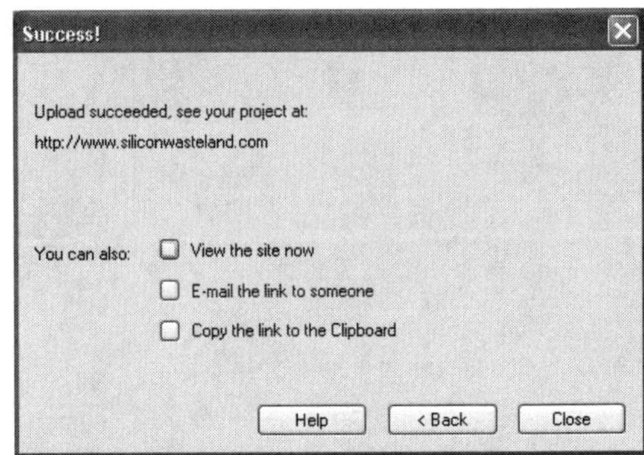

Figure 13.13 After uploading the page, you can view it in your browser, email the link to a friend, or copy the link to the Clipboard (so you can paste it into another application).

Your Own Web Site

All this information about publishing images as Web pages is well and good, but where does one *get* a Web host and site?

Actually, you may already have one that's available to you. The first place to check is with your ISP (Internet Service Provider). As part of a standard account, many ISPs provide a limited amount of space that you can use to create a small site. Call their technical support line to find out if this is the case. Even if free space isn't offered, you may be able to upgrade your account to acquire some space on their Web servers.

If you have ambitions for a greater Web presence and have registered a domain name (like I did for my site), you can use *www.google.com* to search for *Web hosting.* Many hosting services will host a site for you for as little as $8/month. They can also help with domain registrations and transfers.

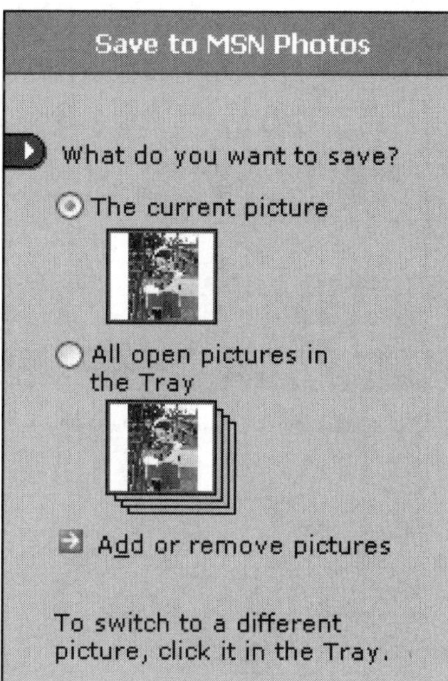

Figure 13.14 Specify whether you want to upload just the current photo or all photos in the Tray.

Sharing images via MSN Photos

You can use MSN Photos, a free Microsoft Web site found at *http://photos.msn.com,* to store and share up to 30 MB of your favorite digital photos.

Before you can use MSN Photos, you'll have to create a free Hotmail account. In addition to letting you use MSN Photos, your new Web-based Hotmail account enables you to send and receive email from any computer that has a browser and an Internet connection. Go to *www.hotmail.com,* and click the New Account Sign-Up tab (if you don't already have a Hotmail account). You will use this new email address and password to sign in whenever you want to use MSN Photos or Hotmail. Although you can upload and share photos directly from the Web site, Picture It! makes it even easier.

To upload pictures to MSN Photos:

1. Open the image(s) that you want to post to MSN Photos.
2. Choose Save to the Web > Save to MSN Photos.

   The Save to MSN Photos pane appears (**Figure 13.14**).
3. *Do one of the following:*
   - ▲ To upload only the picture that is displayed in the workspace, click the radio button for The current picture.
   - ▲ To upload all open pictures, click the radio button for All open pictures in the Tray.
   - ▲ To modify the contents of the Tray by adding or removing pictures, click Add or remove pictures.
4. After selecting an option to upload one or all pictures, click the Next button.

   Picture It! uses your Internet connection to connect to MSN Photos. The Web site appears in the main window.

continues on next page

5. Click the Click Here to Get Started button.

   Thumbnails of the selected pictures are displayed in the main window (**Figure 13.15**).

6. If you're uploading multiple pictures, be sure that each one you wish to upload is checked and then click Continue.

7. In the Choose a folder screen, *do one of the following:*
   - ▲ To upload the photos to an existing MSN Photos folder (such as My Photos), click the folder's icon.
   - ▲ To upload the photos to a new folder, click Create a new folder. In the Create a new folder screen (**Figure 13.16**), name the folder and click Create.

   The photos are uploaded to the designated folder.

8. Click Done to return to Picture It!

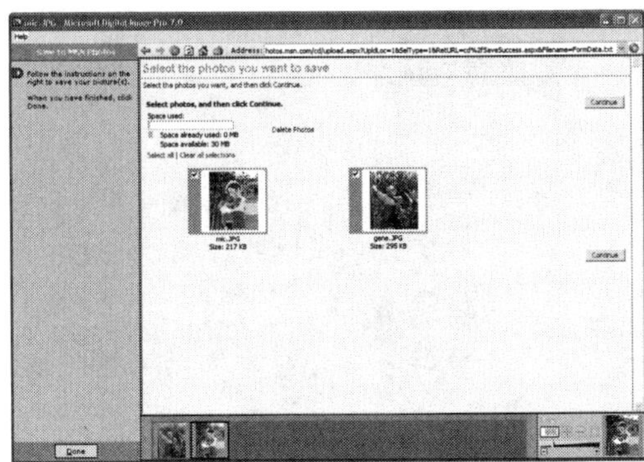

Figure 13.15 Checked images will be uploaded.

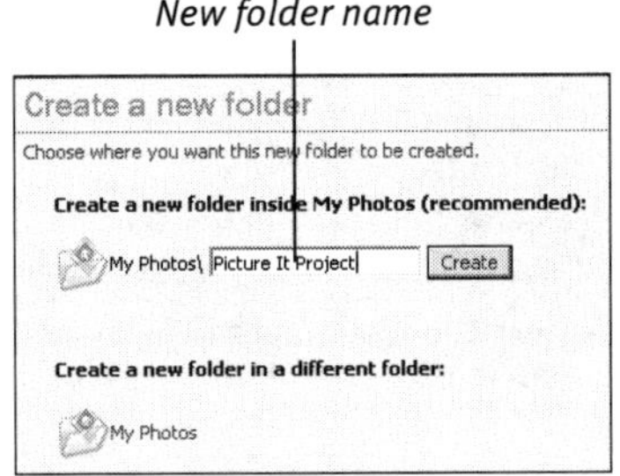

Figure 13.16 To create a new folder, name it and click Create.

✔ Tips

- In Step 3, you can make a different picture active by clicking its thumbnail in the Tray.
- Whether connecting to MSN Photos from Picture It! or from your Web browser, you will be asked to log in to your Hotmail account if you aren't currently signed in. If you have multiple Hotmail accounts, be sure that you are signed in to the correct account. Every account has a separate area in MSN Photos.

To post new photos for others to view:

1. Perform Steps 1–6 of the previous step list.

   The selected photos are uploaded to a new folder named after the current month and year, and the Invite friends screen appears (**Figure 13.17**).

2. In the To line, enter the email addresses of all recipients. When sending to multiple people, separate each pair of addresses with a comma or semicolon.

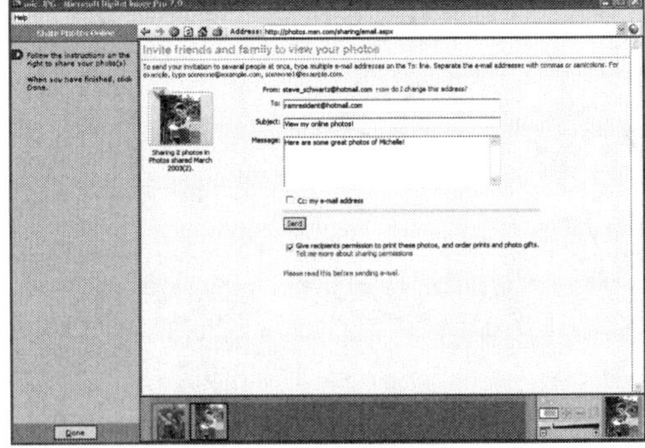

Figure 13.17 Creating an invitation to view your photos is identical to writing a message in your email program.

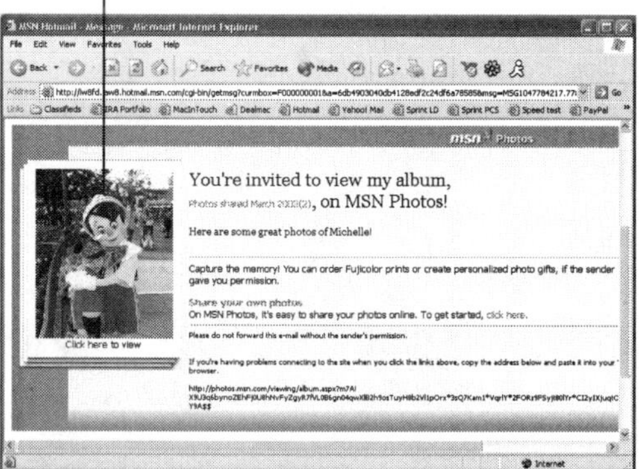

Figure 13.18 When a recipients clicks the photo or text link in this email message, their browser opens to your MSN Photos page.

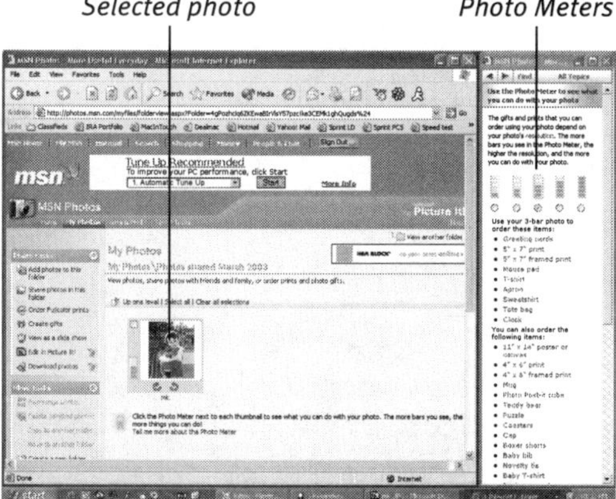

Figure 13.19 Click a Photo Meter for a list of gifts and prints that can be made from the image.

3. Edit the Subject text, if you wish.
4. Enter a message in the Message text box.
5. *Optional:* To receive a copy of this email message, click the Cc: my e-mail address check box.
6. If you want recipients to be able to print the shared photos or order gifts made from them, click the Give recipients permission check box.
7. Click the Send button.

   Each recipient will receive an email message like the one shown in **Figure 13.18**.
8. Click Done to return to Picture It!

✔ Tips

- As mentioned previously, you can also upload photos, manage your photos and folders, and invite others to view them using commands in the MSN Photos site. Use your browser to log into your Hotmail account, go to *http://photos.msn.com,* and click the text links to view and manage your photos.
- At MSN Photos, you can order gift items that feature any of the photos that you've uploaded. When viewing your photos as thumbnails, you'll note that each one has a blue Photo Meter beside it (**Figure 13.19**). The more bars in the meter, the higher the image quality. Click any meter to get suggestions for the types of prints and gift items that can be made from the image.

14 Setting Preferences

Using the Tools > Options command, you can customize your Picture It! experience by changing the program defaults. By setting preferences, you're telling Picture It! how certain operations should be performed and how you'll interact with the program—*until or unless you tell it otherwise.*

The last phrase is key, since it tells you that although preference settings are in effect, you can *still* do things in another way—either by choosing a different option for the current procedure or by changing the preference setting.

In this chapter, you'll learn to do the following:

- Set general preferences
- Set image resolution, compression, and display options
- Set scanner and digital camera preferences
- Set options for plug-in filters
- Choose a default email program to use when sending images from Picture It!

Note that you aren't *required* to alter the preferences. Change them when it will make your work easier or when you find that you're repeatedly resetting a part of the program that could be permanently set as a preference.

In this chapter, the terms *preferences* and *options* are used to mean the same thing.

Setting General Preferences

General preferences don't fall into an obvious category. They don't have much in common with each other, so I consider this a catchall category. While most general preferences can be found in the top half of the Options dialog box (**Figure 14.1**), I'll discuss several others here, too.

To set general preferences:

1. Choose Tools > Options.
2. In the Options dialog box, you can set these general preferences:
   - ▲ *Check for updates online.* When checked, Picture It! will use your active Internet connection to check for and download program updates.
   - ▲ *Require CTRL to zoom with Microsoft IntelliMouse.* This setting only affects you if you have an IntelliMouse or compatible pointing device with a scroll wheel. When unchecked, using the scroll wheel zooms out or in. When checked, using the scroll wheel pages the screen up and down. It zooms only when Ctrl is also depressed.
   - ▲ *Units of measure.* Choose your preferred unit of measurement: inches, millimeters, or centimeters. If you choose a new unit, the rulers change to match.
3. When using Picture It! to send the current project as an email attachment via the File > Send As command, you can specify the email program to use.

   Choose File > Send As > Options. In the Send Options dialog box (**Figure 14.2**), select the email client that you want to use, or select As an attachment in an e-mail message to use your default Windows email client—whatever program that might be.

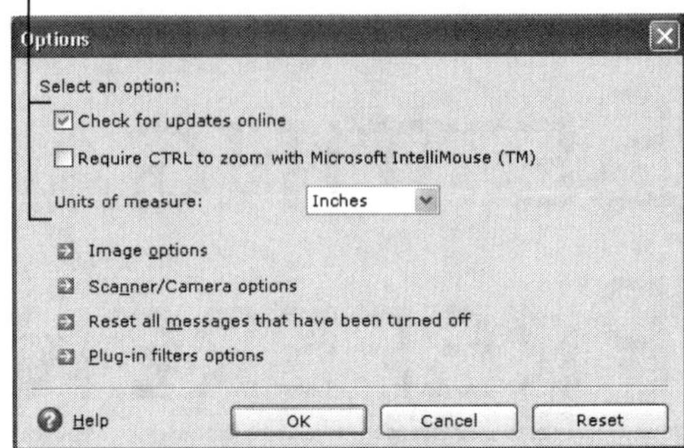

Figure 14.1 The Options dialog box.

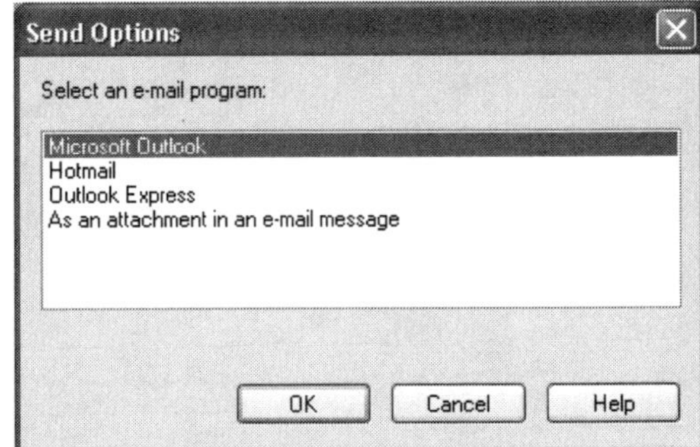

Figure 14.2 Select the program that you want to use when emailing images directly from Picture It!

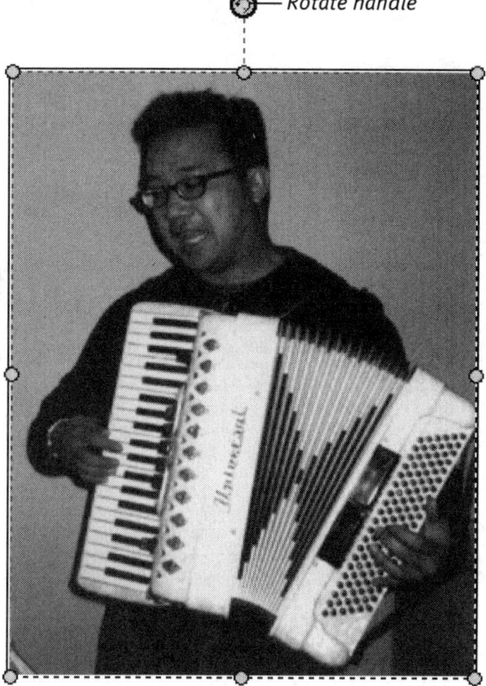

Figure 14.3 With Snap Rotation enabled, it's simpler to rotate objects in 45-degree increments.

4. To simplify the process of rotating objects in 45-degree increments, choose the Tools > Snap Rotation command. (Snap Rotation is enabled when it is preceded in the menu by a checkmark.)

   Snap Rotation affects any object that is rotated with the rotate handle (**Figure 14.3**). When the object is near a 45-degree increment, it snaps to that angle. It does *not*, however, prevent you from choosing other angles; it simply makes it easier to find the 45-degree increments. After changing the Snap Rotation setting, subsequent images that you open will use the new setting.

5. If you've previously disabled one or more warnings or dialog boxes (instructing Picture It! not to display them in the future), you can restore them by clicking the icon labeled Reset all messages that have been turned off (in the Options window).

6. Another way to customize your experience is to selectively disable or enable parts of the Picture It! interface. By choosing any of the top four View menu commands (Common Tasks, Object Handles, Stack, or Rulers), you can hide or minimize these components.

   Each command works as a toggle. When checked, the component is visible or maximized. With the exception of Object Handles, Picture It! remembers the state of these commands from one session to the next.

Setting Image and Display Options

You can set defaults for several image-related options. The *default resolution* is used when you save images and should represent what you intend to do with most pictures, such as display them onscreen (low resolution) or print them on photo paper (high resolution).

The *default compression level* only affects pictures saved to disk in PNG format, a new Web image format. (Images with multiple layers, for example, are often saved as PNG files.) The higher the compression, the smaller the file.

Finally, although not actually a Picture It! option, the program contains a command to open the Display Properties control panel, enabling you to alter the resolution and number of colors displayed on your monitor.

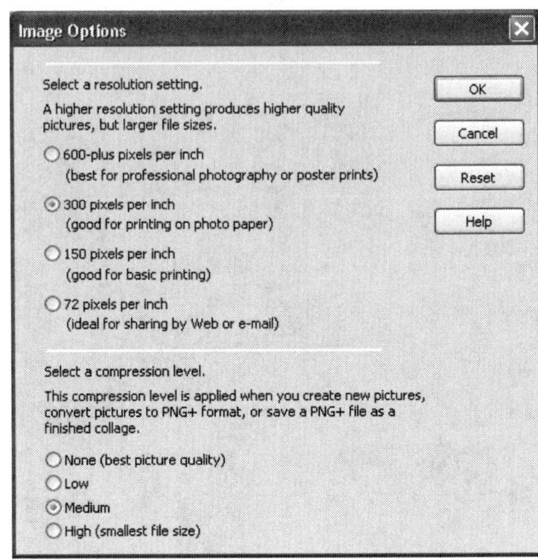

Figure 14.4 In the Image Options dialog box, you can set options that affect saved images.

To set the default resolution and compression:

1. Choose Tools > Options.

   The Options dialog box appears (see Figure 14.1).

2. Click Image Options.

   The Image Options dialog box appears (**Figure 14.4**).

3. In the top half of the dialog box, click a radio button to specify the default resolution to use when saving images.

4. In the bottom half of the dialog box, click a radio button to specify the default compression level to use when saving images in PNG format.

5. Click OK to close the Image Options dialog box.

6. Click OK again to close the Options dialog box, saving the new settings.

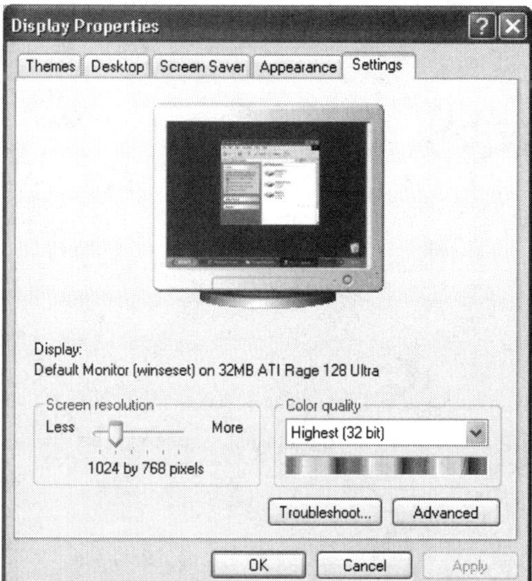

Figure 14.5 Use the Display Properties control panel to set the screen resolution and the number of colors. This is a general Windows setting that affects *all* programs—not just Picture It!

To change the display settings:

1. Choose Tools > Display settings.

   The Display Properties control panel appears, open to the Settings tab (**Figure 14.5**).

2. Make a note of the current Screen resolution and Color quality settings—in case you want to return to them after making changes in this control panel.

3. Set the screen resolution by dragging the slider to the left or right. Available settings depend on your video card and monitor.

   Increasing the resolution has the effect of displaying more information on the screen, but at a reduced size. Pick a resolution that is comfortable for you.

4. Choose a color quality from the drop-down list. Available settings depend on your video card and the screen resolution setting.

   Higher settings enable you to view images in more possible colors. For example, a setting of 16-bit displays thousands of colors.

5. To try out a new setting, click Apply.

   Apply puts the settings into effect without closing the control panel. Depending on how the Compatibility options are set (click the Advanced button to view them), trying the new settings may require you to restart your computer.

6. Click OK to close the control panel, saving the changes.

✔ Tip

- Changing the Color quality setting does not affect the number of data bits in your images. For example, you can work on a 32-bit color scan with Color quality set to 16-bit. If you later view the same image on a system set for 32-bit, the additional color detail will still be there—unless you changed the image's color depth when editing or saving it.

Setting Scanner and Camera Options

When downloading images from a connected digital camera or scanner, you can instruct Picture It! to use computer memory to speed up the transfer process (enhanced mode). If there are problems transferring images into Picture It! using enhanced mode, you can switch to normal mode.

To set scanner and camera options:

1. Choose Tools > Options.

   The Options dialog box appears (see Figure 14.1).

2. Click Scanner/Camera options.

   The Scanner/Camera Options dialog box appears (**Figure 14.6**).

3. *Do one of the following:*
   - ▲ Click an Enhanced (recommended) radio button to use computer memory to speed image downloads from a scanner or digital camera.
   - ▲ Click a Normal radio button if there are problems with enhanced transfers.

4. Click OK to close the Scanner/Camera Options dialog box and save the new settings.

5. Click OK again to close the Options dialog box.

✔ Tip

- Start with enhanced mode for both cameras and scanners. In the world of computers, faster is better—especially when you sacrifice nothing for the additional speed.

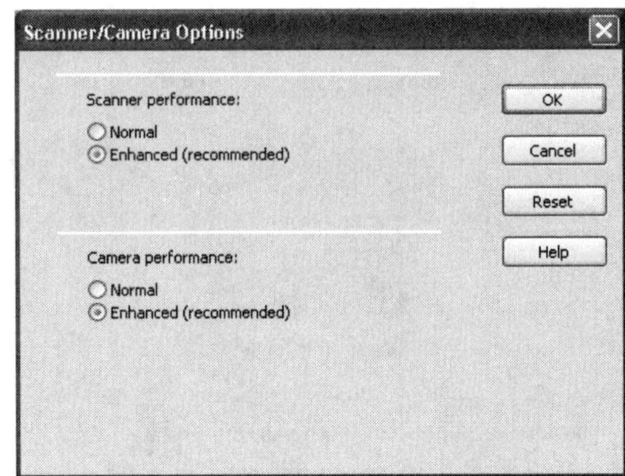

Figure 14.6 Set the data transfer speed in the Scanner/Camera Options dialog box.

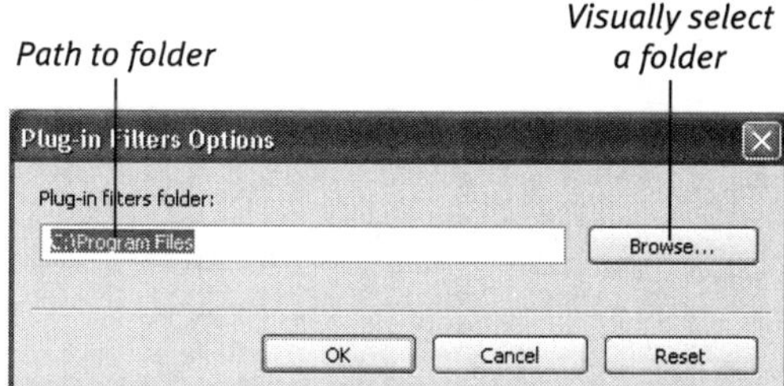

Figure 14.7 Specify the folder in which plug-ins are stored.

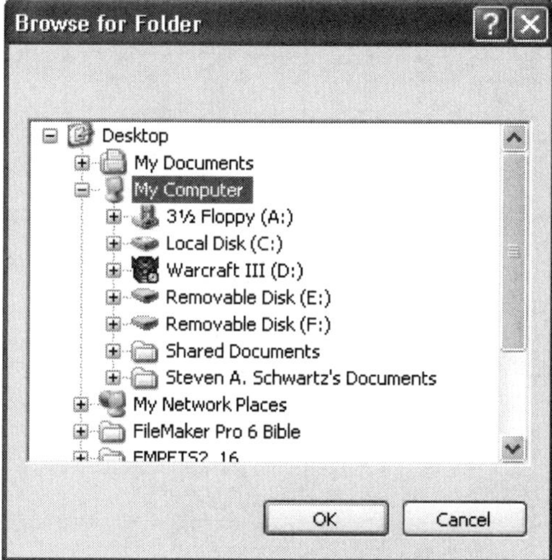

Figure 14.8 Expand folders in this dialog box until you locate the one in which your plug-ins are stored.

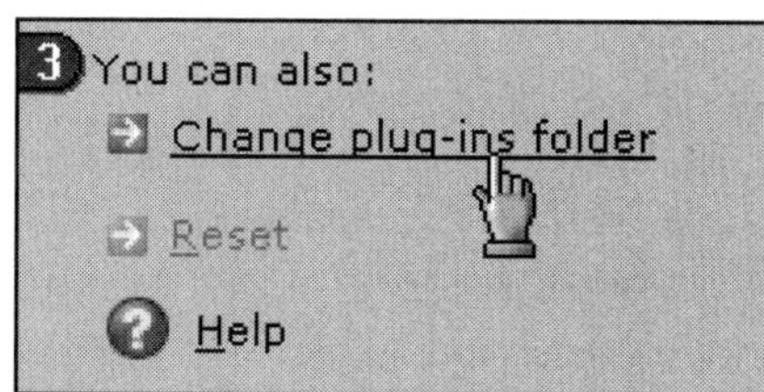

Figure 14.9 You can also change the plug-ins folder by clicking this text in the Plug-in Filters pane.

Setting the Plug-Ins Folder

Digital Image Pro can use standard Adobe Photoshop plug-in filters to expand the program's capabilities. Filters are frequently used to create special effects, for example. To make use of plug-in filters, you must tell Picture It! where they're stored on disk.

To set the plug-in filters location:

1. Choose Tools > Options.

   The Options dialog box appears (see Figure 14.1).

2. Click Plug-in filters options.

   The Plug-in Filters Options dialog box appears (**Figure 14.7**).

3. *Do one of the following:*

   ▲ Type the full path of the folder in which plug-ins are stored.

   ▲ Click the Browse button to select the folder visually (**Figure 14.8**). Highlight the folder name and click OK.

4. Click OK to dismiss the Plug-in Filters Options dialog box and save the setting.

5. Click OK again to close the Options dialog box.

✔ Tips

- Picture It! searches for plug-ins in the designated folder *and* any folders stored within that folder. Pick a folder that encompasses all folders that need to be searched.
- You can also change the plug-in folder by choosing Effects > Plug-in Filters and then clicking Change plug-ins folder (**Figure 14.9**).
- Digital Image Pro can use Photoshop plug-ins, but *not* the ones that come with Adobe Photoshop or Photoshop Elements.
- To find useful plug-ins, search the Web for *Photoshop plug-ins* or *free Photoshop plug-ins.*

INDEX

D

E

G

H

I

J

K

L

M

N

O

P

Q

R

S

U

V

W

X

Z